POSTMODERN
CRIMINOLOGY

CURRENT ISSUES IN CRIMINAL JUSTICE
VOLUME 22
GARLAND REFERENCE LIBRARY OF SOCIAL SCIENCE
VOLUME 1117

CURRENT ISSUES IN CRIMINAL JUSTICE

FRANK P. WILLIAMS III AND MARILYN D. MCSHANE
Series Editors

POSTMODERN CRIMINOLOGY

DRAGAN MILOVANOVIC

GARLAND PUBLISHING, INC.
NEW YORK AND LONDON
1997

Library of Congress Cataloging-in-Publication Data

Milovanovic, Dragan, 1948–
    Postmodern criminology / by Dragan Milovanovic.
        p.   cm. — (Garland reference library of social science ; v. 1117.
Current issues in criminal justice ; v. 22)
    Includes bibliographical references and index.
    ISBN 0-8153-2456-1 (alk. paper)
    1. Criminology—Philosophy.   2. Postmodernism—Social aspects.
I. Title.   II. Series: Garland reference library of social science ; v. 1117.
III. Series: Garland reference library of social science. Current issues in crimi-
nal justice ; v. 22.
HV6018.M55   1997
364—dc21   97-10779
                                                                    CIP

Printed on acid-free, 250-year-life paper
Manufactured in the United States of America

Contents

SERIES EDITORS' FOREWORD

This volume is part of a monograph series in criminal justice and criminology, one of the few such series to emerge over the past thirty years. Some years ago, when we took on the series' editorship, our decision was predicated on the promise that we could help in publishing non–textbook-oriented, meaningful, scholarly work. In the back of our minds was the possibility of getting new ideas, even cutting-edge ideas, into the field. Those hopes were, of course, rather like pipe dreams—things to be wished for, but with little objective chance of succeeding. Imagine our delight when we began receiving manuscripts that were not only well written, but were insightful as well. With this twenty-second volume in the series, we can now say, quite objectively, that pipe dreams have become reality. This series has some extraordinary and cutting-edge work in it, and for that we are deeply indebted to the authors who have made it happen. Editing a series is not an easy task, but our journey with this one has been immensely rewarding.

Dragan Milovanovic's *Postmodern Criminology* is a two-fold creation. First, it allows readers access to a scholar's intellectual travels, a relatively rare happenstance in academic writing. This is valuable because the development of ideas and concepts does not happen easily and is certainly not full-blown, an impression students seem to gain from theory texts. Second, we know of no better documentation of the range of postmodern criminology than Dragan has presented here. This work is both a review of different theoretical concerns and the presentation of an emerging, original, theoretical perspective. In one sense, for scholars in criminology, this is mandatory reading. Whether one prefers "objective" or "subjective" criminology, this volume is at the forefront in the study of criminology. Nowhere else will postmodern ideas be presented with greater clarity, or in more elegant juxtaposition. Finally, it is always impossible to say whether a paradigm revolution is at hand, but this work suggests to us that the field may be getting very close to a new understanding of crime, criminal behavior, and the production of criminological knowledge.

Frank P. Williams III
Marilyn D. McShane

Preface

Postmodern criminology has recently emerged as a perspective that questions many of the core assumptions of modernist thought. The use of its conceptual tools offers the potential for the development of a better understanding of the various configurations of repressive forces and directions for social change. This book discusses some of the key themes in postmodern criminology. It is intended for students as well as those who are more familiar with the subject.

This book was inspired by the lack of published material that deals with both theoretical integrative work, applications, and recent developments in studying postmodern criminology. Published material in postmodern criminology has been scattered in various journals, and a few have appeared in book form with a more singular focus. Accordingly, the time was ripe for a book that introduces a reader to some of the core ideas concerning subjectivity as it is related to discourses and how the discursive construction of social reality takes place. And it was important to indicate how theoretical work can be applied, both in the earlier and in the more recent emerging forms.

During my writings of the 1980s, I felt uneasy concerning my notion of subjectivity. Much of my work had been more of a structural analysis relying heavily on Marx and Weber. But my own experiences (i.e., hanging out with street-corner groups, company point in Vietnam, juvenile counselor in a locked dormitory setting, teacher of inmates in a maximum security jail, worker on a ward of a state mental hospital, participant in the Sandinista revolution in Nicaragua, member of a prison inspection team, among others) constantly resurrected the human being behind the structures, and this was not being adequately expressed in my words. About 1990 I came across the writings of Jacques Lacan. I had seen references to his work in footnotes many times; this indicated to me that Lacan's work was important to the study of postmodern criminology. My first read of *Ecrit* was torturous; my second almost as difficult. The ideas were not connecting. After the third and fourth read, and after some good secondary sources, the ideas started to connect.

Lacan had it right. The subject was intimately connected to the discourse within which it is inserted. A few more readings of *Ecrits* made it clear to me that he was a truly exceptional scholar. Since most of his works (*Seminars*, 26 in total) had not been published, or had not been translated into English, I had to go back to the transcribed versions and do my own translations. (Most of his works still have not been translated into English.) This is indeed a difficult endeavor. My writings in the early to mid-1990s was focused on integrating much of his work.

More recently, I have been intrigued by chaos, topology, and catastrophe theory. Each challenges much of the dominant thought of our age, especially in criminology and law. I have come to realize that an important direction is to integrate Lacan's psychoanalytic semiotics with chaos, topology, and catastrophe theory. Important, too, is critical theory, feminist postmodernist theory, constitutive theory, and the dialogical pedagogy of Freire. This is indeed demanding work. There is much yet to be done. Interested scholars must resist getting turned off by the difficult prose of postmodernist writers. Struggle with Lacan; don't dismiss his prose, for with sustained and focused study, insights will pour forth. I have, over recent years, come across many graduate students who have become disgruntled with the exposure to traditional lines of analysis in criminology and law, and who are in search of something that offers more. Postmodern criminology will surely be one key alternative.

My long-range goal in writing this book is to stimulate discussion between modernist and postmodernist thinkers in criminology and law. The dialogue is necessary. Premature dismissals by modernists have already appeared. The debate is needed.

This book is composed of twelve essays organized into three parts. The first part focuses on theoretical integration; the second, on application; and the third, on emerging postmodern methodologies, integration and application. The most speculative work will be found in part 3 where my current research interests are. Part 2 includes three articles that I co-authored with others. Each of the co-authors, Stuart Henry, Shelley Bannister, and Jim Thomas have broadened the scope of my thinking: Stuart has pointed out the importance of not prematurely totally discarding the past; Shelley, the contradictions with doing activist law; and Jim, the existence of moments of resistance in prison. The first three chapters are on the borders of postmodern analysis. The last two push ahead. Part 1 develops important concepts, distinctions, definitions, and views that are central to postmodernist thought. Previously published work that has been included here has not undergone fundamental revision but has been edited for style consistency.

Acknowledgments

The author is grateful to the following publishers for permission to reprint copyrighted material used in this book:

The journal of *Humanity and Society* for reprinting D. Milovanovic, "Dueling Paradigms: Modernist v. Postmodernist Thought." 19(1): 1-22, 1995.

The journal *Studies in Psychoanalytic Theory*, for reprinting D. Milovanovic, "The Decentered Subject in Law: Contributions of Topology, Psychoanalytic Semiotics and Chaos Theory." 3(1): 93-127, 1994.

The *International Journal of the Sociology of Law* and Academic Press, London, England, Ltd. for reprinting S. Bannister and D. Milovanovic, "The Necessity Defense, Substantive Justice, and Oppositional Praxis." 18(2): 179-98, 1990.

The *International Journal of the Sociology of Law* and Academic Press, London, England, Ltd. for reprinting D. Milovanovic, "Jailhouse Lawyers and Jailhouse Lawyering." 16: 455-75, 1988.

The journal *Social Problems,* and University of California Press for reprinting D. Milovanovic and J. Thomas, "Overcoming the Absurd: Legal Struggle as Primitive Rebellion." 36(1): 48-60, 1989.

The journal *Legal Studies Forum*, for reprinting D. Milovanovic, "Borromean Knots and the Constitution of Sense in Juridico-Discursive Production." 17(2): 171-92, 1993.

The journal *Social Justice*, for reprinting D. Milovanovic and S. Henry, "Constitutive Penology." 18: 204-24, 1991.

The journal *Criminology,* and the American Society of Criminology for reprinting S. Henry and D. Milovanovic, "Constitutive Criminology." 29(2): 293-316, 1991.

I would also like to thank Shelley Bannister, Northeastern Illinois University; Stuart Henry, Eastern Michigan University; and Jim Thomas,

Northern Illinois for their co-authorship in four of the above articles. I have learned much from each of them.

A very special thanks to Joyce Kelly, whose editorial assistance was indispensable. I greatly appreciated her breaking away from her own writing for her assistance on my book project. May your own book project continue to fruition. Your publications have brought to light the struggles of many.

Thanks to Chuck Bartelt, Garland Publishing Inc., who was always there to help me out with the technical aspects of preparing this manuscript. Her professional, knowledgeable and always courteous support made this project progress smoothly.

Thanks to Donn H. Bichsel, Vice President for Development and Public Affairs, who came through with support for this project and alleviated many pending headaches. Thanks, Don, for your timely support; it was very much appreciated.

Introduction

Postmodern criminology has emerged as an alternative perspective to doing critical analysis. It provides new conceptual tools with which to investigate various phenomena in crime, law, and penology. Its robust engagement with the more traditional, modernist perspectives is beneficial in bringing to light the more insidious forms of domination and their possible reduction. Much misunderstanding exists as to many of the conceptual tools provided, and many in the modernist paradigm are quickly dismissive where open debate should prevail. Postmodern criminology is a dynamic perspective, and accordingly, is in a continuous process of change. Whereas the earlier forms of postmodernist analysis, sometimes referred to as the skeptical or nihilistic forms, were appropriately criticized for their excesses, the more mature form, affirmative postmodernism, offers exciting directions for inquiry, discovery, and visions for social change.

Postmodern criminology incorporates a number of perspectives. These include chaos theory, discourse analysis, with Lacan's version of psychoanalytic semiotics being the most prominent, topology theory, catastrophe theory, literary criticism, and constitutive theory. It has also recently been infused with Freire's work on dialogical pedagogy (1972, 1985), Giroux's border pedagogy (1992), and critical theory. Postmodern feminist theorizing, particularly by Cornell (1991, 1993) and Butler (1990, 1992, 1993) have brought the terrain into sharp relief. Critical race theory has contributed the idea of intersections in gender, race, and class biases (Matsuda et al., 1993; Delgado, 1995; Schwartz and Milovanovic, 1996), and the prevalence of multiple consciousness. Postmodernist thought continues to develop in its integration and in its various syntheses. These are indeed demanding scholarly endeavors.

Earlier forms of postmodernist analysis were accused of advocating the "death of the subject" (Held, 1995), and being devoid of the very possibility of creating "foundations" on which to create political agendas for social reform. Some, inspired by their unique readings of Jacques Derrida's work, argued that since no transcendental foundations can arise, all is relative, and therefore, resignation is the only logical outcome. Some of the excesses of the earlier form came in the notion of reversing hierarchies whereby, with success, the form of domination would be reconstituted, be it inadvertently.

But the affirmative forms of postmodernist analysis have countered with the view that the "decidability of the sign" is rooted in socio-historical struggles (Ebert, 1991a, 1991b; Zavarzadeh and Morton, 1990); that political agendas can be based on "contingent foundations," "contingent universalities"—provisional and contingent truths (Butler, 1990, 1992); that "languages of possibility" and "utopian thinking" (Cornell, 1991) have a central place in social reform; that new forms of alliance building will consider the multiplicity of struggles and resistance (Laclau and Mouffe, 1985); that the revolutionary subject (as opposed to the oppositional subject) can be recovered (Freire, 1972, 1985; McLaren, 1994a, 1994b; McLaren and Lankshear, 1994; Henry and Milovanovic, 1996); that a new social "order" coupled with various and changing forms of subjectivity can develop in what chaos theorists refer to as far-from-equilibrium conditions where sensitive and responsive "structures," "dissipative structures," abound (Milovanovic, 1992a; Milovanovic, 1996; Henry and Milovanovic, 1996; see also Unger, 1987); and that the person is a subject-in-process, always, in potentiality of being a border-crosser (Giroux, 1992).

Another polemic has been directed toward the language employed by postmodernists. It is claimed to be too abstract, complex, esoteric, and jargonistic. But the assumptions implicit in this line of critique are left unexamined (Giroux, 1992: 24). Perhaps the consumer society has intruded upon the task of critical reading. Here the commodity is used once and exhausted, then thrown away for another and "better" thrill or contrived need. Reading, too, can come under this grip. The passive reader would prefer to read one-liners devoid of all the nuances often expressed in dependent clauses, and be done with the task. On the other hand, an active reader is an engaged reader; one who actively interacts with the ideas being expressed, deconstructing and reconstructing the text. Here, no closure exists, but rather an infinite play of difference. The consumer reader seeks closure, the definitive read so that the material can be put aside as having been "mastered." The critical and active reader finds only provisional and contingent "truths."

This book brings out these various thoughts. Included here are twelve essays: nine were previously published (Chapters 1-9), three are new (Chapters 10-12), written for this book. Part 1, "Theoretical Integration," includes four articles. This section provides theoretical work on the nature of subjectivity in postmodern analysis. Chapter 1, "Dueling Paradigms," introduces the reader to some of the prominent differences between modernist and postmodernist thought. These are conceptualized along eight continuums: (1) society and social structure, (2) social roles, (3) subjectivity/agency, (4) discourse, (5) knowledge, (6) space/time, (7) causality, and (8) social change. Chapter 2, "The Decentered Subject in Law: Contributions of Topology, Psychoanalytic Semiotics, and Chaos Theory," develops the notion of the decentered subject, a subject intimately connected with discourse. Topology theory is introduced as well as psychoanalytic semiotics. The topological construction of the cross-cap is shown to portray Jacques Lacan's Schema R, the dynamic version of the subject. Chapter 3, "Borromean Knots and the Constitution of Sense in Juridico-Discursive Production," develops Lacan's late views of the borromean knots as portraying the consistency of the psychic apparatus, as well as its usefulness in understanding discursive production in law. It is also integrated with constitutive theory, particularly how "naming" operations create and sustain certain conceptions of reality, and how other "realities" often remain unverbalized, the person being denied opportunities for the embodiment of her/his unique desire. Chapter 4, "Constitutive Criminology: The Maturation of Critical Theory," was written with Stuart Henry, Eastern Michigan University. It develops an alternative approach to traditional Marxist frameworks, and explains the thesis of the discursive codetermination of crime. The notion of a transpraxis as an alternative to "praxis" is offered as a more affirmative form of social struggle. Here deconstruction, reconstruction, theory, and practice go hand in hand.

Part 2, "Application: Doing Affirmative Postmodern Analysis in Law, Crime, and Penology," is a collection of five articles that are more of the "application" form. Chapter 5, "Jailhouse Lawyers and Jailhouse Lawyering," examines the struggles of inmates who have taught themselves law, and practice it while confined. One of the central questions is how the "what happened" is reconstructed in legal discourse. This chapter, as well as chapters 6 and 7, brings to light the dialectics of struggle and how hegemony is maintained. Chapter 6, "Overcoming the Absurd: Prisoner Litigation as Primitive Rebellion," was written with Jim Thomas, Northern Illinois University. It is concerned with investigating whether the jailhouse lawyer is a revolutionary figure, or is better seen as a primitive rebel. Litigation, as discursive production, is portrayed more in terms of existential than revolutionary practice. Chapter 7, "The Necessity Defense, Substantive Justice, and Oppositional Linguistic Practice," was written with Shelley Bannister, Northeastern Illinois University. It raises the question of the radical's dilemma. Do activist lawyers work within the discursive constructions of law, "winning" but inadvertently reconstituting dominant forms, or attempt to introduce political factors, risking not "winning" the case and having the rebel face long imprisonment sentences? The necessity defense is examined for its unique possibility of politicizing the trial and for the development of a more revolutionary discourse. Chapter 8, "Constitutive Penology," was written with Stuart Henry, Eastern Michigan University. It applies constitutive theory to penology. It focuses on the discursive production of meaning constructions in prisons, from policy to justifications. A constitutive penology includes an examination of the discursive co-production of a prison "reality," and how it is often sustained by the very subjects who wish its eradication. Chapter 9, "Topology, Chaos, and Psychoanalytic Semiotics," introduces more recent postmodernist theorizing that makes use of chaos, topology, and psychoanalytic semiotics. This integration and synthesis is then applied to criminology. Especially relevant for application is some recent theorizing in criminology that focuses more on "foreground" rather than "background" factors, such as the sensual, visceral, seductive, adrenalin-charged, passion-driven, pleasure-seeking, and emotional aspects in crime (Katz, 1988; Ferrell, 1995a, 1995b; O'Malley and Mugford, 1994).

Part 3, "Emerging Postmodern Methodologies: Integration and Application," includes three chapters on recent integrative work incorporating chaos theory, catastrophe theory, and psychoanalytic semiotics. It suggests the use of various conceptual tools that may be used in criminological inquiry that move us beyond some of the limitations of conventional, modernist thought. Chapter 10, "Chaos and Criminology: Phase Maps and Bifurcation Diagrams," presents ways of conceptualizing nonlinear, dynamic systems. The phase map and bifurcation diagram are explained and then applied to criminological thought (Matza's *Delinquency and Drift*, 1964), and to the development of replacement discourses by incorporating Lacan's four discourses. Chapter 11, "Chaos, Meta-Modeling, and Criminology: Iterative Loops, COREL and Mandelbrot Sets," first explains how iterative diagrams can better explain dynamic, nonlinear phenomena rather than traditional path-analysis diagrams, and how the Mandelbrot Set captures the idea of deterministic equations producing indeterminate results, and, second, suggests some possible applications in criminology. Chapter 12, "Catastrophe Theory, Crime, and Peacemaking," develops catastrophe theory. First, the "cusp catastrophe" generic model is explained and then applied in doing a postmodern criminology. Second, the "butterfly catastrophe" is explained and then applied in developing a peace discourse that can reduce escalating interpersonal violence. Some limitations are also examined.

The twelve chapters introduce various perspectives in doing postmodern criminology. Exciting times await interested criminologists whether already in the field, or in their graduate studies in search of something better. For the noncriminologist, this book will provide some alternative ways of thinking critically about crime.

xvi

PART 1

Theoretical Integration

CHAPTER 1

Dueling Paradigms
Modernist v. Postmodernist Thought

INTRODUCTION

In recent days, much has been said of a postmodernist analysis in the social sciences. Indeed, a number of comparisons occasionally arise in the literature between modernist and postmodernist analysis, usually as an introduction to some further study. Little, however, has appeared that takes as its primary goal a comparison of the two perspectives. Accordingly, this essay is more didactic and pedagogical in orientation. We have identified eight dimensions as a basis of comparison. Although presented as dichotomies, the differences often fall along a continuum; some tend toward further polarization, others become discontinuities, such as the differences between the centered and decentered subject, the privileging of disorder rather than order, the emphasis on Pathos rather than Logos, etc.

A considerable amount of literature from those who are committed to the modernist approach is of a defensive sort when confronted with the epistemological directions advocated by postmodernist analysis. The first tactic generally is to dismiss its claims as old wine in new bottles, followed by incorporating the postmodernist premises and concepts within the discourse of modernist thought. Much effort, then, is taken to undo the postmodernist's concepts by way of a discursive reorientation, at the conclusion of which modernist thinkers hope to say, "There, I told you so! Old wine in new bottles!" This attempt fails, however, even though in some instances several modernist thinkers did in fact anticipate some aspects of the postmodern paradigm. It is necessary to recognize that postmodernist analysis is indeed premised on radically new concepts, and discursive redefinitions will not help further progressive thought in the social sciences. What we do have are dueling paradigms: the modernist versus the postmodernist.

Modernist thought had its origins in the Enlightenment period. This era was a celebration of the liberating potentials of the social sciences, the materialistic gains of capitalism, new forms of rational thought, due process safeguards, abstract rights applicable to all, and the individual—it was a time of great optimism (Milovanovic, 1992a, 1994a; Dews, 1987; Sarup, 1989; Lyotard, 1984; Baker, 1993).

Postmodernists are fundamentally opposed to modernist thought. Sensitized by the insights of some of the classic thinkers, ranging from Marx, to Weber, to Durkheim, Freud, and the critical thought of the Frankfurt School, postmodernist thought emerged with a new intensity in the late 1980s and early 1990s. "Let us wage a war on totality" states one of its key exponents (Lyotard, 1984: 82). Most of the key concepts of modernist thought were critically examined and found to be wanting. Entrenched bureaucratic powers, monopolies, the manipulative advertisement industry, dominant and totalizing discourses, and the ideology of the legal apparatus were seen as exerting repressive powers. In fact, the notion of the individual—free, self-determining, reflective, and the center of activity—was seen as an ideological construction, nowhere more apparent than in the notion of the juridic subject, the so-called reasonable man in law. Rather than the notion of the individual, the centered subject, the postmodernists were to advocate the notion of the *decentered subject*.

Postmodernist analysis had its roots in French thought, particularly during the late 1960s and early 1970s. Here, with the continued disillusionment with conventional critical thought, a transition from Hegelian to Nietzschean thought took place. Deleuze, Guattari, Derrida, Lyotard, Baudrillard, Foucault, Kristeva and many others were to emerge bearing the banner of postmodernist thinking. Feminists from the postmodern tradition were to become key thinkers. Such theorists as Irigaray, Moi, and Cixous were to apply much of this thought to gender construction. The central figure in developing alternative notions of the subject, the determining effects of discourse, and the nature of the symbolic order was Jacques Lacan.

New-wave postmodernist thinkers are likely to draw from chaos theory, Godel's theorem, catastrophe theory, quantum mechanics, and topology theory. Novel conceptions of space, time, causality, subjectivity, the role of discourse, desire, social structure, roles, social change, knowledge, and the nature of harm, justice, and the law were developed and continue to be developed in postmodernist thought. The call is for the abandonment of a center, privileged reference points, fixed subjects, first principles, and an origin (Sarup, 1989: 59).

This essay will outline the differences between the modernist and the postmodernist paradigm. As Thomas Kuhn said many years ago, paradigms tend to crystallize around key validity claims that become premises for scientific thought. "Normal science" tends to work out the implications of this general body of knowledge(s) through, for example, deductive logic. Occasionally, as in the case of postmodernist thought, a revolutionary new science with entirely new premises develops and becomes the body of knowledge from which new questions are asked and entirely new discoveries are made.

MODERNIST VERSUS POSTMODERNIST THOUGHT

To clarify some of the more salient differences, we have selected eight dimensions for comparison. These dimensions include the nature of: (1) society and social structure, (2) social roles, (3) subjectivity/agency, (4) discourse, (5) knowledge, (6) space/time, (7) causality, and (8) social change. This essay will highlight the major differences that have emerged by the early 1990s. Accordingly, we will list the dimensions and comment briefly on each. We should add, whereas the modernist assumptions seem more descriptive, the postmodernist add a prescriptive dimension. Contrary to many modernist critics, postmodernism is not fatalistic, cynical, and nonvisionary; rather, what the new paradigm offers is a more intense critique of what is, and transformative visions of what could be.

1. Society and Social Structure

Key Concepts:
Modernist: equilibrium; homeostasis; tension reduction; order; homogeneity; consensus; stasis; normativity; foundationalism; logocentricism; totality; closure; transcendental signifiers; structural functionalism.
Postmodernist: far-from-equilibrium conditions; flux; change; chance; spontaneity; irony; orderly disorder; heterogeneity; diversity; intensity; paralogism; toleration for the incommensurable; dissipative structures; antifoundationalism; fragmentation; coupling; impossibility of formal closure; structural dislocations/undecidability; constitutive theory.

Commentary
a. *Modernist Thought.* Much of the dominant literature of modernist thought can be traced to the work of structural functionalism or totalizing theory. Theorists such as Durkheim, Luhmann (1985) and Parson, stand out as exemplary. A good part of this literature rests on an underlying homeostatic, tension-reduction, or equilibrium model. Freud, for example, rests his views on some conception of tension-reduction as the operative force in social structural development. Perhaps we can trace much of this to Newtonian physics and its influence. The central question is one of order. It is seen as desirable without further explanation. In fact, some, such as Parsons, define deviance in terms of distance from some assumed acceptable standard of normativity.

Modernist thought is focused on totalizing theory — the search for overencompassing theories of society and social development. Some discoverable foundation was said to exist. At the center, a logos was said to be at play; whether, for example, as in Weber's forces of rationalization, Freud's homeostasis, or as in Hegel's Absolute Spirit. These logics slumbered in anticipation of their correct articulation. These were the transcendental signifiers that were discoverable.

Much of the often-mentioned consensus paradigm, too, can be placed within the modernist paradigm. Thus metanarratives are still replete with assumptions of homogeneity, desirability of consensus, order, etc.

b. Postmodernist Thought. Postmodernist thought, although still emerging, and which initially found its basis in its critique of modernism, has found grounding in the insights of chaos theory, Godel's theorem, catastrophe theory, quantum mechanics, emerging cosmological insights, topology theory, and Lacanian thought—to name a few.

Postmodernists begin their analysis with privileging disorder rather than order. Their starting point is *paralogism*: privileging instabilities (Lyotard, 1984). Accordingly, this model begins with far-from-equilibrium conditions as being the more "natural" state, and places a premium on flux, nonlinear change, chance, spontaneity, intensity, indeterminacy, irony, and orderly disorder. No permanent stable order is possible or even desirable. No center or foundation exists. Godel's theorem (1962), describing the impossibility of formal closure, dictates that the search for an overall, all-encompassing totalizing theory is an illusory exercise. In fact, as we shall show below, since no precise center exists, or since no possibility exists for precisely specifying initial conditions, then, the process of iteration will produce disproportional and unanticipated effects.

"Dissipative structures" are offered as relatively stable societal structures that remain sensitive and responsive to their environment (Baker, 1993; see also Unger's suggestion for the establishment of criticizable institutions, 1987; see also Leifer on organizational transformations, 1989). This concept implies both relative stability as well as continuous change (i.e., order and disorder). Contrary to structural functionalism and its privileging of homeostasis, postmodernists see the desirability of ongoing flux and continuous change captured by the notion of far-from-equilibrium conditions. It is within these conditions that dissipative structures flourish.

Accordingly, some have offered the notion of *structural coupling* and *constitutive theory* to explain the movement of information between structure and environment (Luhmann, 1992; Hunt, 1993; Jessop, 1990; Henry and Milovanovic, 1991, 1996). Implied is the coexistence of multiple sites of determinants whose unique historical articulations are never precisely predictable. Due to inherent uncertainties in initial conditions, iterative practices produce the unpredictable. Here, the focal concern is on tolerance and support for the incommensurable. Assumed is the existence of perpetual fragmentation, deconstruction, and reconstruction. Advocated is the facilitation of the emergence of marginalized, disenfranchised, disempowered, and other excluded voices.

Noteworthy in the analysis of societal structure by way of postmodernist analysis is Unger's work on an empowered democracy (1987), even if he didn't explicitly state his affinity with postmodernist thought. In his offerings, orderly disorder should be privileged. During the 1960s and 1970s, the development of the conflict paradigm in the social sciences marked some movement toward the postmodernist approach, but the promise fell short.

Chaos theory is increasingly becoming a key element in postmodern analysis. The founding figures include Ilya Prigogine, Henri Poincare, Mitchell Feigenbaum, Benoit Mandelbrot, and Edward Lorenz (see the overview by Briggs and Peat, 1989; Gleick, 1987; Stewart, 1989). We find application of chaos theory to psychoanalysis (Deleuze and Guattari, 1987; Milovanovic, 1992a, 1993a); to literature (Serres, 1982a, 1982b; Hayles, 1990, 1991); to criminology (T.R.Young, 1991a; Pepinsky, 1991); to law (Brion, 1991; Milovanovic, 1993a); to psychology (Butz, 1991, 1992a, 1992b); to sociology (Young, 1991b, 1992; Baker, 1993); to business and management (Leifer, 1989); and to political science (Unger, 1987). Others such as Charles Sanders Peirce anticipated some dimensions of this approach (see especially his essay on the doctrine of chance and necessity, 1940: 157-73; and his notion of *pure play* or *musement*, 1934: 313-16).

Nietzschean and Lacanian thought, rather than Hegelian thought, are inspirational to postmodernist thinkers. Feminist postmodernists traced to the former have perhaps contributed the most important insights. Julia Kristeva, Luce Irigaray, Helene Cixous, and Toril Moi, to a considerable extent, have borrowed ideas from them in their elaboration of given phallocentric social structures and their possible alternatives (a useful overview is found in Sellers, 1991; Grosz, 1990; for an application in law, see Cornell, 1991, 1993; Milovanovic, 1994a: Chapter 6, 1994b).

2. ROLES

Key Concepts:
Modernist: role-taking; socialization; integration; centripetal; closure; static; dichotomies; system serving; primacy to the "me"; limit attractors; symphony orchestra player.

Postmodernist: role-making; role-jumbling; variability; centrifugal; openness; porous boundaries; testing boundaries; primacy to the dialectic between the "I-me"; privileging the "I"; strange attractors; torus; jazz player.

Commentary:
a. Modernist Thought. The modernist view tends to rely on a Parsonian construct of a role in which centripetal forces of society socialize the person into accepting the obligations and expectations that pertain to him/her. This, then, becomes the question of functional integration. Accordingly, roles tend to become dichotomized—male/female, employer/employee, good guy/bad guy, etc. In the specified balance of the I-me that many social theorists advocate (Durkheim, Mead, etc.), great weight is placed on the dominance of the "me," that part of the self that dresses itself up with the persona demanded by the situation, struts upon the stage, and plays its part with various degrees of success to various audiences. A person is relegated to role-taking. The operative metaphor we offer is a member of a symphony orchestra.

b. Postmodernist Thought. Postmodernists see things differently. Roles are essentially unstable and are in a dialectical relationship between centrifugal and centripetal forces. And this is desirable. Whereas roles in the modernist view would be similar to what chaos theorists refer to as *limit attractors* (they tend toward stereotypical closure), roles in postmodernist analysis would be very much like *torus* or *strange attractors*. A strange attractor can appear as two butterfly wings where instances of behavior may occur in one (i.e., a person's conduct is situated in the illegal underworld), and in the other (i.e., a person's conduct is in the legitimate world). Where the two cross, maximal indeterminacy prevails. When instances of behavior are plotted in *phase space* (a diagrammatical depiction), what appears over time is some degree of global patterning (the distinct wings of the butterfly), but at any instance, that is at any specific location, variability and indeterminacy prevail (from quantum mechanics' uncertainty principle, one cannot at the same time predict location and momentum). There exists, in other words, local indeterminacy but a relative global stability, an orderly disorder. A person's fate is relegated to role-making (Young, 1994).

In George Herbert Mead's framework, role-making would indicate the active contribution of the "I." Unger's notion of *role-jumbling* would be another example (1987). Harraway's idea of a postmodernist identity would be another (1991). Others have advocated a simultaneous disidentification and identification with various discursive subject positions, a process by which reidentifications are produced (JanMohammed, 1993; McLaren, 1994a). "It is...a process of forming affiliations with other positions, of defining equivalences and constructing alliances" (JanMohammed, 1993: 111). In fact,

Lacan's view is that the person is decentered and is always subject to imaginary and symbolic play, and therefore a stable *moi* is illusory. Stability can only be maintained by the impositions of external forces (i.e., manipulative powers of political forces and the advertisement industry; the violence of a phallocentric symbolic order, etc.). For the postmodernist view, the call is to be a jazz player and poet.

3. SUBJECTIVITY/AGENCY

Key Concepts:
Modernist: centered; the individual; transparent; reflective; self-directing; whole; positivistic; the "oversocialized" conception; juridic subject; homo-duplex; homo-economicus; homeostatic; passivity; the "good," interpellated, spoken subject; transcendental self; cartesian; *cogito, ergo sum*; logos; rational man; conscious, autonomous being; desire centered on lack.
Postmodernist: decentered subject; polyvocal; polyvalent; *parlêtre*; *l'être parlant*; pathos; subject-in-process; schema L and schema R; subject of desire; activity; subject of disidentification; assumption of one's desire; effects of the unconscious; positive/productive desire; will to power.

Commentary:
a. Modernist Thought. Modernist thought has privileged the idea of the individual, a person who is assumed to be conscious, whole, self-directing, reflective, unitary, and transparent. In its extreme we have what had been characterized in the 1960s by Dennis Wrong and picked up in the critical literature as the "oversocialized conception of man." Other conceptions cling to a homo-duplex view in which human nature is said to be a balance of egoism and altruism. Here individual desires are said to be in need of synchronization with given sociopolitical systems. Alternatively, we have homo-economicus. The Enlightenment period was one in which the individual or the centered subject was discovered. This conception of the transcendental self, the cartesian subject, has been incorporated in the legal sphere as the juridic subject, the reasonable man/woman in law. Nowhere better has it been expressed than in *Cogito, ergo sum*.

Desire, for the modernists, is inscribed on the body; it is *territorialized* (Deleuze and Guattari, 1987). As Foucault would point out, the desiring subject becomes a body of passivity and economic/political utility (1977). Desire must be tamed, captured within the coordinates of various dominant discourses. Here desire begins with a lack, the price it pays for its inauguration into the Symbolic Order, and the biography of the self is one in which repetition drives the organism in its attempt to fill the void (see also Dews, 1987: 132, 135). In the more passive form of adaptation, the person is driven toward homeostasis, tension-reduction, catharsis, etc. The subject is said to be interpellated into her/his discursive subject-positions necessitated by the imperatives of a smoothly functioning socioeconomic political order. Thus we have the *interpellated* (Althusser, 1971), *spoken* (Silverman, 1982) or the *good* subject (Pecheux, 1982). In the more active form of adaptation, expressions of alienation, despair, resistance and opposition produce the oppositional subject caught within the "discourse of the hysteric" (Lacan, 1991a; Milovanovic, 1993a).

b. Postmodernist Thought. Postmodernist thought has offered the idea of the decentered subject. The subject is more determined than determining, is less internally unified than a desiring subject caught within the constraints of various discourses and their structuring properties. Kristeva has referred to the person (Bartlett and Kennedy, 1991a: 387-9) as the subject-in-process; Lacan, *l'être parlant* or the *parlêtre* (the speaking being, or the speaking); and much African-American feminist analysis in law, for example, has argued for the polyvocal, polyvalent nature of consciousness (Harris, 1991: 235-62; Matsuda, 1989; Williams, 1987, 1991; Bartlett and Kennedy, 1991a: 387-9).

Perhaps the clearest exposition of the decentered subject has been provided by Lacan in his schema L (1977). This four-cornered schema proposes two diagonally intersecting axes: one represents an unconscious/symbolic axis, the other the imaginary axis. Here the subject is drawn over all four corners of this schema; s/he is simultaneously caught in the working of the symbolic and imaginary axes. The unconscious/symbolic axis has at one end of the pole the grammatical "I"; at the opposite end, the Other, the sphere of the unconscious structured like a language. The second axis, the imaginary axis, has at one end the imaginary construction of the self (*moi*); the opposite end that of the *other*, the entity through whom the self establishes itself as a coherent (be it illusory), whole being. Lacan's more dynamic models of Schema L appear as the "graphs of desire" and Schema R (1977; see also Milovanovic's expose, 1992a; on Schema R, see Milovanovic, 1994a).

The modernist's view of the subject often centers on the idea that desire emerges from "lack," and is predicated on the need for keeping desire in check—its free-flowing expression being said to be inherently subversive or disruptive in ongoing social activity. The postmodernists add that the desiring subject is imprisoned within restrictive discourses; at one extreme in *discourses of the master*, where subjects enact key master signifiers producing and reproducing the dominant order; at the other, in the *discourses of the hysteric*, where despairing subjects find no adequate signifiers with which to embody their desire (Lacan, 1991a; Bracher, 1988, 1993; Milovanovic, 1993a, 1993b). Oppressive discursive structures interpellate subjects as supports of system needs (Althusser, 1971; see also Silverman's analysis of the manipulative media effects, 1983). In either case hegemony is easily sustained.

Postmodernists offer both a more passive and a more active form of disruptions. In the more passive form, we have the notion of disruptive voices, such as in the notion of *délire*, a disruptive language of the body (Lecercle, 1985, 1990); or in *minor literature* and the *rhizome* (Deleuze and Guattari, 1986, 1987); or in the notion of *noise* or the *parasite* (Serres, 1982a: 65-70; Hayles, 1990: 197-208); or in the nonlinear discursive disruptions of the *enthymeme* that intrudes on any linear discursive constructions (Knoespel, 1985); or, finally, in Lacan's notion of an alternative form of *jouissance*, a jouissance of the body, a view that initiated much debate over the desirability of an *écriture féminine* (Lacan, 1985: 145). In the more active form, postmodernists offer a dialogically based pedagogy whereby the cultural revolutionary or revolutionary subject enters a dialogical encounter with the oppressed in coproducing key master signifiers and replacement discourses that more accurately reflect the given repressive order (see Lacan's discourse of the analyst in combination with the discourse of the hysteric, Milovanovic, 1993a; see also Freire, 1985; McLaren 1994a; Aronowitz and Giroux, 1985).

For postmodernists, desire can "be conceived as a forward movement, a flight towards an object which always eludes our grasp, the attempt, never successful but never frustrating, to reach the unattainable by exploring the paths of the possible" (Lecercle, 1985: 196). Here desire, contrary to merely responding to lack and being a negative, conservative force, is seen as equated with positive processes (Dews, 1987: 132, 135-6), a will to power, defined as "the principle of the synthesis of forces" (Deleuze, 1983: 50). Nietzsche, not Hegel, is the key figure. Deleuze and Guattari's notion of the *rhizome* brings out the nonlinear paths taken by desire seeking expression at each level of semiotic production (Milovanovic, 1992a: 125-33).

For postmodernists, desire is liberating, joyous, ironic, playful, and a positive force. Ultimately, the "hero" (or Nietzsche's *overman* as opposed to the *common man* [woman]), must avow her/his desire and act in conformity with it (Lacan, 1992: 309, 319-21; Lacan, 1977: 275; Lee, 1990: 95-9, 168-70; Rajchman, 1991: 42-3).

4. DISCOURSE

Key Concepts:
Modernist: instrumental; uniaccentual; global; neutral; dominant; master/university discourse; primacy to paradigm/syntagm; major literature; readerly text; production/reproduction; referential signifier and text;

privileging of master signifiers and "natural" categories; privileging noun forms.

Postmodernist: multiaccentual; fractal signifiers; regime of signs; discourse of the hysteric/analyst; linguistic coordinate systems; discursive formations; borromean knots; capitonnage; symptoms; *objet petit (a)*; primacy to the semiotic axes — metaphor/metonymy, condensation/displacement; minor literature; writerly text; nonreferential text; hyperreal; cyberspace; verb forms.

Commentary:

a. Modernist Thought. The Modernist paradigm assumes that discourse is neutral; it is but an instrument for use to express rationally developed projects of an inherently centered subject. In fact, some transcendental signifiers exist at the center of social structure and phenomena that are discoverable. Assumed, most often, is an ongoing dominant discourse that is seen as adequate for providing the medium for expression, whether for dominant or subordinate groups.

The couplet, the signifier (the word), and the signified (that which it expresses) are said to stabilize and crystallize in conventional understandings (uniaccentuality). Signifiers are more often said to be referential: they point to something outside themselves, to some "concrete" reality (naturalism). Modernists are more likely to assume these natural categories rather than treating them as semiotically variable concepts (the Sapir-Whorf linguistic relativity principle anticipated many of the insights of postmodernist analysis). Modernist discourse celebrates the noun rather than the verb forms (Bohm, 1980). It is much more likely to make use of master signifiers such as prediction, falsification, replication, generalization, operationalization, objectivity, value freedom, etc.; these are "givens" in investigations (Young, 1994).

Modernists are more likely to focus on the most conscious level of semiotic production. Consciously constructed discourses are coordinated by two axes: the paradigmatic axis, which is a vertical structure, if you will, that provides word choices, a dictionary of sorts. The horizontal axis, the syntagmatic axis, stands for the grammatical and linear placement of signifiers. The two axes work together to produce meaning. Debates that do question the nature of dominant discourses often are centered on the differences between an oppressive master discourse versus an ostensibly liberating discourse of the university (on the nature of the four main discourses—master, university, hysteric, and analyst, see Lacan, 1991a; Bracher, 1988, 1993; Milovanovic, 1993a). The evolution of history, for the modernist thinker, is often seen as the progressive victory of the discourse of the university over the discourse of the master.

Discursive production, in modernist thought, is much more likely to produce the *readerly text* (Barthes, 1974; Silverman, 1982) and *major literature* (Deleuze and Guattari, 1986). This text is a linear reading (or viewing) with the organizing principle of noncontradiction. Its goal is closure. Its effect is the production and reproduction of conventionality. Interpreters and viewers are encouraged to assume conventional discursive subject-positions and fill in the gaps by use of dominant symbolic forms.

b. Postmodernist Thought. Postmodernist thought does not assume a neutral discourse. There are many discourses reflective of local sites of production, each, in turn, existing with a potential for the embodiment of desire in signifiers and for the constructions of realities. The sign, composed of signifier and signified, finds its natural state as being in flux. The signified is multiaccentual, the site of diverse struggles (Volosinov, 1986). The paradigm-syntagm semiotic axis is only the most manifest level of semiotic production, the most conscious. Two other levels have been identified and work at the unconscious level: the condensation-displacement semiotic axis, and the metaphoric-metonymic semiotic axis (Milovanovic, 1992b, 1993b).

Desire, it is argued, begins at a deeper level of the psychic apparatus and undergoes embodiment—for Freud, "figuration"; for Lacan, essentially "fantasy," $ \$ \lozenge a $ —by the contributory work ("overdetermination") of these two axes—they are the coordinating mechanisms which provide temporary anchorings to the floating signifiers found in the Other, the sphere of the unconscious—, finally reaching the level of a particular historically rooted and stabilized discourse or linguistic coordinate system. It is here where final embodiment must be completed in the paradigm-syntagm semiotic axis (i.e., a particular word or utterance is vocalized). It was Freud who began this analysis with his investigation of *dream work* as the "royal road to the unconscious." It was Lacan who added the metaphoric-metonymic semiotic axis. Much of the investigation of the effects of language by modernists is focused merely on the surface structure of paradigm-syntagm (in law, for example, see Greimas, 1990; Jackson, 1988; Landowski, 1991).

Postmodernists identify the *violence of language* (Lecercle, 1985, 1990). Linguistic repression and alienation are the results of historically situated hegemonic discourses (see also the notion of the *regime of signs* of Deleuze and Guattari, 1987, and their notion of *minor* versus *major literature* 1986; see also Foucault's notion of discursive formations and the *epistemes* 1973; Milovanovic's notion of *linguistic coordinate systems* 1992a, 1992b; Pecheux's notion of discursive formations, 1982).

Critically, as we have previously said (1992a), Lacan has offered four intersubjectively structured discourses (1991a; Bracher, 1988, 1993; Milovanovic, 1993a; Arrigo, 1993a, 1993b). Desire, it is argued, has various forms of embodiment in these structured discourses. Different discourses may, on the one hand, be manipulative and repressive in the expression of desire; and, on the other, offer greater possibilities of expression to these same desires.

Postmodernists would celebrate the *writerly text* (Barthes, 1974; Silverman, 1982). This text is seen as being more subversive than a readerly text. Encouraged in the viewer/interpreter is "an infinite play of signification; in it there can be no transcendental signified, only provisional ones which function in turn as signifiers" (Silverman, 1982: 246). For the writerly form, deconstruction of the text is celebrated with the purpose of uncovering hidden or repressed voices (consider feminist's celebration of investigating "her/story" rather than history). This strategy, the postmodernists would say, is particularly important in a contemporary society characterized as producing the nonreferential and autonomous *hyperreal* (Baudrillard, 1981), and the new order of *cyberspace* (Gibson, 1984).

Similarly, Deleuze and Guattari (1986) have offered the idea of *minor literature,* which tends toward a deterritorialization, manifest in the carnivalesque genre or other forms expressive of *délire* (Lecercle, 1985), such as in the writings of E.E.Cummings, Franz Kafka, and James Joyce. In this spirit, David Bohm (1980) has advocated the privileging and the further development of the verb over the noun form; this would allow us to transcend the limiting metaphysics and metanarratives embedded in subject-verb-object discursive forms (consider, too, Benjamin Whorf's investigations of the Hopi language, 1956).

5. KNOWLEDGE

Key Concepts:
Modernist: global; dominant; discourse of the master and university; grand narrative; totalizing; binary (as in law); logos; education as liberating; Truth; privileging scientific knowledge; absolute postulates; axiomizability; deductive logic; banking education; closure.
Postmodernist: local; repressed voices; constitutive processes; metanarratives; power/knowledge; fragmented; contingent and provisional truths; Pathos; discourse of hysteric and analyst; knowledge for sale; education as ideology and functional; narrative knowledge; noise, the parasite; enthymemes; the rhizome; *délire*; incompleteness; undecidability; dialogic pedagogy; abduction.

Commentary:
a. Modernist Thought. Enlightenment thought tended toward a totalizing Truth centered on an ostensibly discoverable logos. Driven by formal rational methods, one inevitably dominant and globalizing thought would result.

Lyotard, for example, has explained how *scientific knowledge* has usurped *narrative knowledge* (1984; see also Sarup, 1989: 120-1; Hayles, 1990: 209-10; see also Habermas' point concerning the establishment of new *steering mechanisms* based on power and money that fuel *purposive rational action*, 1987). Narrative knowledge, on the other hand, is based on myth, legend, tales, stories, etc., which provided the wherewithal of being in society (see also Habermas' idea of communicative or symbolic communication, 1987). Whereas scientific knowledge tends toward closure, narrative knowledge embraces imaginary free play.

Lacan has provided the mechanism for the production of knowledge and the reconstitution of Truths in his analysis of the *discourses of the master and university*. For the former, knowledge and ideology are embedded in dominant discourse. Since this discourse is the one which is seen as relevant and since subjects must situate themselves within it, they too are subject to its interpellative effects (Althusser, 1971; Milovanovic, 1988a). Thus conventional knowledge is more likely to be reconstituted by way of the *readerly text*, *major literature*, or the *discourse of the master and university*.

The search for Truth by the modernists was inevitably guided by the ideal of establishing Absolute Postulates from which all other "facts" can be explained by linear, deductive logic. Efficiency and competency in the educative process are geared toward a *banking education* whereby conventional master signifiers or their derivatives are stored to be capitalized (Freire, 1985).

b. Postmodernist Thought. Postmodernists, on the other hand, view knowledge as always fragmented, partial, and contingent (see also, Sarup, 1989; Dews, 1987; Lyotard, 1984). It always has multiple sites of production (Geertz, 1983). It is derived from a dialogic pedagogy where novel signifiers are coproduced in the process of critique and the development of a *language of possibility* (Freire, 1985). It is more likely to reflect Pathos, human suffering, than Logos. Since there are many truths and no over-encompassing Truth is possible (following Godel's undecidability theorem, 1962), knowledge defies closure or being stored passively as in a banking education. In fact, following chaos' idea of iteration, the unpredictable and unanticipated are likely to continuously appear.

Postmodernists celebrate local knowledge. Dominant and global knowledge always subverts voices that otherwise seek expression, either directly or indirectly; by the demand that all desire must be embodied within dominant concepts, signifiers, and linguistic coordinate systems, or by way of translation (intertextuality) from their more unique concrete form into abstract categories of law and bureaucracy. Postmodernists, however, view local knowledge(s) as not necessarily subsumable under one grand narrative or logic (Godel's theorem).

Postmodernists view subjects within a social formation as thwarted in their attempts to be true to their desires. Even so, "space" does exist for possible articulation of desire. The destabilizing effects of *noise*, the *parasite*, the work of the *rhizome*, *minor literatures*, the nonlinear disruptions of *enthymemes*, and the subversive *writerly* text always threaten dominant forms of knowledge. Denied subjects may be oppositional, as in the discourse of the hysteric; or revolutionary, as in the discourse of the analyst/hysteric (Milovanovic, 1993a, 1993b).

For postmodernists, knowledge is always both relational and positional (Kerruish, 1991). Accordingly, standpoints are always situated in social relations and within ideologies (p. 187). Power and knowledge are intricately connected and hierarchically arranged (see Dew's useful discussion of Foucault, Nietzsche, Lyotard, 1987). To enter a discursive formation (legal, medical, scientific, political, etc.) is to enter the logic and rationality embedded within it (Foucault, 1973; Pitkin, 1971); thus, truth is discourse-specific.

Feminist postmodernist analysis has been poignant as to the explanation of the construction of the phallic Symbolic order, gender roles, and possible alternative knowledges (see especially Cornell, 1991, 1993; Brennan, 1993). Investigations on the contribution of the imaginary sphere and its possible impact on reconstructing myths have been illuminating (Arrigo, 1993b, 1993c). Constitutive theory has also offered the notion of replacement discourses (Henry and Milovanovic, 1991; Milovanovic, 1993a, 1993b). This new knowledge is based on contingent and provisional truths, subject to further reflection and historicity.

The notion of *abduction* offered by Charles S. Peirce is more accurately reflective of the postmodernist epistemology than deductive logic. Here, Absolute Postulates or major premises never achieve stability; rather, creative free play guides the formulation of tentative propositions. As Nancy Fraser and Linda Nicholson have said, postmodernist critique:

> floats free of any universalist theoretical ground. No longer anchored philosophically, the very shape or character of social criticism changes; it becomes more pragmatic, ad hoc, contextual, and local...[t]here are no special tribunals set apart from the sites where inquiry is practiced, [but only] ... the plural, local, and immanent (cited in Bartlett and Kennedy, 1991b: 388).

6. SPACE/TIME

Key Concepts:
Modernist: three-dimensional space; integral; homogeneous; striated space; Newtonian mechanics; Euclidean geometry; Cartesian coordinates; quantitative; differential equations and continuities; reversibility of time.
Postmodernist: multidimensional; smooth; fractal; imaginary; quantum mechanics/relativity; implicate (enfolded) order; non-Euclidean geometry; holographic; topology theory; qualitative; twister space (imaginary); cyberspace; nonlinear; nonreversible time.

Commentary:
a. Modernist Thought. Modernist thought rests on Newtonian mechanics. This classical view in physics rests on notions of absolute space and time. This in turn is connected with the existence of determinism within systems: if we know the positions, masses, and velocities of a particle at one time we can accurately determine their positions and velocities at all later times (Bohm, 1980: 121).

Newtonian physics and Euclidean geometry, with its use of Cartesian coordinates, is the map or blueprint of space on which modernists construct the social world. It is what Deleuze and Guattari refer to as *striated space* (1987: 488): it consists of space with whole-number dimensions where constant direction can be describable and end-states predictable. Drawing from Descartes' coordinate grid of an x-axis perpendicularly intersecting with a y-axis, a point could be located anywhere in two-dimensional space (similarly with 3-D space, with an added z-axis). Thus the equation, $y = 3x$, can be identified on this graph. At one stroke geometry and algebra are linked. And Newton refined this further with his calculus with its differential equations. Now a continuous change in one variable can be shown to produce a calculable change in the other. And just as time flows forward, it can flow backward in a predictable way: the romantic past, the "good old days," can be re-created.

This model has been incorporated in the social sciences. A person's life course, for example, could be plotted with precision if we could discover appropriate determinants. This is the basis of positivism. It is by a *striated space* (Deleuze and Guattari, 1987) that science progresses and by which desire can be territorialized on the body (1986) by a political economy. But striated space needs its discrete variables with whole-number dimensions.

b. Postmodernist Thought. Postmodernists see things differently. Quantum mechanics, non-Euclidean geometry, string theory, twister space, topology theory, and chaos theory, to name a few of the most prominent approaches, have offered alternative conceptions. The question of a dimension and prediction becomes problematic.

Nuclear physicists, for example, faced with trying to reconcile general relativity theory with quantum mechanics, have come up with infinities. By adding space dimensions to their equations, these begin to drop out of the equation. At 10-D in one model and 26-D in another, they disappear (Peat, 1988; Kaku, 1994). The 3-D model we see is perhaps just an explicate order with the rest of the dimensions rolled up tightly (compactified). This compactified order is the *enfolded* or *implicate order* (Bohm, 1980), said to have its origins moments after the Big Bang.

Chaos theory has developed the idea of *fractal* dimensions. Rather than having whole dimensions we can refer to a space with 1½ dimensions, 1¾, etc. (A point has a dimension of zero, a line a dimension of one; a plane, two; a volume, three.) A coastline, for example, can have a fractal dimension between one and two. So, for example, contrary to the Boolean logic of doctrinal legal analysis, truths are always fractal in form. Deleuze and Guattari have developed the idea of a *smooth space,* which is continuous, not discrete. The notion of fractals is in accord with smooth space (1987), and, as we shall show below, fields. It is within smooth space that becoming occurs; but progress and conventional science is done in striated space (p. 486; see also Bergson, 1958; Serres, 1982a, 1982b).

Yet others, such as the noted mathematician Penrose, have constructed a view of space in terms of imaginary numbers, a *twister space* (Peat, 1988: Chapter 8; Penrose, 1989: 87-98). Chaos theorists, such as Mandelbrot, made use of complex numbers in the form of $z = x + iy$, where i is an imaginary number (the square root of -1). By further plotting $z = z^2 + c$ and by taking the result and reiterating by the use of the same formula, they were to find enormously complex and esthetically appealing figures (see Penrose, 1989: 92-4). Yet others have relied on the hologram to indicate how inscriptions of phenomena are encoded and how they can be revealed with their multidimensional splendor (Bohm, 1980: 150; Pribram, 1977). Finally, we note the field of topology, the qualitative math which offers alternative ways of conceptualizing phenomena without the use of math. Here, in what is often called the "rubber math," figures are twisted, pulled, and reshaped in various ways. Breaking and gluing are not legitimate operations. Breaking produces entirely new forms. Much current thinking in nuclear- and astrophysics relies on topology theory (Peat, 1988; Kaku, 1994).

Lacan has made use of topology to explain such things as the structure of the psychic apparatus by using borromean knots, Mobius bands, the torus, and projective geometry (the cross-cap) (see also Milovanovic, 1993b, 1994c; Granon-Lafont, 1985, 1990; Vappereau, 1988; for an introduction to topology theory, see Hilbert and Cohn-Vossen, 1952; Weeks, 1985; for non-Euclidean geometry, see Russell, 1956). In fact, in 4-D space the borromean knot of Lacan is no longer knotted. The cross-cap, which topologically portrays the working of schema R and how desire is embodied as a result of the effects of the Symbolic, Imaginary, and Real Orders, can also be presented in 3-D or 4-D space (Milovanovic, 1994c; Hilbert and Cohn-Vossen, 1952). It is not without effect when we move from 3-D to 4-D space (Rucker, 1984; Banchoff, 1990; for the contributions of non-Euclidean geometry and 4-D space on cubism in art, see Henderson, 1983). Much needs to be done in the analysis of the effects of these novel conceptions.

Thus, for the postmodernists, several notions of space are currently being explored and incorporated in their analysis of the subject, discourse, causality, and society: multiple dimensional (Peat, 1988), fractal (Mandelbrot, 1983), holographic (Talbot, 1991; Bohm, 1980: Pribram, 1977), enfolded/implicate order (Bohm, 1980; Bohm and Peat, 1987), cyberspace (Gibson, 1984), hyperreal (Baudrillard, 1981), smooth space (Deleuze and Guattari, 1987), twister space (Penrose, 1989; see also Peat, 1988), and topological (Lacan, 1976, 1987a; Peat, 1988; Granon-Lafont, 1985, 1990; Vappereau, 1988; Milovanovic, 1993b, 1994c; Lem, 1984). T.R. Young has been succinct in indicating the relevance of these notions in that an alternative space is open for the development of conceptions of "human agency in ways not possible in those dynamics privileged by Newtonian physics, Aristotelian logic, Euclidean geometry and the linear causality they presume" (1992: 447). And there can be no return to the nostalgic "good old days": time is irreversible; since initial conditions are undecidable, then, with the passage of time and iteration, there can be no return to some decidable state.

7. CAUSALITY

Key Concepts:
Modernist: linear; proportional effects; positivism; determinism; classical physics; I. Newton; "God does not play dice"; certainty; grand theorizing; predictability; future fixed by past; particle effects.
Postmodernist: nonlinear; disproportional effects; genealogy; rhizome; chance; contingency; quantum mechanics; uncertainty; iteration; catastrophe theory; paradoxical; discontinuities; singularities; field effects.

Commentary:
a. Modernist Thought. Modernist thought rests on the determinism of Newtonian physics. It appears most often in the form of positivism. Modernist thought would assume that given some incremental increase in some identified cause or determinant, a proportional and linear increase in the effect will result. The basic unit of analysis is particles (i.e., assumed autonomous

individuals, social "elements," and discrete categories) and their contributory effects. The use of cartesian coordinates, whole-number dimensions, calculus, etc., in a few words, striated space, is what makes possible a highly predictive mathematics. Even Einstein refused to accept much of quantum mechanics that came after him, particularly the notion that God plays dice.

b. Postmodernist Thought. Postmodernists see things differently. Chaos theory, Godel's theorem, and quantum mechanics stipulate that proportional effects do not necessarily follow some incremental increase of an input variable. Uncertainty, indeterminacy, and disproportional (nonlinear) effects are all underlying assumptions and worthy of inquiry in explaining an event (genealogy). In the extreme, a butterfly flapping its wings in East Asia produces a hurricane in Warren, Ohio. Key thinkers here are Edward Lorenz, Benoit Mandelbrot, and Stephen Smale (see the excellent overview by Gleick, 1987; Briggs and Peat, 1989). In fact, in the extreme, something can emerge out of nothing at points identified as *singularities*; this is the sphere of order arising out of disorder.

Two current approaches within chaos theory are making their impact: one, focused more on order that exists in an otherwise apparently disorderly state of affairs (Hayles, 1991: 12; see Feigenbaum, 1980; Shaw, 1981); the second, focused more on how, in fact, order arises out of chaotic systems— order out of disorder or self-organization (Hayles, 1991: 12; 1990: 1-28; see also Prigogine and Stengers, 1984; Thom, 1975). A growing number of applications is taking place. See particularly Unger's application in his prescription for an empowered democracy (1987).

The notion of iteration is a central concept of postmodernism. Simply, it means recomputing with answers obtained from some formula. Continuous feedback and iteration produces disproportional (not linear) effects. Derrida has applied it to how words obtain new meaning in new contexts (1976; see also Balkan, 1987); in law, for example, the "original intent" of the "founding fathers" undergoes modification over time and can not be reconstructed. The point being made is that because of minute initial uncertainties—however small, consider Godel's theorem—, when iteration proceeds these are amplified, producing indeterminacies (Hayles, 1990: 183; Lyotard, 1984: 55). Thus, rather than celebrating global theory, chaos theorists and postmodernists look to local knowledges, where small changes can produce large effects (Hayles, 1990: 211). In other words, postmodernists see otherwise small contributions as having profound possibilities. Yes, one "small" person's actions can make a difference! One person's involvement in a demonstration, petition signature, act of civil disobedience, or "speaking up," can, in the long run, have greater effects than anticipated.

Causation can be attributed to field rather than particle effects (Bohm, 1980; Bohm and Peat, 1987). Borrowing from Bohm's insights concerning the *quantum potential* and the *enfolded order* where all is interconnected, rather than focusing, as the modernists do, on particles, points and point events, all of which are narrowly spatiotemporally defined (analogously, consider the subject in traditional positivistic sciences: an object, located socioeconomically, who has engaged in some act at a particular time and place), the unit of analysis, for postmodernists, should be a field with its moments, duration, intensities, flows, displacements of libidinal energy. Moments, unlike point events, have fluctuating time-space coordinates that defy precise measurement (Bohm, 1980: 207). Within this field, heterogeneous intensities can affect movement, even if they are not immediately discernible or linear and/or local. Nonlinear and nonlocal factors, therefore, even at a distance, can have a noticeable effect (Bohm and Peat, 1987: 88-93, 182-3). Research awaits in drawing out the implications of moving from 3-D to 4-D space, i.e., what is knotted in the former becomes unknotted in the latter (Rucker, 1984; Kaku, 1994; consider Lacan's borromean knot in 4-D space, as discussed in Milovanovic, 1993b).

In the postmodern view, certainties that do appear are often the creation of subjects: Nietzsche has shown, for example, how a subject in need of "horizons" finds *semiotic fictions* that produce the appearance of a centered subject; Peirce, anticipating chaos, has shown how free will is often created after the event as the "facts" are rearranged to fit a deterministic model and individual authorship (1923: 47); legal realists, in the early part of this century, have shown that what creates order in legal decision-making is not syllogistic reasoning and a formally rational legal systems, but *ex post facto* constructions; and so forth. For postmodernists, especially Nietzsche and Foucault, it is the "fear of the chaotic and the unclassifiable" (Dews, 1987: 186) that accounts for the order we attribute to nature.

8. Social Change

Key Concepts:

Modernist: evolutionary; Darwinian; rationalization; linear; Absolute Spirit; dialectical materialism; praxis; Hegel; reaction and negation; reversal of hierarchies; reduction of complexity; stable premises for action; history as progress; variation, selection, and transmission; oppositional subject; discourse of the hysteric.

Postmodernist: genealogy; transpraxis; standpoint epistemology(ies); Pure Play/musement; rhizome; disidentification; play of the imaginary; dialectics of struggle; affirmative action; deconstruction and reconstruction; proliferation of complexity; premises of action based on tolerability; overcoming panopticism;

dépensé, mimeses; multiplicities of resistance to power; assuming one's desire; dialogism; conscientization, language of possibility; revolutionary subject; discourse of the hysteric/analyst.

Commentary:
a. Modernist Thought. Modernist thought often sees change in terms of evolutionary theory, in various versions of Darwinian dynamics, particularly in terms of some "invisible hand" at work, or some working out of a logic, as in the Absolute Spirit of Hegel, or in forces of rationalization as in Weber, or in dialectical materialism as in Marx. What often underlies these approaches is some linear conception of historical change. Perhaps praxis is the upper limit of modernist thought.

In the most liberal modernist view, Hegel's master-slave dialectic is a key parable of change. It is premised on reaction-negation dynamics. The slave (the oppressed) only creates value by a double negation. Nothing new is offered. The limits of an alternative vision remain tied to the initial logic of the major premise of the master-slave dialectic that falls on the side of the master. At best we have the oppositional subject who finds her/himself in the discourse of the hysteric, sometimes slipping into nihilistic and fatalist stances — in neither case offering anything new; at worst, a subject that inadvertently recreates the dominant repressive order (hegemony).

Modernist thought that often takes the form of evolutionary theory of change attempts to account for three phenomena: variation, selection, and transmission (Sinclair, 1992: 95; Luhmann, 1985: 249; see also Sinclair's critique of evolutionary theory of law, 1987). Luhmann's analysis is instructive. He tells us that the continuous differentiation of society tends to produce an *excess of possibilities* (1985: 237; see also Manning's application to police bureaucracies and how diverse voices are channeled into "relevant" categories, 1988). Given this creation of excesses, law, Luhmann claims, functions to reduce complexity so that subjects may plan within certain discernible horizons which, in turn, produce predictability in social planning. Social change is therefore a linear affair with continuous adjustments of social institutions to continuous processes of differentiation.

b. Postmodernist Thought. Postmodernist thought focuses more on nonlinear conceptions of historical change, genealogical analysis, and transpraxis, a materialistically based politics that includes a language of critique and possibility (Freire, 1985; McLaren, 1994a; Aronowitz and Giroux, 1985). Postmodernists are in general agreement that, in studying historical change, much room must be made for the contributions of contingency, irony, the spontaneous, and the marginal. Nietzsche, once again, is the dominant thinker (1980; see also Love, 1986; Deleuze, 1983).

Nietzsche's version of the master-slave dialectic is key for postmodernists. Here, rather than reaction-negation dynamics as in Hegel, an inherently conservative approach, Nietzsche's position advocates active change. This includes deconstruction and reconstruction as inseparable elements. This has been captured by the idea of a transpraxis rather than a praxis (Henry and Milovanovic, 1991, 1993b; Milovanovic, 1993b).

Most prominent in recent days are feminist postmodernist theorists who have built on various versions of Lacanian psychoanalytic semiotics as well as those who have developed a standpoint theory aided especially by numerous productive critiques. Accordingly, Cornell has identified the contributions of the imaginary and the rethinking of the myth (1991, 1993; Cixous, 1986; Arrigo, 1993a); Cornell (1991: 147) and Grant (1993: 116) have noted that given ideologies "leave some critical space" or "slippage" (in this context Peirce's notion of *musement* or *pure play* is also relevant [1934: 313-16]); Kristeva has focused on the idea that semiotic processes that are situated in the form of the *readerly text* of Barthes are faced with semiotic overflow at privileged moments specified as the subversive triad: "madness, holiness and poetry" (cited in Grosz, 1990: 153); Pecheux has focused on the notion of dis-identification (1982); Irigaray on *mimeses* (1985; see also Cornell's commentary, 1991: 147-50); Lacan on the discourse of the analyst (1991a; see also Bracher, 1993); Milovanovic on the revolutionary subject (composite of the hysteric and analyst, 1993a) and on knot-breaking (1993b).

Some current trends in postmodernist analysis draw out the implications for social change from Freire (1985), whose work lies between modernist and postmodernist analysis. The wherewithal of the revolutionary subject and social change may be fruitfully situated in the integration of Lacan's work on the discourse of the hysteric/analyst with Freire's notion of *conscientization* rooted in social struggles over signification. In this integration, structure and subjectivity, material conditions and ideology, the macro and the microsociological, critique and visions for change, undecidability and decidability, can be reconciled. The signifier can be rooted in the concrete, historical arena of struggles; it can attain provisional decidability and a *contingent universality* in producing utopian visions of what could be, and contribute, by way of a dialogic pedagogy, to the subject-in-process (generally, see, McLaren, 1994a; Ebert, 1991a; Zavarzadeh and Morton, 1990; Butler, 1992).

Postmodernists, too, are concerned with the possible negative and unintended effects of struggles against oppression and hierarchy. Reaction-negation dynamics may at times lead to what Nietzsche referred to as *ressentiment* as well as to new master discourses, forms of political correctness, exorcism (Milovanovic, 1991b), and dogma. Transpraxis, however, has as a central element the privileging of reflexivity of thought and the specification of contingent and provisional foundational political positions for social change (i.e., contingent universalities can become the basis for political alliances and agendas for change, McLaren, 1994a).

Among ethical principles that may come into play, for the postmodernists, perhaps Lacan's idea of "assuming one's desire" will become a key one. Faced with the passivity of the *common man* (woman), Lacan advocates that the *hero* is the one who does not betray her/his desire; meaning, s/he will act in conformity with it and not embrace the offerings of manipulative powers that offer an abundance of substitute materials, or what Lacan referred to as *objets petit(a)* (Lacan, 1992: 309, 319-21; Lacan, 1977: 275; Lee, 1990: 95-9, 168-70; Rajchman, 1991: 42-3). Here, the productive use of desire is advocated, not one based on lack, tension-reduction, and stasis. Thus a sociopolitical system that maximizes the opportunities for avowing one's desire is a good one; conversely, hierarchical systems, whether under the name of capitalism or socialism, that systematically disavow subjects' desire, are bad ones. Elsewhere, a postmodernist definition of crime/harm has been offered based on harm inflicted (Henry and Milovanovic, 1993a).

Postmodernists faced with the question of variation, selection, and transmission, opt for the development of the greatest variation, the most expansive form of retaining local sites of production, and the most optimal mechanisms for transmission. Accordingly, faced with an increasingly differentiating society with "excesses in possibilities," and the modernist's call for ways of reducing complexity—the most extreme form being in pastiche (Jameson, 1984; Sarup, 1989: 133, 145), an imitation of dead styles as models for action—, the central challenge of the postmodernist alternative is to create new cultural styles that privilege chance, spontaneity, irony, intensity, etc., while still providing some dissipative horizons within which the subject may situate her/himself.

CONCLUSION

This essay has presented some of the salient differences between modernist and postmodernist thought. Contrary to modernist critics, a new paradigm is upon us. And it is neither fatalistic nor nihilistic; nor is it without visions of what could be. We were especially concerned with the possibilities of a new transpraxis and the development of replacement discourses. It might be argued that the postmodernist paradigm may take on the form of a *normal science* and tend toward closure. But, unlike the modernist enterprise, there are intrinsic forces that militate against closure and stasis.

The Decentered Subject in Law
Contributions of Topology, Psychoanalytic Semiotics, and Chaos Theory

INTRODUCTION

Consider the everyday reality of decaying slums, polluted air, violence in the streets, dysfunctional families, exploitive workplaces, manifest gender and race discrimination, and the brutalizing machinery of the criminal-justice apparatus. Oppose these to the exotic fauna and flora that is provided by the postmodern epistemology. Could this new excursion into the postmodern produce an epistemological break from conventional paradigms in the social sciences, particularly in the sociology of law? Or is it a fad, a bottling of old wine in new containers? This article represents a foray into the realm of the imaginary. We shall see very quickly that epistemological breaks necessitate a new vocabulary and a centering in a new discourse. A constitutive perspective in law is especially well-suited for assimilating many of the ideas of postmodernist's key scion, Jacques Lacan.

In a recent exchange between Joel Handler and his critics in *Law and Society Review* (Vol. 26, No. 4, 1992), much discussion centered on the transformative potentials of postmodernist thought. Our focus is in developing some of the key concepts behind a critically informed psychoanalytic semiotics that may indeed be the basis for theorizing a potential replacement discourse. Contrary to Handler, and more in agreement with Winter (1992: 792), we stress that all too often sympathetic leftists are quick to assimilate postmodernist thought to traditional categories, which become the basis of critique. This misses entirely the point of postmodernism. The more compelling task before us is to engage the key theoretical developments offered by postmodern thought on its own terms (see also McCann, 1992: 734). The debates in *Law and Society Review* nowhere, for example, cited Lacan's work and its impact on the development of postmodernist thought, even though many of the key contemporary thinkers within this field (i.e., Deleuze, Guattari, Foucault, Kristeva, Irigaray, Lyotard, Derrida, Baudrillard, and many others), the first wave if you will, had attended the Seminars offered by him in the 1950s, 60s, and 70s, and/or drew directly or indirectly from them. The second wave of inspired postmodernists were to focus heavily on these French intellectuals.

Our approach here is to first come to terms with the incredibly far-ranging and insightful notions offered by Lacan as to the desiring subject in relation to language (topology theory will be seen as an essential element for exposition and for discovery), then to indicate how some of their categories are useful in examining issues in law (i.e., images and words that are said to "cause" violence), and finally to offer some thoughts as to the potential contribution to the development of a replacement discourse(s) and an emancipatory transformative politics (feminist *standpoint epistemology* will be seen as an especially fruitful beginning and the notion of "contingent universalities" as overcoming some of its limitations). We first want to situate our approach via the Handler debate begun in *Law and Society Review*.

POSTMODERNISM AND TRANSFORMATIVE POLITICS

Handler has done a great service in bringing attention to postmodernism and its relation to transformative politics. He, however, in presenting a *Reader's Digest* form of postmodernism, has done a disservice to its central ideas.

Handler tells us that: (1) the new social movements (i.e., feminist, gay and lesbian, environmental, antinuclear, peace) have emerged in the last twenty years and demand careful nondogmatic analysis and prescriptions based on it; (2) the two central ideas of a postmodernist epistemology concern the notion of the decentered subject and the need to reconceptualize the notion of hegemony; (3) absent a foundational position such concepts as deconstruction render progressive change impossible; and (4) postmodernism has not come up with an alternative vision of community, polity, and the economy. We agree with the first (see Laclau and Mouffe's clear analysis as to the new social movements, 1985), profoundly disagree with his analysis concerning the next two, and only partly agree with point four.

Let us briefly deal with the question of the decentered subject and its relation to hegemony. We will have more to say in the sections below. Handler has misunderstood the relationship between the desiring subject and discourse. He tells us "...discourse theory is not really theory. Rather, it is a method or process for raising questions and criticizing the presumptions of theory" (1992: 723). It is this and much, much more. Handler's position already assumes a transcendental, centered subject. He does not see the intimate connection between discourse and the desiring subject. We cannot separate the subject from the discourse in which s/he finds herself. Much follows this insight.

As to point three, Handler's position, as Winter (1992) quite correctly points out, is imprisoned in the logic of the 1960s form of opposition. However, Winter comes perilously close in falling into the same trap when he tells us that "[t]here is no better foundation for our values than our own actions" (1992: 807). Action is constituted by desire, values, ethics, logic, visions, and a form of rationality. But all these are embodied and embedded in discourse. In fact, language has a strong performative dimension that therefore militates against any clean separation of action from discourse. We shall see, for example, that cognitive framing activities—fantasies, according to Lacan—are indeed action-in-process. Lacan's definition of the subject as the "speaking being" (*l'être parlant* or *parlêtre*), therefore seems quite appropriate. A desiring subject frames her visions within a discourse, be it an oppositional one. At play are the interactive effects of imaginary and symbolic structures immersed within a changing sociohistorical political economy (the basis of primordial sense data and part of the unverbalized Real Order of Lacan). Without an understanding of the nature of the relationship of the subject to discourse, one cannot accurately describe hegemony nor develop prescriptive visions for change. Elsewhere, for example, we have indicated how certain groups inadvertently participate in hegemonic constructions and reconstructions (i.e., "jailhouse lawyers," Milovanovic and Thomas, 1989; Milovanovic, 1988a; "activist lawyers," Bannister and Milovanovic, 1990; criminologists, Henry and Milovanovic, 1991; see also Part 2 of this book). We need not only change material conditions of existence but also the structure of discourse itself (elsewhere, for example, we have argued that Lacan's *discourse of the master* and *university* often support hegemony and that a synthetic *discourse of the analyst/hysteric* need to be engendered, 1991a; 1993b).

Handler's fourth point, that the new Left that has relied on postmodernist thought has failed to come up with progressive visions of polity, economy, and community, is at best only partly correct. Handler assumes that transformations take place linearly and abruptly. McCann quite correctly indicates that progressive politics already has had some successes and that perhaps "analysts should study, or at least speculate about, whether specific episodes of resistance have been (or might be) *contained* or *magnified* into more defiant actions involving greater numbers of fellow citizens" (1992: 744-5). McCann's position indicates that struggle is ongoing, reflexive, critical, and nonlinear. Many within the new social movements are naively embracing pop versions of postmodernism, and using these misconstrued concepts to center their praxis. Anticipating Handler's critique, elsewhere we have developed some speculations for an alternative order by looking at the contributions of Unger, but in combination with chaos theory and the critical insights of a materialistically grounded, psychoanalytic semiotics

(Milovanovic, 1992a: chapter 6; 1993b). Feminist standpoint epistemology (Bartlett and Kennedy, 1991a) provides an important beginning understanding of a potential grounding; Butler's (1992) suggestion for "contingent universalities" overcomes some of the criticisms directed toward the potential slippage into essentialism and reversal of hierarchies; and Cornell's (1991) analysis of the wherewithal of alternative imaginary constructions provides a basis of "utopian thinking."

Most importantly, the new social movements that are informed by concepts emerging from postmodernist thought are too often doing solidarity politics without adequate theoretical analysis. Thus cooptation, conversion, deflection, hegemony, etc., are too readily the result. Hadn't Marx himself said of praxis that theory and practice must go hand-in-hand? "Reversal of hierarchies" often reconstitutes the form of domination; marxist dogmatism often leads to "schmarxism" (Milovanovic, 1991b), or the *discourse of the master* (Lacan, 1991a; Milovanovic, 1993b); *ressentiment* (Nietzsche) often leads to leftist forms of exorcism, political correctness, or "revenge politics" (Cornell, 1991); well-intentioned, humanistic practitioners often inadvertently reconstruct dominant conceptions of reality in their very struggles against repressive structures; the successful mobilization of policy-making resources by oppressed groups often further (be it inadvertently) empower and legitimize the state (i.e., "Let's get tough with polluters, abusers, racists, corporate offenders, etc., by tougher terms of imprisonment"). All this, perhaps, comes from the strong aversion to theory by the Left, most particularly in the U.S. Pragmatism, translated into solidarity politics, without an informed theoretical base, often militates against the development of novel visions of a transpraxis (Henry and Milovanovic, 1996). Accordingly, this article first lays out some of the key concepts of the relationship of the desiring subject with discourse. Topology theory has been useful in this pursuit.

TOPOLOGY AND PSYCHOANALYTIC SEMIOTICS

Topology theory is often called the *rubber math* or a *rubber sheet geometry* (for a lucid introduction, see Weeks, 1985; the key main progenitors have been mathematicians Stephen Smale and Henri Poincare.). It has to do with how different shapes can be stretched, pulled, twisted, bent, deformed, and distorted in space without at the same time, changing their intrinsic nature. That is, it studies continuous properties. A piece of clay, for example, can be stretched into different shapes, but break off a piece and it is no longer continuous with its original nature. Thus a doughnut is similar to a cup in that each has a hole in it. But a sphere and a two-holed doughnut are topologically not equivalent (tearing and regluing surfaces to make them resemble each other are disallowed operations in topology theory). Cutting operations produce specific effects. Accordingly, topology theory engages in qualitative operations as a counterpart to quantitative operations such as +, -, =, etc. Representations of these qualitative operations appear, for example, as the torus and the Mobius Band. For Lacan, topology theory is not metaphor nor analogy, but rather homology: these operations precisely define the dynamics of the desiring subject in relation to discourse.

Lacan, in the 1960s and 1970s, was to make heavy usage of topology theory in his exposition of the nature of the desiring subject in discourse (*l'être parlant*). Rather than relying on the sphere, the traditional symbol of unity and totality, Lacan saw the essential inscription of the subject best portrayed by the surfaces of the torus, Mobius band, *cross-cap*, Klein bottle, and borromean knots (Lacan, 1962, 1966-1967, 1972, 1974-1975, 1975-1976; see also Granon-Lafont, 1985, 1990; Nasio, 1987). Here we would like to briefly present one of these topological constructions—the *cross-cap* (which subsumes the Mobius band)—in indicating its value for a better understanding of the desiring subject. In the final section we will provide some applications to selected areas. But first a brief overview of Lacan's idea of the decentered subject depicted by his Schema L (figure 1) (Lacan, 1977; see also the following secondary sources for some precise definition of terms: Ragland-Sullivan, 1986; Lee, 1990; Marini, 1992; Sarup, 1992).

Figure 1. Schema L

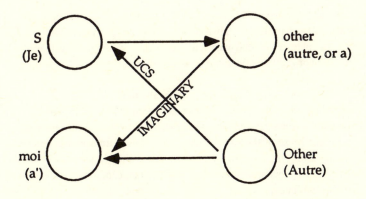

Lacan's conception of the subject has an inter- and an intrasubjective dimension. Here: *S* stands for the grammatical subject, a presence of an absence (i.e., with the appearance of the personal pronoun as a representative of the subject, the subject of production disappears, represented by its signifiers); O is the Other, the domain of the unconscious structured like a language (a repository of signifiers coordinated by metaphor and metonymy); a' is the ego or *moi*, the imaginary construction of self; and a, the other, including objects of desire. The *moi* seeks recognition by the other; the other, then is an object and source of desire. The S (or the grammatical I in discourse), receiving its message from the *Other* in signifiers, gives temporary stability to the fleeting identifications of the *moi*. The quadrilaterally defined subject, in turn, finds its being and meaning within the confluence of three orders: the Imaginary (specular images of self and others), the Real (primordial sense data that is beyond symbolization), and the Symbolic, the sphere of language and culture.

What activates the psychic apparatus is periodically experienced gaps (*manque-à-être*), which lead the subject to *suture*, or stitch over this felt sense of incompleteness; with success this leads to closure, a felt, but always illusory sense of *plenitude* (or completeness) and *jouissance* (elation, happiness, or enjoyment) that periodically covers over the inherent lack or hole in being. This hole in being is the result of the inauguration of the child into the Symbolic Order, offering, through discourse, mastery and control, but at a cost of a permanent separation, or castration from the Real. Story-telling in the courtroom, for example, involves a complex interplay of the three orders producing, in the end, a static and believable version of what may have happened. Story-telling, then, reflects the production of fantasy. (Elsewhere we have indicated that it is precisely because we inadvertently and advertently infuse energy and form to our constructions that they exist in reified form. See Henry and Milovanovic, 1991, 1996). Lacan's model, in distinction to Freud's homeostatically driven one, always leaves open end-states, due to, for example, the play of the imaginary and the illusory nature of objects of desire being capable of fully satisfying the desiring subject.

THE MOBIUS BAND, THE CROSS-CAP, AND SCHEMA R

Understanding subjectivity and reality construction in law necessitates coming to terms with framing devices or mechanisms used by the psychic apparatus in order to make sense of the world. For Lacan, these "frames" are essentially fantasy, the effects of primarily imaginary and symbolic processes, but also rooted in real sociohistorical and political economic conditions. Thus Lacan's model situates fantasy production within inter- and intrasubjective processes within contexts. (Elsewhere we have developed the notion of the "quintrivium," which details the five elements of meaning construction, 1992a.) In order to explore this in more detail, we shall present some of the essential insights of Lacanian topology theory portraying the desiring subject in relation to discursive production.

Mobius Band

A Mobius strip can be constructed by simply taking a strip of paper, placing a twist in it, and joining the ends (figure 2). In 2-D space, a traveler does not traverse from an *inside* to an *outside*; rather, one should imagine an object that is soaked through the strip (i.e., consider a porous piece of paper soaked through by ink). When a traveler traverses this strip the traveler will return in a mirror (reverse) form; the mobius strip, then, is characterized as nonorientable, as being orientation-reversing. When Lacan states that a message always returns to the sender in inverted form (1977: 85, 312), he is making reference to the internal production of sense in discourse.

The Mobius band has been presented in Lacan's algorithm for metaphor (1977), one of the two semiotic axes said to coordinate signifier production within the unconscious. It indicates how a primary signifier "crosses the bar" to the unconscious, replaced with a substitute signifier (S` now stands for S). Consider such metaphors as "she is a dynamo." One signifier is being replaced by another, which in turn, with a complete traversing of the Mobius band, reappears. The "crossing of the bar," the movement along the Mobius band, is the "spark" in the creation of meaning (Lacan, 1977: 157-8, 164, 166). It also represents how a signifier represents the subject for another signifier (i.e., S` for S).

Figure 2. The Mobius Band

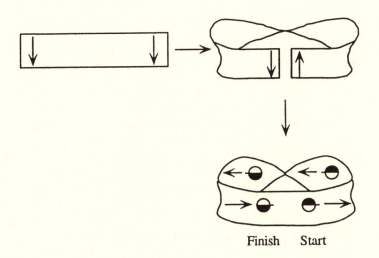

Finish   Start

For example, let's briefly indicate how "exchange-value" comes to stand for "use-value" in Marx's commodification thesis. We start with the algorithm for metaphor: $f(S'/S)S \approx S(+)s$; or rewritten: $S/S' \bullet S'/x \rightarrow S(1/s)$; or:

$$\frac{\text{exchange-value}}{\text{use-value}} \bullet \frac{\text{use-value}}{\text{unknown signified}} \rightarrow \text{exchange-value} \quad \bullet \quad \frac{1}{\text{idea of use-value}}$$

By crossing out the two use-values what remains is the exchange-value over the idea of use-value, or the replacement of the unique by an abstraction. We could do the same with the development of the juridic subject, the "reasonable man/woman in law." The operations are homologous. Here, the uniqueness of being human, or somewhat equivalent to use-value (abilities, needs, temperament, etc.) disappears and the substitute is the exchange-value, the abstraction, the juridic subject in law, which now comes to stand for the subject (S' for S).

Cross-Cap

The *cross-cap* (figure 3a) is an exemplary topological construct portraying the functioning of the subject in relation to objects of desire. The *cross-cap*, in three or four-dimensional space, is derived from non-Euclidean geometry. By attaching the boundary of a disk to the boundary of a Mobius band (explained below), we arrive at the *cross-cap*, a form of a projective plane within projective geometry (for an introduction to projective geometry, see Russell, 1956: 117-47; Banchoff, 1990: 194-8; Weeks, 1985; Hilbert and Cohn-Vossen, 1952: 298-321). What results is a unilateral surface that is *nonorientable*: an "inside" and an "outside" are indistinguishable, and it is not possible to distinguish an object on the surface from its reflected image in a mirror (Hilbert and Cohn-Vossen, 1952: 313-18). Discursive production is essentially fantasy, $ \$ \lozenge a $. This matheme is read as: $\$$, the desiring but barred subject; $\lozenge$, alternatively, the stamp (*losange*), the cut (*la coupure*), or operator (*poincon*); and a, the *objet petit (a)*, or object of desire.

Fantasy represents the relation of the subject to its objects of desire. "[F]antasy plays a double role. It supports desire, and offers it its objects" (Juranville, 1984: 189; my trans.). But it does not maintain it (ibid.: 189, 193). Desire is a response to the essential and insurmountable gaps engendered by the inauguration of the subject into the Symbolic Order. Fantasy offers a momentary answer to the essential lack in being of the desiring subject. Words (embodied signifiers) can be viewed as one specification of an object of desire, or *objet petit (a)*; they are elements for the suturing process; their materialization offers a jouissance, or *jouis-sens*, an enjoyment in sense.

Discursive production (i.e., law-talk) can be seen as an interplay of different levels of the psychic apparatus portrayed by the *cut, la coupure du huit interieur*, made in the *cross-cap*. As Lacan states it: "the subject begins with the cut" (1966: 9; my trans). If one uses scissors and cuts out a figure eight by englobing the central point twice (figure 3b, point E) of a *cross-cap* (Lacan refers to this traced path as the *huit interieur* or the *double boucle*), the surface will separate into two parts: the central part, or the disk that contains the central point, a singularity; and the peripheral structure, looking like a double leaf (*double oreille*), the Mobius band (figure 3c). (Enigmatically, the *cross-cap* which is globally single-sided and nonorientable, with the cut is transformed into one object that is unilateral and non-orientable, and another that is bilateral and orientable.)

Figure 3. The *Cross-Cap*

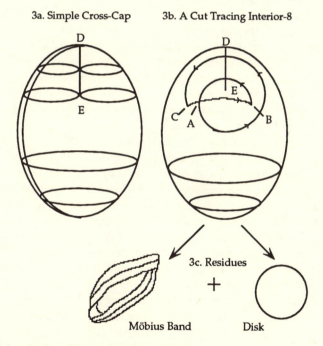

3a. Simple Cross-Cap   3b. A Cut Tracing Interior-8

3c. Residues

Möbius Band   Disk

(Adopted, with modifications, from Nasio, 1987: 208)

The disk is identified with *objet petit (a)*, the object of desire. It is constructed around a central hole, a gap (*le trou*), which signifies the imaginary phallus, symbolized as (φ).[1] The disk, in 3-D space, should be better envisioned as a sea-shell that spirals toward this point, or point-hole (*point-trou*). The Mobius band, will be identified with the subject. The subject shows itself in these paradoxical cuts.[2]

Each figure-8 "cut" traced on the *cross-cap* englobing the central point detaches a Mobius band, which represents a snapshot or a frame of the field of reality (*le champ de la réalité*). "This field," according to Lacan, "will now be merely the representative of the phantasy of which this cut provides the entire structure" (1977: 223). Fantasy is a momentary but effervescent framed perception of *reality*. Lacan's Schema R (figure 4) is the flattened version of the Mobius band (figure 2). It reflects the simultaneous separating and joining of the subject to its objects of desire, $S \diamondsuit a$, topologically portrayed, again, by the notion of the cut. In discursive production this process produces a certain sense that is unique to the subject (Granon-Lafont, 1985: 125). It is to the overdetermining effects of a political economy, however, that we must look in order to delineate the determinants of the various manifest elements and their articulations in these schemas (see also chapter 3, this book).

The *cross-cap*, in four-dimensional space (4-D), produces a unilateral surface with no singularities or boundaries. In our more intuitive 3-D space, the segment D-E in figure 3b appears as a line of self-intersection; in 4-D space no such self-intersection exists (Hilbert and Cohn-Vossen, 1952: 323). A traveler, for example, that follows a surface will perceive no boundaries and will return from a journey along the surface of the *cross-cap* in inverted form. The *cross-cap* is constituted by the Mobius band.

The central point of the *cross-cap* is a singularity which encompasses all the possible intertwining and intersecting lines of the *cross-cap*; in other words, all straight lines converge on and diverge from this central point. It provides stability for the subject. The imaginary phallus is this point of convergence and divergence where the divided subject, S, and the objects of desire (a) simultaneously join and separate from themselves. The symbolic phallus, (Φ), the end result of all these processes, is the more manifest aspect of these interplays, being at the base, for example, of discursive production. It is ubiquitous in manifest signifiers.

Whereas the subject, topologically portrayed by the Mobius Band, always must be perceived in relation to its specular images (of its objects and of the other), in Lacan's mathemes, *i(a)*, the *objet petit (a)* is not specularizable. The *objet petit (a)* is always permeated with images of the imaginary phallus, in Lacan's mathemes: -φ(a). In fact, the ego can be depicted as: m◇-φ(a) (see Nasio, 1987: 97). All signifiers are stamped and subsumable under the symbolic phallus Φ.

Further, two movements can be distinguished: the movement of the S toward a, symbolized as $S > a$, and the movement of (*a*) toward S, symbolized as $\mathcal{S} < a$; together symbolized in Lacan's mathemes as $\mathcal{S} \Diamond a$ (Lacan has also referred to this as the alienation and separation behind the *fading* of the subject). In a phallocentric Symbolic Order, what gives consistency to the subject is the effects of the imaginary phallus; put in another way, the imaginary phallus provides a degree of stability and contributes toward a degree of periodic permanence in the sliding identifications of the ego and anchorings (*capitonnage*) of signifiers to particular signifieds.

A number of signifiers, however, have more lasting effects; these master signifiers (S1) have their source in early childhood and receive additional stabilization by the overdetermining effects of the political, economic, and ideological. Of course, all this also implies that something other than the imaginary phallus can provide this stabilizing function (we will develop this implication in the last section). To better explain this we move briefly to his equally enigmatic Schema R, which is the more dynamic form of Schema L and is portrayed in 2-D space.

Schema R and the Cross-Cap
The *flattened* version was presented by Lacan in *Écrit* (1977: 197). By reducing the surface of the Mobius band to a single line (*ligne sans points*), we arrive at the *huit interieur* produced by the cut following the figure eight (Lacan, 1973: 38-9; Nasio, 1987: 215). We could also envision closing up the central space of a Mobius band until the central void becomes an apparently one-dimensional point (or point-hole, *point-trou*). This *point* outside the Mobius band, *un point hors-ligne*, is better conceived of as an enfolded order in 4-D space, acting much like astrophysicists' notion of the black and white hole. The resulting figure of this collapsing operation is the *cross-cap* (Granon-Lafont, 1985: 79; Nasio, 1987: 214).

All this represents the opening and closing of the unconscious and the appearing and disappearing (*aphanisis*) of the subject. To understand the complexities, one must see it in the context of the structure of the *cross-cap* in relation to Schema R (figure 5). One notes that the *cross-cap* in figure 5 has undergone a small vertical cut following the line of intersection (for a detailed derivation, see Hilbert and Cohn-Vossen, 1952: 314-17; Granon-Lafont, 1985: 83). This is done to indicate how in fact a Mobius band type twist exists, the dotted lines between I and i, and m and M.

Figure 4. Schema R   Figure 5. The Cross-Cap and Schema R

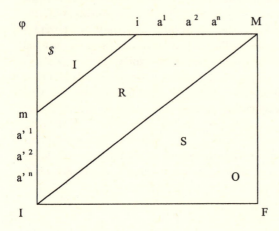
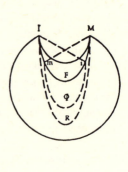

Where:

φ, small phi = the imaginary phallus ("in which the subject identifies himself…with himself as a living being");

Φ, large phi = the symbolic phallus, the signifier of *jouissance*, seen in the *cross-cap* as a singularity (small and large phi are distinguishable, see Lacan, 1991b: 277-307);

i = specular image(s), imaginary;

m = ego (imaginary);

a' = ideal ego(s);

a = object(s) of desire, including the imaginary other(s);

M = mother ("signifier of the primordial object");

F = law-of-the-father;

I = ego-ideal, alternatively, I(O);

$ = divided subject;

I = Imaginary Order (imagoes, sphere of imaginary constructions);

S = Symbolic Order (culture, language);

O = Other (the unconscious "structured like a language," coordinated by metaphor and metonymy);

R = the perceived field of reality, *le champ de la réalité* (framed by the Symbolic and Imaginary Order).

(For an accessible explanation of terms, see Mueller and Richardson, 1982: 211-2, 245, 255, 259)

Identifactory Axes

Two identifactory axes exist: with other, and with self. (1) The axis i-M represents specular images of objects of desire and the other; i.e., we have i-a^1, i-a^2, i-a^n...i-M; the primordial form is established during the *mirror stage* of infant development. In law, for example, the juror engages in fleeting identifications with a host of images of the other, $S\rightarrow$i(a^{1-n}). "Is s/he a person who could possibly do such a thing?" (And in the inverted form: "Am I the kind of person who could do such a thing?") Here, therefore, are a multitude of aggressive and narcissistic relations in movement. Many of these preconstructions of type-of-persons (as objects), however, are constituted elsewhere.

Consider, for example, *EEOC v. Sears* (1988), a Federal Appeals court decision. Lawyers for Sears successfully argued that women were disproportionally represented in certain positions not because of discrimination but because women lacked "interest" in particular positions. Accepted by the court was expert testimony that established the normative orientation of women as nurturing, humane, focused on relationships, and adverse to the capitalist competitive work ethic. Williams sees *Sears* as providing "a dramatic academic language in which to dignify traditional stereotypes" (1991: 102). Elsewhere, Winter (1992: 815-16), applying a cognitive approach to law, has indicated how "meaningfulness...is a function of stabilized and standardized mental frameworks that enable conventionalized interpretations under most circumstances."

(2) The axis m-I represents an imaginary identification by the subject of the kind of person that would appear likable; thus we can specify $S\rightarrow$m($a^{`1}$, m-$a^{`2}$, m-$a^{`n}$...m-I); said in yet another way, these are others the subject desires to be like. In law-finding practices, the subject is encouraged to assume the discursive subject-position of the juridic subject, the "reasonable man/woman in law." (The word "role" is too limiting a term.) In a study of jailhouse lawyers, for example, it was observed that inmate jailhouse lawyers often identify with their free-world counterparts (Milovanovic and Thomas, 1989; see also chapter 6, this book). Thus we have $S\rightarrow$m($a^{`j}$).[3]

Implied, too, is the omnipresence of some valued gaze. But whose gaze? Having assumed a particular discursive subject-position, I(O), the person is further subject to a projected approving or disapproving gaze. (The notion of a discursive subject-position is a more accurate conceptualization than the notion of a "role," which downplays the significance of the structuring and performative characteristics of discourse and signifiers. For a good discussion of a "role," see Winter, 1992: 972-91.) Consider an activist lawyer. An inherent dialectic of struggle exists between desiring to present a politicized version of "what happened" [i(a)] and identifying with a projected approving political gaze [m(a`)], and the imperatives of juridic procedural constraints disallowing broader political elements, severely restricting the production of a politicized version of the "what happened" and diminishing, in the process, the possibility of the activist lawyer favorably identifying with the projected approving eye of groups in struggle (see also Bannister and Milovanovic, 1990; see also chapter 7, this book).

To add to an already complex movement, the various possible lines from a'^{1-n} to a^{1-n} imply that the subject is being "doubly articulated." Since a twist exists in the Mobius band, what this also says is that the *other* comes full circle to represent the loci from which the ego's own conception of self is constituted (see, for example, Lacan, 1977: 85-6). Put in another way, the *other* is the object and cause of desire. Critical cinema theory has been clear as to the effects of political economy on the development of culturally induced objects of desire and appropriate idealizations of self (see Silverman, 1982; Williamson, 1987). In our final section we shall see how, in law, certain images have been perceived to be the "causes" of violence.

If this is not complex enough, we must also look to the lower triangle of Schema R, I-M-F (note, F can be equivalently replaced by O, the Other, or S, the Symbolic Order; it is the point where all three coincide). The Other is the locus of signifiers that come to represent the subject. In Lacan's formulation, the law of metaphor and metonymy are responsible for the creation of a chain of signifiers, which is the basis of sense (1977: 164-7). Elsewhere we have extended this semiotic axis to three, respectively from the more conscious to the unconscious levels: paradigm-syntagm, metaphor-metonymy, and condensation-displacement (Milovanovic, 1992b; see also chapter 3, this book). To be brief, while the imaginary interplay unfolds in the top triangle of Schema R, the bottom triangle indicates that signifiers are being embodied with desire. Since the contemporary Symbolic Order is phallocentric, then all signifiers will be colored with the law-of-the-father (F) (see also Caudill, 1992a: 34; 1992b). Is it no wonder, then, why we have a privileging of *(his)tory* over *(her)story*? Legal narrative constructions, then, are bound by: the recognized signifiers constituted in law (paradigm) and their acceptable (legal) linear constructions (syntagm); the imaginary interplay of aggressivity and narcissism between the ego and the other; and the discursive subject-positions within which a subject takes momentary residence. What this implies, too, is that law-making and law-finding practices are inherently phallologocentric.

Interior-8 and the Signifier
Let us provide the notion of the figure-8 cut done upon the *cross-cap* (figure 3b) to the domain of the signifier. Again, what is produced is a Mobius band. The Mobius band is used by Lacan to portray the specular nature of the subject, how signifiers return in inverted form (essentially repetition), and

how the *inside* (the unconscious) comes to be the *outside* (the conscious). For Lacan, the signifier is that which represents the subject for another signifier.

The signifier and the subject are intimately connected. The signifier "insists" in signifying chains: it tends toward repetition (Lacan, 1977: 153; Nasio, 1987: 205-208); it seeks to unfold its dimensions into consciousness (for a precise example, see Lacan's seminar on the "Purloined Letter," 1988; see also Winter's example of the "performative dimension" of discourse applied to being a college professor, 1992: 797). It is the signifier that produces effects on the subject. Thus rather than searching for stable signifieds, Lacan suggests that we view signifiers as existing in signifying chains, each affecting the other in a forward direction (the anticipatory dimension, in figure 3b, A→B); but only with a punctuation does a retroactive, intuitive grasping (from B→A) of the sense of the whole utterance become finalized, and only at that point does each signifier take on value in relation to each of the others in context (point C), essentially producing a new value for the signifier that previously materialized at point A (Lacan, 1967: 132, 137; Nasio, 1987: 202-211; see also the discussion on the "elementary cell of speech production," chapter 3, this book). As Granon-Lafont poignantly states, "[a] signifier never returns except as another signifier, it represents a subject, for an other signifier" (1985: 37; my trans.). The exact movement—displacement and substitution—of a signifier, and hence its sense, is governed by Lacan's algorithm for metaphor and metonymy (1977: 164). Using topology theory we may say that a signifier undergoes a journey but always returns in inverted form. The Mobius band represents the surface on which this transversal takes place. How is this possible?

The interior-8 traces the movement of the signifier. "A signifier signifies something in a given moment, in a certain context of discourse, but one does not know how to give to a signifier its signified at the same time" (Granon-Lafont, 1985: 37; my trans.). The key to this dilemma rests with the idea of *repetition*. Lacan, following Freud, has said that repetition is "the insistence of speech which returns in the subject until it has said its final word, speech that must return, despite the resistance of the ego which is a defense, that is, the adherence to the imaginary misconstrual of identification with the other. Repetition is fundamentally the insistence of speech" (1993: 242). Thus, a signifier returns as *L'un en plus*, a more-than-one (at point C), or simply, a new signifier incorporating a trace of its past (portrayed by line D-E on the *cross-cap*, the point of the fold) (see Lacan's seminar, *La Logic du Fantasm*, of 15 February, 1967). Consider the example "a man is a man" (Granon-Lafont, 1985: 37). Clearly, the sense of the second signifier, "man," is different from the first, even while incorporating a trace from the first. There has been a passage in time and space, and a return. Point C, then, stands for the closure in the movement of repetition. With the return of the signifier, a more-than-one results, the new meaning with a trace of the past. The same is true for the subject. Since the signifier represents the subject for another signifier, the subject should be viewed as a subject-in-process, always presenting a trace of its past. But repetition is what gives constancy to the sense-in-process. The Mobius band, the interior-8, thus portrays the two different moments in the repetition of the signifier, the closure of the movement of repetition as finished product, and the effects on the subject. It is by way of the cut that we operationalize terms and processes within a structure.

Now let's relate this to Schema R. Figure 5 situates Schema R on the *cross-cap*. Again, at the precise moment when the figure-8 cut is completed, two distinct parts are created: the Mobius band, representing the subject of the unconscious, and the disk representing *objet petit (a)* (figures 3b and 3c). The divided subject appears dialectically: in its objects of desire producing meaning at the cost of pure being, outside of meaning. The "line," D-E, which is more of a twist or fold (Granon-Lafont, 1990: 92; Lacan refers to it as *le dessus-dessous*, or over/under), is a critical topological structure. This *line of suture*, or *auto-intersection*, has important properties: it is that unmeasurable point in time where the conscious subject begins to materialize, a product of the discourse of the Other; it is the occasion for the momentary manifestation of fantasy, a framing of the field of reality. It is also that moment when the subject identifies itself with that which speaks it, with that which it desires (Lacan, 1981: 273; Granon-Lafont, 1985: 88).

At the moment where the mapping of the subject in relation to *objet petit (a)* has taken place (Schema R), "the experience of the fundamental fantasy becomes the drive" (Lacan, 1981: 273; 1977: 314), made manifest in its "grammatical artifice(s)," and thereby the fantasy becomes the basis of social action (see also Lee, 1990: 76, 148-54). Put in another way, this is the dynamic underlying the notion of the performative dimension of language. Note that when we close the *cross-cap* (figure 5), point I matches with i and m with M (keep in mind the twist). At this point we have a second singularity in the *cross-cap*.

The primal singularity is at the base-point of this "line" (D-E). At point E, we find the central hole (*le trou*), a hole in being (also referred to as a *point-trou*). The symbolic phallus, Φ, however, is what provides a sense of constancy; thus, in a phallocentric symbolic order, all is permeated with the coloration of the phallus. What this all means is that every snapshot of "reality" is through-and-through fantasy, composed of a number of relations in movement. Thus when we fantasize, i.e., engage in imaginary and discursive production, there is a momentary relation established between the specular image of objects of desire, $i(a^{1-n})$, and the ego and its idealizations, $m(a'^{1-n})$. What holds the fantasy together in a momentary stable and coherent manner is the symbolic phallus, signifier of the lack in the Other. It is this that provides *jouissance*, a sense of potency, control, mastery, and power, and for the observer, the perception of the centered subject engaged in "willful" and self-directing activity. For the divided subject it is a moment when the essential gap in being is denied (i.e., by way of *suture*); here, a sense of *plenitude* results. For the other in a social encounter, it is a moment for the possibility of recognition, empathy, understanding, and for the possibility of coordinated social action.[4]

Legal Sphere and Schema R

Let's take an example in law, the so-called juridic subject. Weberian and Marxian legal scholars have well-delineated the wherewithal of the abstract bearer of rights in a competitive capitalist mode of production and in its changing nature in a monopoly form (see Milovanovic, 1987; 1989b). Here, a polymorphous, polyvalent subject with diverse drives, desires, temperamental traits and proclivities is provided with: (1) an imaginary ego with which to identify $m(a'^j)$, the reasonable man/woman in law; (2) acceptable signifiers with which to construct narratives $i(a^{1-n})$ and their acceptable syntactical form in a legal Symbolic Order (where both, in a phallocentric order, are permeated by the phallus, i.e., $m \diamondsuit \text{-} \varphi(a)$; and (3) the promise of *jouissance* and *plenitude* with the suturing of periodic unexplainables in the ebb and flow of social and human encounters and in the construction of sense from nonsense. Fantasy, therefore, is a historically determined construct in a political economy. The available "cuts" may be infinite, but the modal types will surely be circumscribed by the determinants of a political economy and its effects on the articulation of the different levels of the divided subject. Capital logic, for example, with its avatar, the law of equivalence, in privileging the production of replaceable parts, privileges, too, replaceable fantasies. In law, race, gender, and class specificities, i.e., multiple consciousnesses, or $ \$ \rightarrow m(a'^{1-n})$, are replaced by universalizing abstractions such as the juridic subject, $m(a'^j)$.

A recent U.S. Appeals Court decision affirming a lower federal district court (*U.S. Ex Rel Hunley v. Godinez*, 784 F. Supp. 1992) poignantly shows the dilemma. A jury was deadlocked eight to four for conviction of a suspect for burglary. That evening, a burglar broke into four of the juror's sequestered quarters, two of whom at the time were voting against conviction (and one of these jurors was the foreman). Many of the circumstances of the burglary of the trial reappeared. The jury then voted unanimously for conviction after one hour of deliberation. The Federal District Court overturned, noting that the burglaries "placed at least four jurors in the shoes of the victim." The court noted approvingly an affidavit provided to the court by a noted criminologist that stated that even though the jurors denied any bias after the verdict, what was at work was an "unconscious bias." What the court in fact did was to say that the jurors no longer identified with the "reasonable man/woman" in law, the appropriate imaginary identification, $m(a^{\cdot j})$, or, ideally, I(O). Nor with an appropriate imaginary other, i(a). Here, the imaginary other was in fact the juror who may have been in the same position as the murdered victim of the burglar. Nor, finally, with the locus of available signifiers unique to the juridic discursive region, in constructing an acceptable legal text (fantasy) by which guilt or innocence could be ascertained. Hence they were "irrational" in their decision, presumably because their identification was more with the plight of the victim associated with the original burglary (and an alternative knotting of signifiers to signifieds in a narrative construction). Here the allowable fantasy ($\$\diamond a$), was given a permissible range in law. What all this indicates is that the complexity of the human condition is given the promise of understandability and explainability in law, thus providing a sense of control, mastery, and omnipotence for the subjects (i.e., the appearance of the centered subject in law), and provides a basis for continuous "rational" decision-making (i.e., by means of syllogistic reasoning) in subsequent judicial litigation.

Up to this point we have provided a framework for a psychoanalytic semiotics. We would like now to briefly take note of chaos theory, an emerging critical element of the postmodern perspective, after which we will be in a position to apply these insights to three areas of study under the overall framework of constitutive theory.

CHAOS AND ORDERLY DISORDER

The postmodern sciences have been identified as a search for instabilities (Lyotard, 1984: 53-67). Chaos theory, one of the more recent threads, has been applied to literature (Serres, 1982a; Hayles, 1991), social sciences (Deleuze and Guattari, 1987; Lyotard, 1984), psychoanalysis (Butz, 1992a, 1992c), organizational theory (Leifer, 1989), criminology (T.R.Young, 1991a, 1991b, 1997), and law (Arrigo, 1993a; Brion, 1991; Milovanovic, 1993a). It is an epistemological break from classical thought (for a lucid introduction, see Briggs and Peat, 1989; Stewart, 1989). (We shall have more to say about its possible integration in Part 3 of this book.) Along with Godel's theorem and catastrophe theory, it fundamentally questions the deterministic universe of Newton and the positivistic sciences. Here we would like to briefly mention some of the main thrusts of chaos theory, and then, in the next section, we will see how this paradigm along with psychoanalytic semiotics can provide alternative fantasies for discoveries of an alternative order. Hence, our justification for the use of chaos theory rests on its usefulness as a tool for discovery, for expository purposes, and as a pathway toward a possible transpraxis.[5]

Briefly, chaos theory offers the following: (1) that initial conditions are indeterminable—there exists no precision in defining initial conditions; (2) since initial conditions are indeterminable, iterations will compound the initial uncertainties; (3) these iterations can, at some point in the future, produce disproportionate effects (i.e., the oft-used example of a butterfly flapping its wings in Southeast Asia "causing" a hurricane in Florida)—the point being that even an apparently insignificant variable can make a difference; (4) that mapping dynamic systems produce different "attractors"— limit, cycle, torus, and strange attractors — with the former two being closed and cyclical, and the latter two combining elements of global stability with local instability and uncertainty; (5) that space can be *fractal* (having fractional dimensions), and thus binary logic and dualisms overlook complex phenomena; (6) that classical physics' and the positivistic science's celebrated notion of equilibrium conditions must be supplanted by the notion of *far-from-equilibrium* conditions, where flux, diversity, interpenetrating effects, and change are the normal conditions; (7) that far-from-equilibrium conditions provide the context where bifurcation points are ubiquitous (a phenomena mapped by an apparently stable limit or cycle attractors can very easily change into a somewhat unpredictable torus attractor, and to an even more unpredictable strange attractor); (8) that the search for stabilities in the universe as a methodology (reflecting unexamined metaphysical truth-claims) can be fruitfully supplanted by the search for instabilities, and, finally, (9) that order can exist within an apparently disorderly system. Hence, chaos theory can be seen as a science of orderly disorder.

Although Lacan was unfamiliar with chaos theory, many of the conceptual tools offered by chaos are quite compatible. Some initial forays at integration have taken place by those heavily influenced by Lacan. See, for example, Deleuze and Guattari's offering of an alternative conceptualization of space (1987: 474-500) and of the nonlinear psychic pathways of desire in their notion of the *rhizome* (ibid.: 3-25). See also Lyotard's claim that postmodernism is a search for instabilities, and that chaos is one of its pillars (1984: 53-60). Using an example from law, Balkin has shown how a signifier iterated in different contexts produces a different sense (1987; see also Winter's discussion of the role of imagination which militates against any "fixed or linear" discursive production [1992: 816]; Hayles has also developed a useful integration of chaos theory with postmodernist thought [1990: 175-86]). It is precisely because of this that such legal ideals as "original intent" of some "founding fathers" cannot be the measurable and definitive criteria for the meaning of a legal signifier. Signifiers that appear in discursive production, then, are always more-than-one (*L'un en plus*).

DISCUSSION: EXEMPLIFICATIONS, REPLACEMENT DISCOURSE, AND TRANSFORMATIVE POLITICS

In the final section, we would like to first provide some possible lines of critical analysis following the conceptualizations offered by Lacan, and, second, offer some views toward the development of a replacement discourse and a transformative politics that draws from psychoanalytic semiotics and chaos theory.

EXEMPLIFICATIONS: TOOLS FOR CRITICAL INQUIRY

Let us first turn to exemplifications in two areas: legally defined images and words as "causes" of violence, and the ontology of the gendered subject.

Images and Words as "Causes" of Violence

Court decisions are exemplary for indicating the applicability of a critically informed psychoanalytic semiotics. We will concentrate on the notion of "fighting words" and "pornographic images" that are said, in law, to "cause" violence. The former more implicates the bottom triangle of Schema R, the sphere of the Symbolic Order; the latter, more the top portion of Schema R, the sphere of the Imaginary Order.

i. *Words*. The U.S. Supreme Court has specified the scope of First Amendment rights of freedom of expression: "the government may not prohibit the expression of an idea simply because society finds the idea itself offensive or disagreeable" (*Texas v. Johnson*, 491 U.S. 397, 414, 1989). However, the limit to unprotected expression rests on the notion of "fighting words," which encompasses two definitions: words "which by their very utterance inflict injury" and words which "tend to incite an immediate breach of the peace" (*Chaplinsky v. New Hampshire*, 315 U.S. 568, 1942; more recently, see *R.A.V., Petitioner v. City of St. Paul, Minnesota*, 1992; see also Gellman, 1991). Operationally, in *Chaplinsky*, it was noted that words that could be constitutionally prohibited were those "such as have a direct tendency to cause acts of violence by the person to whom, individually, the remark is addressed....The test is what men of common intelligence would understand would be words likely to cause an average addressee to fight" (p. 573).

Implicit here, of course, is the *performative* dimension of signifiers (see Lee, 1990: 75-9, 89-90; for an application to law, see Winter, 1992: 795-97, 800, 812; see also Deleuze and Guattari's notion of *mot d'ordre*, or "order-words," 1987: 76; see also critical race theorist's analysis of "words that wound," Matsuda et al, 1993). For one of the clearest renditions of these effects, see Lacan's analysis of Poe's short story, the "Purloined Letter" (1988). Here Lacan shows how the circulation of the letter, or signifier (the content, or signified unknown), amongst three structured discursive subject-positions is a parable of the effects of the signifier.

Let us return to figure 5 and situate the dynamics of this prohibition. We are again in the realm of the construction of fantasy, in this case with an eye toward acceptable and unacceptable fantasies (i.e., constitutionally permissible "cuts"). Clearly, given the idiosyncrasies of being human, the class of words that may provoke any particular individual to retaliate at a point in time may be infinite. It might nevertheless be that certain words (a subset) do have a higher probability of invoking a violent reaction in certain contexts (i.e., "yo' mama" invoked in certain street-corner settings). What the court has done to resolve the issue, however, is to invoke the "reasonable man/woman" standard, here the "average addressee."

In other words, the *moi* and its identifications (a'^{1-n}) is intricately connected with the imaginary other (a^{1-n}) along an axis in Schema R. This axis lies on a Mobius band. In addition, the axis from the imaginary phallus to the law-of-the-father (i.e., the underlying paternalism or *parens patriae* of the State) stabilize this relation. Signifiers that are anchored (*point de capiton*) in this setting, the syntagmatic construction of which find limits within some linguistic code, indeed are inherently connected with the whole constellation of factors: imaginary identifications (narcissism, aggressivity); contextually assumed discursive subject-positions; the effects of phallologocentrism; and the legal linguistic code (syntagmatic axis), the basis of which provides narrative coherence (i.e., through the process of *suture*). All this provides the appearance of the centered subject in a self-determining capacity and becomes the basis of linear syllogistic reasoning in law (i.e., narrative coherence, Jackson, 1988).

All this, too, indicates the wherewithal of the delineation of a range of permissible fantasy productions, or "frameworks" in law. Indeed, this is a constitutive process. What is being offered are the elements out of which constitutionally permissible, narratively coherent texts can be produced. In this sense, a higher court's opinion constitutes a stable meaning system within which different subjects, assuming the juridic discursive subject-position, must operate; that is, they must draw elements from juridical articulations in narrative constructions. By assuming preconstructed discursive subject-positions and by making use of predefined signifiers in suturing gaps, the subject is being *interpellated*, or if you will, constituted in a linear, predefined manner. Following Barthes and Silverman, what is being constructed is the "spoken subject" (Silverman, 1982). Foucault has quite correctly pointed out the nature of this power-subject relationship: "[t]he individual is an effect of power, and at the same time, or precisely to the extent to which it is that effect, it is the element of its articulation" (1980: 98).

Let us approach the same problem from a constitutive approach in law (see also Henry and Milovanovic, 1996). The very legal opinion meant to control ethnic intimidation crimes is, ironically, constitutive (codeterminous) of the very problem at hand. Laws directed at vulnerable disenfranchised groups, for example, inadvertently send the message that these groups are indeed weak, that they are disliked by a significant number of others, that perhaps there is even some basis to this dislike, and that they therefore must become dependent on the state for protection (i.e., *parens patriae*) (Gellman, 1991: 385-8). With this recognition, the vulnerable group may also become doubly so: here to majority groups as well as to the state, which holds out the possibility of withdrawing its support at some point in time. Indeed, the court's articulation of social problems provides symbolic value and raises a certain awareness in the populace, good or bad, where it may not have existed (ibid.). It gives stability to possible permissible "cuts" that can be done. In this view, legal decision-making is a constitutive element in the construction of social problems. Subjects are being pacified and brought within the loci of the forces of the state and technobureaucratic apparatuses, even while being offered a momentary respite from other forms of exploitation and control. What are stabilized are imaginary constructions of self and others, and a core set of master signifiers that come to articulate the subject.

ii. *Images*. Let's turn now to a recent Canadian legal decision, *R. v. Butler* (1992), which was concerned with establishing a constitutionally understood linkage between obscenity and harm to society. After reviewing the social science literature on the nature of the causal links, and noting their inconclusiveness (p. 503), the Court nonetheless stated that "images that people are exposed to bear a causal relationship to their behavior" (p. 502).[6] The effects of pornography coupled with violent themes, the court said, "reinforce(s) male-female stereotypes to the detriment of both sexes. It attempts to make degradation, humiliation, victimization, and violence in human relationships appear normal and acceptable" (p. 493). Continuing, it tends to portray women "as objects for sexual exploitation" (p. 497). "Women...are deprived of unique human character or identity and depicted as sexual playthings, hysterically and instantly responsive to male sexual demands" (p. 500).

All these concepts and ideas can be placed on our Schema R. What the court is saying, in short, is that some "cuts" are constitutionally impermissible. Put in another way, the court, as a disciplinary institution, is engaging in the *territorialization of desire* (Deleuze and Guattari, 1987; in Foucault's terminology, it is disciplining bodies, 1977; Deleuze, following Foucault, has referred to this as the cartography of the "diagram," 1988; in other characterizations, Habermas has referred to this process as the constitution of a new modal form of a steering mechanism for interactive encounters, 1984; and in Goodrich's read of Legendre, law works on the emotional body and soul, 1990: 268).

The Court noted that it is the community standards "as a whole" that ought to be considered as to what constitutes impermissible pornography, and that the court must determine if exposure to this pornography produces harm, defined as that which "predisposes persons to act in an antisocial manner, as for example, the physical or mental mistreatment of women by men..." (p. 485). The court dismissed the argument that a particular audience's view was the measure (pp. 476-8); the minority view, however, saw "tolerance" centering on particular audiences and the question of time, manner, and place of expression (pp. 514, 518-20). The Court has further solidified the value of global over a local knowledge.

Let us again refer to Schema R and the *cross-cap*. Focusing on the upper triangle of Schema R, the Imaginary Order, we can see how the court is articulating permissible values of terms. It is delineating the boundaries beyond which certain "cuts" are impermissible due to the immediate contribution to violence they are said to have. Referring to the bottom triangle, what underlies the phallocentric Symbolic Order is the law-of-the-father, a paternalism that makes ubiquitous appearances. Here we are in the domain of unconscious semiotic production—the semiotic axis of metaphor-metonymy, and the constellation of stabilized master signifiers (S1), knots in being (static forms of borromean knots), or symptoms (See Milovanovic, 1993b; see also chapter 3, this book). Together—the Imaginary and Symbolic Orders— codetermine fantasy production. (Of course the domain of the Real Order, the generator of raw, primordial sense data, remains ubiquitous with effects.)

It would seem to follow that if we accept the logic of the courts' decisions above, that, moving in the opposite direction, certain words and images should be celebrated for their contributions toward subjects better assuming their idiosyncratic desires and for collective development. (Lacan has referred to this as the ethics of the "well-spoken," 1987b: 45; see also Lacan, 1992: 309-310, 319-21; Lee, 1990: 161-70.) Courts, in other words, are predominantly in the reactive-negative mode: in a Nietzschean critique of Hegel's version of the dialectic between master and slave, the latter does not create new values but must always react to the master. Implicit within the courts' reasoning, whether recognized or not, are often alternative visions for human emancipation. One of the challenges, then, is the creation of institutions which celebrate the affirmative, productive, and positive side (Nietzsche, 1980; Deleuze, 1983: 147-98; Milovanovic, 1991a; see also Dews' analysis of Lyotard's, Deleuze's, and Guattari's work of the late 1960s and early 1970s on the poetics and libidinal economy of the unconscious, 1987).

Elsewhere, theorists have specified one critical element of constitutive criminology/law: the effects of media in providing distorted images of crime and justice (Barak, 1993; Benedict, 1992). The media's coverage of rape, for example, often portrays the victim in the imagery of a provoking female or the attack by a monster. Benedict has concluded that "reporters tend to impose these shared narratives—which are nothing but a set of mental and verbal clichés—on the sex crimes they cover like a cookie-cutter on dough, forcing the crimes into proscribed shapes, regardless of the specifics of the case or their own beliefs" (1992: 24). She insists on the idea that these discourses and their conceptual categories must themselves be changed. Zita, focusing on the pornographic industry, notes that "[t]he pornographic apparatus is a social practice which imposes certain codes on the bodies of women, and can result in texts and images which produce effects in battered, raped or murdered women" (1987: 39-40; see also Bracher's account, 1993: 83-102). (For a more general analysis see Newman's account of how the media links justice to violence by way of connecting primitive iconographies of good versus evil in such media hits in popular culture as Batman and Robin, 1993). What all this indicates is that the sphere of the Imaginary finds relatively stabilized categorical expression reflecting some segments of the population at the expense of others.' The mechanisms or "diagrams of power" (Deleuze, 1988: 34-44) can be pin-pointed on Schema R. The subject finds him/herself within a Symbolic and Imaginary Order always already replete with narratives and attendant imaginary constructions. Reality construction must be situated within these coordinates.

THE GENDERED SUBJECT AND THE STRANGE ATTRACTOR AT THE CENTER OF BEING

The examination of the wherewithal of gendered subjects, too, could be more clearly elucidated. But postmodernist feminist analysis has major implications for other situated subjects who find themselves constructing and reconstructing dominant conceptions of reality while simultaneously disavowing them.

Let's return to Lacan's dense and insightful article entitled "A Love Letter" (1985; see also Melville 1987; Lee 1990: 172-86) that shows some clear possibilities for an alternative basis of subjectivity. Here Lacan presents his seemingly outlandish statement: "woman does not exist." He tells us:

For man: (1) $\forall x \bullet \Phi x$ For woman: (3) $\overline{\forall x} \bullet \Phi x$

      (2) $\exists x \bullet \overline{\Phi x}$ (4) $\overline{\exists x} \bullet \overline{\Phi x}$

The first "algorithm" means that for man (the *masculine discursive subject-position*), all x is a function of the phallus. Put in another way, all discursive production answers to the phallus as it is incorporated in the dominant Symbolic Order. The second algorithm means that there is an x that is not a function of the phallus. Lacan makes it clear that the male *or* female can take up the phallic function: sex and gendered roles are not inherently connected. Hence, algorithm two above indicates man *not* taking up the phallic function. Algorithm three states that for woman (the *feminine discursive subject-position*), not all x is a function of the phallus. In other words, women are not totally determined by the phallic symbolic order. Algorithm four means that there is not an x that is not a function of the phallus.

Persons assuming the masculine discursive subject-position experience a phallic jouissance within the phallic symbolic order. Women, on the other hand, are not imprisoned within this function; they have a privileged access to a bodily jouissance. However, there is no language that embodies this form of jouissance—it is unspeakable. Hence, "woman does not exist"; she is essentially lacking within the dominant phallic symbolic order, she is *pas-toute*. She does, however, experience another jouissance beyond the phallic function. Lacan gives examples of the words of the poet or mystic (see also Lecercle's analysis of *délire*, 1985). At best, this sense can only be half-said/articulated (*mi-dire*). One feminist jurisprudential approach indeed has grounded its epistemology and praxis on the experiential dimension of oppressive feminine experiences, but with a qualification centered on the contingent and provisional nature of commitments that are always subject to critical evaluation and possible revision (Butler, 1992; Bartlett and Kennedy, 1991a; see also Currie, 1993; Arrigo, 1993b). However, the Imaginary dimension must also be integral to transformative politics.

Cornell's (1991) brilliant polemic and synthesis of Lacan's psychoanalysis, postmodernist feminist's perspectives, and Derrida's deconstructive epistemology have emphasized the imaginary elements for potential change. She, however, only partially works through the Symbolic dimension. After all, it was Lacan's vision that the two orders are implicated. Nevertheless, she has provided a profound analysis of alternative imaginary constructions, particularly by building on Irigaray's idea of *mimesis* (ibid.: 147-52) and Cixous' idea of "retelling of the myth" (ibid.: 178) in developing the wherewithal of an "utopian thinking" (ibid.: 169). As she explains: "utopian thinking demands the continual exploration and re-exploration of the possible and yet also the unrepresentable" (ibid.). In other words, the imaginary constituted by metaphoric and metonymic condensations and displacements always implies a "slippage," an excess (what Lacan refers to as *le plus de jouir*) that is especially manifest in myths.

In recreating myths we are in the position of creating an "elsewhere." According to Cornell's read of Cixous, "[w]e re-collect the mythic figures of the past, but as we do so we reimagine them. It is the potential variability of myth that allows us to work within myth, and the significance it offers, so as to reimagine our world and by so doing, to begin to dream of a new one" (ibid.: 178). In this way an affirmative politics of the feminine can begin to emerge that is also utopian in trying to point to an elsewhere (ibid.: 182, 200). As she states:

> consciousness-raising must involve creation, not just discovery. We need our poetry, our fantasies and our fables; we need the poetic evocation of the feminine body in Irigaray and in Cixous if we are to finally find a way beyond the muteness imposed by a gender hierarchy in which our desire is "unspeakable" (ibid.: 201).

We hasten to add, again, that Cornell's philosophical treatise sides with the subject, a reductionism that without more does not lead to social change. What is conspicuously missing is the catalyst for social change. We want to take her insights and develop a social transpraxis. Necessarily, the Imaginary and the Symbolic must be essential elements in this transformative politics, both relatively constrained by the effects of the Real Order that remains beyond accurate symbolization. In our final section we will develop some thoughts on how this synthesis might be the basis of a transformative politics.

In the topology of the *cross-cap* and Schema R, what the above analysis suggests is that a qualitatively new constellation of "cuts" or fantasies may appear based on alternative valuations of elements, with local unpredictability but with global order. And here lies, then, the potential for an alternative subject to develop and an alternative discourse to materialize (see, for example, Bartlett and Kennedy's call for a "feminist practical reasoning," 1991a). The revolutionary subject, one engaged in transpraxis, is one who would begin to articulate the jouissance of the Other, will begin, that is, to find an alternative source for the embodiment of desire in *objets petit (a)* (i.e., words). This alternative discourse, however, would best flourish in *far-from-equilibrium* conditions, with the strange attractor constitutive of the locus of being.[7] This implicates necessary and fundamental changes in the political economic order (See, for example, Braidotti, 1990: 95; Arrigo, 1995b).

DEVELOPMENT OF A REPLACEMENT DISCOURSE AND A TRANSFORMATIVE POLITICS

In the previous sections we have addressed the question of the decentered subject. We have indirectly critiqued those such as Handler (1992), who would simply assimilate postmodernist categories into conventional theorizing and transformative politics and find in dismay that postmodernist thought falls short in its promise. Here we would like to briefly address Handler's third criticism concerning the relationship of postmodernist thought to the issue of foundational positions that support transformative politics, and his fourth point concerning alternative visions of polity, economy, and community.

In our view, one of the most important initial approaches that grounds postmodernist thought is "standpoint" theory offered from feminist thought (Bartlett and Kennedy, 1991a). As she has it, "standpoint epistemology identifies woman's status as that of victim, and then privileges that status by claiming that it gives access to understanding about oppression that others cannot have" (ibid.: 385). Further:

> The positional stance acknowledges the existence of empirical truths, values and knowledge, and also their contingency. It thereby provides a basis for feminist commitment and political action, but views these commitments as provisional and subject to further critical evaluation and revision...the positional knower conceives of truth as situated and partial (ibid.: 389).

What this interventionist strategy indicates is that alienated, repressed, disenfranchised, and marginalized subjects have had their voices denied in mainstream discourse (global knowledge); in other words, they remain *pas-toute*. Bartlett is indicating a direction for change. However, she falls short in providing the social and psychic transformations that take place. Although an important start, she falls short of convincingly arguing how changes in the Symbolic and Imaginary Orders would follow. Without more, her standpoint epistemology could easily slip back into "revenge politics" (Cornell, 1991), reversal of hierarchies, and, with it, inadvertently reconstitute previous forms of domination, perpetuate hegemony, and so forth. Additionally, critical race theorists have pointed out that there are diverse standpoints that may exist and hence, diverse epistemologies. And further, standpoint epistemology without more falls short because even the disenfranchised must situate themselves in a dominant discourse to construct narratives and thereby inadvertently reconstruct the dominant Symbolic Order.

Two refinements of standpoint epistemology have been recently developed. First, we may more sensitively refer to it in the plural: standpoint(s) epistemology(ies) and all that it implies. And, second, Butler's (1992) offering of the notion of "contingent universalities" moves theorizing away from essentialist arguments.

Elsewhere, we have indicated that Lacan's *discourse of the master* in combination with the *discourse of the hysteric* can be conceived as the basis of the cultural revolutionary who in fact may collaborate with the oppressed in engendering change (Milovanovic, 1992a, 1993b, 1993c; see also Unger's conception of the cultural revolutionary, 1987, and Freire's pedagogy underlying literacy campaigns, 1972, 1985; Henry and Milovanovic, 1996).[8] In other words, in Lacan's two discourses what is indicated is a path toward the development of new master signifiers (S1) (key signifiers that ground the subject's meaning constructions), which better embody the uniqueness of historically and socially situated oppressed groups in a local knowledge (S2). We drew from Paulo Freire's work on the pedagogy of the oppressed in combination with Lacan's two discourses to indicate how key master signifiers can be produced by disenfranchised subjects, not superimposed top-down by intellectual imperialism, but by a collaborative effort of the cultural revolutionary and the oppressed. Here, celebrated is the discursive production of those whose voice has been denied. This transformative politics has everything to do with privileging local knowledge, even its very construction.

In other words, we argue *with* Bartlett and her notion of privileging the position of the oppressed, but add that a catalyst, the cultural revolutionary, is necessary, who collaboratively develops a new constellation of master signifiers that better represent (embody) the desiring subject. This, in turn, may become the basis of a relatively stable discourse reflecting a local knowledge. But due to the work of the Imaginary that Cornell so brilliantly lays out, this is always a provisional truth, a historically and contingent knowledge subject to change. Hence, a "contingent universality" (Butler, 1992) has much similarity with the idea of "dissipative structures" developed by chaos theory.

The production of provisional truths is actively engendered by those who previously were silenced (*pas-toute*). With the development of a new body of master signifiers that better embody desire within historical contexts, a new, relatively stable but constantly changing discourse sensitive to contingencies and nonlinear historical developments could be established, a replacement discourse. The various "cuts" of Schema R would be infused with alternative imaginary and symbolic content and hence, R, the perceived field of reality, fantasy, could be the basis of qualitatively different forms of social actions, such as those predicated on what Martin Buber referred to as I-thou rather than I-it reciprocities.

Consequently, rather than privileging a global knowledge and truth we see a plurality of forms of consciousness and discourses that are more responsive to local contingencies. This is not to say there are no foundations, but it is to say that they are provisional. Change would be endemic to this replacement discourse, or more appropriately, replacement *discourses*. Accordingly, we would, following Julia Kristeva's conceptualization, have a *subject-in-process* and, we add, a "reality"-in-process. This approach could also be a guard against the negative effects in the dialectics of struggle where previous forms of hierarchy are inadvertently reconstituted. Referring to our elaboration of Schema R, we envision alternative suturing operations between the Symbolic and Imaginary Orders that are more open, spontaneous, contingent and reflective of historical and social nuances.

FAR-FROM-EQUILIBRIUM CONDITIONS AND A NEW BASIS OF BEING

Let us briefly move on to the question of a vision of polity, economy, and community. It is here that the Real Order will certainly have effects. A useful direction can be developed by the conceptualizations of chaos theory, the transformative agenda of Unger, and concepts offered by a critically informed psychoanalytic semiotics developed above.

Chaos theory offers some important insights as to the necessary milieu out of which more sensitive and responsive social structures could take form. A necessary condition within which the development of alternative master signifiers and body of knowledge could take place is the existence of *far-from-equilibrium* conditions within which *dissipative structures* abound (Prigogine and Stengers 1984; Briggs and Peat 1989; Jantsch 1980; Leifer 1989; Marchante, 1992; Henry and Milovanovic, 1996: 203-11).

Dissipative structures—whether examined at the level of semiotic forms, texts, organization of psychic economy, management practices, or social structure—are characterized by their sensitivity and responsiveness to perturbations, however slight, hence their receptivity to continuous change. In other words, a static, bureaucratic society (i.e., equilibrium conditions) hinders the free development of new master signifiers and body of knowledge; similarly, textual production is hindered in a *readerly text* (Silverman 1982). It reinforces the development of the unilateral discourses of the master and university (i.e., point and limit attractors). It minimizes the engagement of bifurcation points, which could be the point for the development of new, more sensitive orders within which subjects exist. It reduces the number of possible discursive subject-positions within which a subject may take up residence, substantially circumscribes the forms within which desire may be embodied (i.e., signifiers), and circumscribes the possible "cuts" or fantasies that may materialize.

Alternatively, in an order characterized as being in far-from-equilibrium, a new flow of desire would be evident. Here, random psychic fluctuations as well as more focused coordination of psychical states (Freud once referred to the latter as "attention") would find *rhizomatic* pathways (Deleuze and Guattari, 1987) along which desire flows, continuously intersected by a perpendicular *line of continuous variation* that provides a wide range of possible variances (i.e., the *writerly text*—Silverman, 1982: 246-49; or a *minor literature*, Deleuze and Guattari, 1986). Rather than restrictive expression we see continuous variation, a writerly textual production, a privileging of minor literature. At the most conscious level of semiotic production, one coordinated by the paradigm-syntagm semiotic axes, a replacement discourse would allow only temporary knottings of signifiers to signified; all is contingent, subject to iterative variations, and, hence, the privileging of the subject-in-process. Here, greater free-play is provided for fantasy, as well as for the significantly greater development of alternative forms for the embodiment of desire (i.e., signifiers), multifarious discursive subject-positions within which to reside, and an omnipresent pluralistic gaze reflecting diverse segments of the population (see, for example, Matsuda's call for "multiple consciousness as jurisprudential method," 1993).

Given a rigid, bureaucratically structured society increasingly tending toward ossification, stasis, self-referentiality, formal rationality, and self-reproduction (equilibrium conditions) (see, for example, Habermas, 1984), transpraxis will be a difficult achievement. Generated knowledge (S2) and master signifiers (S1) strongly preclude alternative forms of rationality and more complete embodiment of desire. The *objet (a)*, in other words, will find incomplete expression, or alternatively, will be the object of manipulative political and economic practices. If, however, we argue with Roberto Unger's recent suggestion for an *empowered democracy* (1987; see also Milovanovic 1992a: 243-55; Henry and Milovanovic, 1996: 235-41), we do see the possible basis for a pragmatically grounded replacement discourse, one offering in every way what Lacan has referred to as *mythic knowledge* and new forms of master signifiers (S1) that resist closure. In the Lacanian schema, the subject here will find embodiment in signifiers that provide fuller and more genuine expression of desire, a manifestation of the will to power.

What far-from-equilibrium conditions foster are: alternative discursive subject-positions, ideal-egos, or $\$\rightarrow m(a^{1-n})$; an expanded range in the conceptualization of others and objects with which to identify, $\$\rightarrow i(a^{1-n})$; an ego-ideal that idealizes multifarious and multivalent forms of social and individual existence, I(O); alternative signifiers within which desire is embodied, including master signifiers (S1) that are more open and receptive to change; a political economy where primordial sense data (the domain of the Real Order) is qualitatively different from that generated in hierarchical structures (consider the images that the Canadian court stipulated as the cause of violence); and the appearance of diverse "cuts," and with them fantasies, which collectively provide a relative order at the *global* level (i.e., a subject that is somewhat predictable) but with *local* unpredictability (i.e., the spontaneous subject, the *subject-in-process*)—here we implicate the torus and strange attractor as indicative of the collective "cuts" taking place.

CONCLUSION

We have provided a journey through unconventional topological terrain. What has been explored is the potential for the development of new master signifiers, a *subject-in-process*, and a new body of knowledge that excludes tendencies to ossification, stasis, equilibrium, and permanent stability. The new semiotic forms would reflect variability, chance, spontaneity, becoming; the new vocabulary would encompass such notions as far-from-equilibrium conditions, stochastic bifurcation points, dissipative structures, strange attractors, semiotic iterations, fractal geometry and nonlinear developments. The new vocabulary situates us in an alternative paradigm within which desire finds alternative expression. We are not offering a blueprint, but some alternative directions to prevailing discourses of the master and often their disguised form, the discourses of the university.

NOTES

1. Lacan has said: "In order to clarify all that I would like to say I will say to you that it is in articulating the function of this point [central point] that we are able to find all sorts of useful formulas which permit us to conceive of the function of the phallus at the center of the constitution of the object of desire" (Lacan, 6 June, 1962, unpublished: my translation).

2. If now we do a lengthwise cut on the Mobius band, we produce a new paradox. Prior to this cut, the Mobius band had a half-twist, was a surface with a single side with no distinction between inside and outside, and was mirror-reversing (nonorientable), retaining its specular image. After this cut, the figure becomes a band with four half-twists, with two sides (similar to an ordinary band), has an inside and an outside, and is not mirror-reversing. Interestingly, and not without significance, if we once again cut this band lengthwise, two separate but knotted surfaces result (Granon-Lafont, 1985: 114-6, 121-2). Thus the knot of fantasy is also formed by two pieces of string: the simple loop of a disk intertwined with the 8-interior of the Mobius band.

3. Translational nuances have at times created some confusion. Thus *objet petit a* is sometimes translated as a or o; the Other as A or O; the moi as m or e; the ideal ego as o' or a', etc.

4. It is this dynamic, too, that lies behind the constitutive processes in theorizing in criminology, penology, and law (Henry and Milovanovic, 1991).

5. We say "transpraxis" instead of "praxis" because the former is rooted more in the Nietzschean ideal of an affirmative value-creating metaphysics, not the more conservative Hegelian reaction-negation dynamics that lies behind the creation of value for the slave in his classic master-slave dialectic.

6. As to actual proof, the court said "it is sufficient in this regard for Parliament to have a reasonable basis for concluding that harm will result and this requirement does not demand actual proof of harm" (p. 505).

7. See also chapter 3, this book.

8. See also chapter 3, note 2, this book.

Borromean Knots and the Constitution of Sense in Juridico-Discursive Production

INTRODUCTION

A critical perspective in law and criminology can be constructively augmented by a psychoanalytic semiotic view rooted in postmodern thought, particularly drawing inspiration from Jacques Lacan. A new direction could be defined as constitutive law and criminology (see chapters 4, 8, this book; Henry and Milovanovic, 1996). This view suggests that thinking about law should be reconsidered as the coterminous discursive production by human agents of an ideology of the rule of law that sustains it as a concrete reality. Although some initial forays have appeared, a contribution to the question of agency is still in the process of development. Accordingly, this article explores the contributions of Lacanian thought, particularly his late development of topology theory, and, more specifically, the borromean knots. This could potentially lead to a macro/micro integration. The construction of an alternative, more liberating "replacement discourse" that allows desire fuller embodiment will be seen as implicit in this integration and will be developed somewhat in the final section.

MACRO-MICRO INTEGRATION: CONSTITUTIVE PERSPECTIVE ON LAW

Approaches in the sociology of law that seek to identify law as simply an outcome of macro- or of microcontexts should be rejected. Rather, we will argue that coproductive activity by agents both produce and reproduce juridical-ideological phenomena. Law, in this view, both reflects dominant social relations and constitutes them (Henry and Milovanovic, 1991). Driven by purposive rational constructions and reproduced by syllogistic reasoning within relatively stabilized linguistic coordinate systems, law provides key master signifiers (S1) that are determinative of social relations. In other words, law has the power to frame politics and legal processes, and hence shape political possibilities. Dominant social relations, in turn, continuously infuse juridic constructions with energy through use, while providing, especially during crises, new material for incorporation.

In all this, we hasten to add, voices from the disenfranchised, marginal, oppressed, and exploited are denied their effective contributions in semiotic production and in the stabilization of alternative linguistic coordinate systems within which more liberating embodiments of desire may materialize. Nor are relatively stabilized discursive subject-positions offered that provide greater opportunity for the play of spontaneity, chance, randomness, irony, and continuous variation. In this sense, subordinates are *pas-tout(e)*, not all, not complete in the dominant Symbolic Order. As we shall see below, they are more often relegated to the *discourse of the hysteric,* and hence further marginalized or, in their haste to overcome the gaps in being, resigned to suturing operations that are modal forms of the *discourse of the master* and in more refined form, the *discourse of the university* (see also Milovanovic, 1993a, 1993b; see also chapter 2, note 8, this book).

How to overcome this cyclical and hegemonic reproduction of dominant reality? Let us first briefly summarize some key Marxian conceptualizations of the relationship between the "base" and "superstructure," noting some of their deficiencies, and then move on to the synthesis of constitutive theory with Lacan's idea of the borromean knots.

MARXIST-INSPIRED VIEWS

Marxist views in the sociology of law have been the beginning points for illuminating analysis. In most cases, however, they lack a necessary component of semiotic analysis, a bonafide conception of agency, and an understanding of the intimate connection between the two.

Several Marxist views have evolved. First, the instrumental Marxist view in law would argue that the economic sphere is the primal causal agent behind all phenomena, be it law, crime, definitions of crime, public policy, development of consciousness, morals, ethics, and so forth (figure 1a). This view was substantially criticized during the 1970s, and by the early 1980s grew into disfavor. The second approach is the structural approach that developed during the early 1980s. Here, the essential argument is that several relatively autonomous spheres exist—economic, ideological, political, juridical—and contribute, in a concerted manner to the development of phenomena. Thus, specifying the causal agents is an exercise in attempting to state the particular articulation of these relatively autonomous spheres within historical conditions. Any phenomena, then, is overdetermined by a number of disproportionally impacting spheres.

After some polemics during the 1980s, several subcategories have been delineated. The commodity-exchange perspective, or the so-called capital-logic school, still places decisive weight with the economic sphere, although it does indicate that commodity-exchange in a competitive capitalist marketplace produces certain phenomenal forms such as the juridic subject, formal equality, and generally, the law of equivalence (figure 1b), which then affects socioeconomic relations. A second variant of the structural version is the structural interpellation perspective rooted more in Althusser and Poulantzas. Here, the superstructure is the primal or decisive causal sphere. Subjects are said to be interpellated as spoken subjects by the juridical-ideological sphere (Figure 1c).

Figure 1. Critical Perspectives of Base-Superstructure

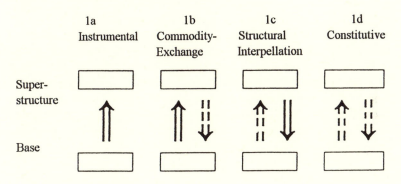

In all these Marxist perspectives what is lacking is a bonafide statement concerning agency and a sensitivity to nonlinear historical developments. Instrumental Marxists relegate the subject to Bentham-like utilitarian existence; commodity exchange views subjects merely acting out the logic of the movement of capital; structural interpellationists see subjects as merely "supports" of hegemonic groups. Ironically, all three, ostensibly concerned with the human condition, have been insensitive to the multidimensional nature of agency.

Constitutive theory begins with certain strengths of the structural interpellation view (figure 1d), but recognizes inherent limitations within it. (For a fuller explanation of constitutive theory, see chapters 4, 8, this book; see also Henry and Milovanovic, 1996.) The necessary element in overcoming the above deficiencies is semiotic analysis and the use of nonlinear conceptions of historical change, suggested, for example, by Nietzsche, Foucault, and chaos theory. Postmodernist analysis, particularly one rooted in the insights of Lacanian psychoanalytic semiotics, offers us much potential for better conceptualizing the nature of the desiring subject in relation to discursive production. Constitutive theory, however, offers an organizing structure that applies semiotic analysis as a key element.

OPPOSITIONAL AND REVOLUTIONARY SUBJECTS

Increasingly, in a social formation, we see the tension between, on the one hand, the constituted subject (alternatively: the "interpellated," "spoken," or "good subject")[1] and, on the other, the resisting subject (i.e., ranging from the less politically aware oppositional subject to the politically articulate, revolutionary subject). Lacan's offering of four structured discourses has been instructive in these conceptualizations.[2] Elsewhere, drawing from Lacan, we have indicated (1993c) that the *discourse of the master*[3] (Lacan, 1991a; Arrigo, 1993a; Bracher, 1993; Milovanovic, 1992a, 1993a, 1993b), or its more hidden form, the *discourse of the university*,[4] is the modal form of subjectification in hierarchical social formations, be they "capitalistic" or "socialistic." The oppositional subject (i.e., the alienated, frustrated, and revolting subject), one without a fully articulate transformative politics, can be depicted by the Lacanian *discourse of the hysteric*.[5] The revolutionary subject, or perhaps more precisely, the cultural revolutionary, we shall show below, can be seen as constituted by the discourse of the hysteric and analyst[6] and is one who begins to be driven by an articulate transformative agenda.

Marxist analysis has indicated how subjects become constituted by the discourse of the master and university, but yet often revolt in the form of the discourse of the hysteric, a discourse by itself devoid of any potential for transformative politics or new visions of what could be. At best, the Marxian/Hegelian conceptualization of historical change can merely indicate that dialectical materialism will propel the disenfranchised (the "slave" in Hegel's master-slave dialectic, or the proletariat in Marx's version) to revolt, or to engage in the discourse of the hysteric. But careful examination will indicate that this is merely reactive-negative dynamics: nothing new is being offered. In fact, many of the more contemporary Marxists or postmodernists who seek help from Derrida have too quickly embraced the idea of "reversing hierarchies" as the solution. With but little reflection we can see how, on the one hand, this merely reconstitutes forms of domination (see also, Milovanovic, 1992a; Henry and Milovanovic, 1991; Bannister and Milovanovic, 1990), and, on the other, the subject of Nietzsche's *ressentiment* (Deleuze, 1983; Groves, 1991; see also chapters 5, 6, 7, this book). Elsewhere (1993a), we have indicated that a cultural revolutionary, a hybrid of Lacan's discourse of the hysteric and *discourse of the analyst*, provides a direction illuminating the necessary changes that must take place in discursive formations.

We hasten to disagree with both Lacan and Bracher (1993) that the *discourse of the analyst*, in *itself*, offers the direction, for, as both indicate, this discourse can easily slip back into, and historically has slipped back into, the discourse of the master. Accordingly, in our view, a perpetual oscillation between the discourse of the hysteric and analyst, tantamount to what chaos theorists have termed a "strange attractor" (see note 21), is desirable and would produce the cultural revolutionary. Applying the borromean knots, below we will also provide a novel conceptualization of how new signifiers may develop within more stable structures. Some of the insights from Chaos theory have also shed productive light on the milieu within which this could take place (i.e., far-from-equilibrium conditions, see Milovanovic, 1992a: Chapters 5, 6; Arrigo, 1993a; Henry and Milovanovic, 1996).

LACAN'S PSYCHOANALYTIC SEMIOTICS

According to Lacan, the interactive effects of three main orders lie behind phenomena: the Imaginary, Symbolic, and Real. The Imaginary Order is the sphere of imagoes, of imaginary constructions of self, others, and possible objects that offer the potential for the fulfillment of desire (*objet petit a*). These are essentially illusory, but give us hope of mastery in otherwise incomprehensible situations.[7] The Symbolic Order is the sphere of language, culture, and sociocultural prohibitions. The Other, an unconscious sphere, is the sphere within which signifying production, coordinated by the tropes of metaphor and metonymy, takes place. The Other as the "treasure of signifiers" is where signifiers "float" awaiting anchorage (*capitonnage*) to particular signifieds. And, in Lacan's enigmatic definition, a signifier is that which is the subject for another signifier.

The Lacanian desiring subject, then, is represented in discourse by signifiers who speak it. The speaking being (*l'être parlant*, or *parlêtre*) is divided, represented in Lacan's mathemes as a slashed subject or $. It exists on two levels: the level of discursive production and the level of discourse itself. At the level of discursive production, meaning "falters, slips and slides," always subject to the effects of desire seeking expression, always "insisting." Periodic punctuations provide temporary joins to particular signifiers: it is this that produces particular meaning (Lacan, 1977). In Lacan's mathemes:

$$S(\emptyset) \rightarrow \$ \diamond a \rightarrow s(O) \rightarrow \text{signifying chain; or: S-S-S-S-S/s.}$$

What this means is that the inherent-lack-in-being [$S(\emptyset)$] of the *parlêtre* ($), a condition in which signifiers exist temporarily without anchorage (*point de capiton*) within the Other (O), periodically leads to fantasy production ($\diamond a$), culminating in a punctuation [s(O)], a temporary and unstable knotting of a signifier to a particular signified (S/s). S-S-S-S-S/s represents a "signifying chain," an utterance. Ultimately, of course, embodied signifiers must find expression within particular linguistic coordinate systems coordinated by the paradigm and syntagm semiotic axis to produce a narratively coherent text (B. Jackson, 1988). It is this process that produces idiosyncratic sense.

The final Lacanian Order is the sphere of the Real. It represents the phenomenal world of sense perception, beyond any accurate reflection in symbolic constructions.

In the Lacanian construct, desire is mobilized periodically due to the inherent lack-in-being of the subject, which was the cost born by the child in its inauguration into the Symbolic Order and all that it has to offer: control, mastery, understanding, and the basis for social action.[8] Henceforth, contradictions, contrarieties, and anomalies faced mobilize desire whereby the subject, $, attempts to *suture*, or stitch over the gaps in being. This search for objects of desire (*objet petit a*) implicates the Symbolic and Imaginary Order. Existing value-laden signifiers within particular linguistic coordinate systems (legal, oppositional, pluralistic, etc.) offer linguistic forms for the embodiment of desire. The creation of sense overcomes the felt lack in being, an experience that Lacan referred to as *jouissance* (or *jouis-sense*, enjoyment in sense; in the French, the term also has connotations of an orgasm).[9] This is essentially fantasy, or in Lacan's mathemes, $◇a. Sense production, then, entails the interplay of the Imaginary and the Symbolic Order with the Real always in the background, but nevertheless insisting.[10]

BORROMEAN KNOTS

Lacan's late works (1972-1977) focused on topological constructions of borromean knots (1972, 1973, 1975-1976, 1976-1977; see also Granon-Lafont, 1985, 1990; Juranville, 1984; Skriabine, 1989; Soury, 1980; Chaubard, 1984; Ragland-Sullivan, 1990a, 1990b). Lacan attempted to provide an alternative mapping of the psychic apparatus and sense production. These constructions are neither metaphors nor analogies to the workings of the psychic apparatus: they are offered as homologies. His reasons for the use of topology theory are two-fold: for expository purposes and as a means of discovery. It is these borromean knots that provide an explanatory mechanism of constitutive processes taking place, producing and reproducing hierarchically constituted discursive formations. The constitutive theory of law will provide a useful schema in understanding the processes of sense production in signifying practices. Also illuminated will be possible directions for reconstituting discursive regions in the form of a replacement discourse.

STRUCTURE AND FUNCTION OF BORROMEAN KNOTS

Remarkably, little in Western thought has engaged the insights generated by Lacan on the borromean knots. From 1962 to 1972, the Mobius band and *cross-cap* were key topological constructs for Lacan.[11] From the middle of

1972 to about 1977, the borromean knot became dominant (after 1977, Lacan's productivity and creativity were reduced dramatically due to deteriorating health). In between, beginning in 1969, the notion of the four discourses was to be a transitional step to increasingly abstract and difficult conceptualizations.

The idea of a knot, however, was already appearing in Lacan's seminars in 1962. In short form, a borromean knot is defined by two or more loops or rings knotted by another (each ring represents one of the Lacanian Orders); cut one, and all disentangle. (Figure 2 below is a 2-D portrait; a 3-D portrait would more accurately indicate how the three circles are intertwined. Note, for example, that in the 3-D version there is an under-over, interlocking form of the rings.) The borromean knot depicts the interconnectedness of the psychic apparatus, portraying how it in fact maintains *consistency*.

Figure 2. Borromean Knot, 2-D.   Borromean Knot, 3-D.

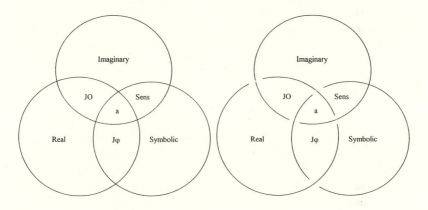

Here,
a = *le plus-de-jouir* (the more than enjoyment, the left out)[12]
JO = jouissance of the Other; bodily jouissance
Jφ = phallic jouissance
Sens = meaning unique to the speaking being (*l'être parlant*)
R.S.I. = the three orders: Real, Symbolic, Imaginary

A ring (actually a torus), unlike a sphere, is not a container and thus something appearing within the borromean intersections is both in and outside of it; the notion of "inside" and "outside" becomes problematic (Sarup, 1992: 113). Ragland-Sullivan has precisely commented on this enigma: "the space structured around the joins of these orders would be inferred into discourse as a topology of fixed positions and effects in the Other which operates language and perception, ensuring that neither discourse nor perception be purely linear, nor purely conscious" (1990a: 58). Consider, too, Marini's observation that the theory of the borromean knots implies that the subject is "mis-situated between two and three dimensions," which finds expression in Lacan with his idea of *dit-mension* (1992: 242; see also his seminar to the North American community of 1 December, 1975, p. 42). In chaos theory, this would be represented by the idea of a *fractal*, depicting fractions of dimensions. Clearly, Lacan had an entirely novel conception of space, one in opposition to Newtonian physics. Unfortunately, he was not acquainted with chaos theory; some theorists inspired by him, such as Deleuze and Guattari (1987), have indeed explored some illuminating directions with this insight.

From 1972 to 1977 Lacan was to develop numerous pictures of the borromean knots. He would construct a borromean knot as a set of interlocking rings whereby cutting one would let loose the others. He would then construct several of these, producing a ring of such knots, a borromean ring. For Lacan, it was a representation of the functioning of the psychic apparatus. This conceptualization was to replace his earlier idea of a signifying chain. It is within this chain that the "letter [signifier] insists" (Lacan, 1977: 146-78).[13]

Let us relate the borromean knots to fantasy. Fantasy production, as we have indicated, can be traced to the essential lack in being of the subject (see also Chapter 2, this book). Lack, in turn, "is iterated with specific effects in each of the Lacanian topological orders" (Rapaport, 1990: 243). The cumulative result (symbolized by the knots) or fantasy, representing the appearing and disappearing of the subject, also becomes the basis of social action.

It should also be noted that two forms of *jouissance* appear: phallic jouissance (Jϕ) is located at the intersection of the Real and Symbolic Orders—it is the upper limit of jouissance that exists within a given phallocentric Symbolic Order. However, an *unspeakable* jouissance exists that is beyond the phallus at the intersection of the Real and Imaginary, called alternatively a *supplementary*, *bodily*, or jouissance of the Other (JO) (Lacan, 1985: 142-4; Juranville, 1984: 335). And here exists the potential for the development of alternative knottings, and thus, understandings.

Let us provide an example, the narrative: "Jones willfully inflicted gross bodily harm on Fred." Here, each signifier takes on value within a discursive whole; in its apparent linear construction, each completed signifier anticipates the next (the anticipatory dimension) and only with the punctuation is there a return to the beginning (Lacan's *retrograde*), providing the whole a precise sense. In figure 3, we note that the divided subject now appears at the bottom left. Here the subject is represented in discourse by her/his signifiers. The discursive chain now stands for the presence of an absence, whereby the signifier is the subject for another signifier. We should add that the paradigm-syntagm level of semiotic production is only the most manifest level experienced in actual dialogical encounters within particular linguistic coordinate systems (here we are at one with Bernard Jackson's narrative coherence model, 1988); at a deeper level, however, desire begins to be embodied by the effects of condensation-displacement (discovered by Freud) and takes on additional embodiment via metaphor-metonymy (Lacan's contribution following Jakobson's work on aphasic disorders) (see figure 4).[14]

Figure 3. Elementary Cell of Speech Production (Lacan, 1977: 303)

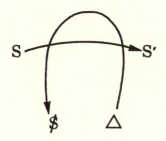

Figure 4. Semiotic Grid

More conscious	Paradigm	Syntagm
↑ ↓	Metaphor	Metonymy
More unconscious	Condensation	Displacement

Each signifier embodying desire (see also Freud's idea of "figuration") finds its coordinates in the semiotic grid. This consists of the following axes: paradigm-syntagm (at the conscious level), metaphor-metonymy (at the unconscious level), and condensation-displacement (at the most fundamental and unconscious level of the working of the unconscious).[15] Each manifest signifier is but the loci of complex processes (i.e., the interactive effects of the three orders: Real, Symbolic, and Imaginary), which have reached an anchoring point, a knotting (*capitonnage*) that maintains degrees of consistency. Master signifiers, S1, are the core identificatory signifiers.[16] It is this knotting that produces an idiosyncratic sense for each speaking being (*l'être parlant*). Some of these knots, or constellations of knots, attain greater permanence within the psychic structure: these belong to the order of the symptom (*le synthome*), and become the basis of "repetition," or as Lacan has it, the source of the periodic manifestation of the "letter insisting" (1977: 146-78). They become relatively stable points from which jouissance is experienced. In sum, Lacan's notion of structure is unique: it "is both anticipatory and retroactive; static and dynamic; prediscursive and discursive; regulatory and disruptive" (Ragland-Sullivan, 1990a: 58).

The topology of the borromean knots—its opening, closing, stasis, and transformation—in relation to the disciplining mechanisms of a political economy becomes the key in understanding change. Consider, for example, the *cuts* engendered during revolutionary upheavals, especially in contemporary Eastern Europe and the former Soviet Union, and with it the appearance of the good (i.e., more liberating articulations of the three Orders), the bad (i.e., divisive nationalistic and ultra-right-wing movements), and the ugly (i.e., ethnic hatred and campaigns of "ethnic cleansing").

THE SYMPTOM (*LE SYNTHOME*)

In late 1975, Lacan, then in his mid 70s, discovered the fourth Order, that of *le synthome,* or *le sinthome,* Σ (see the seminar delivered on *Le Synthome,* 16 December 1975).[17] Lacan attributed the discovery of the symptom to Karl Marx, whom he read when he was twenty (Lacan, *RSI*, 18 February 1975: 106). During his seminar of December 9th and 16th, 1975, he tells us that he had scratched his head for two months pondering the possibility of the fourth tie. He drew considerable inspiration from two friends who were mathematicians, Michel Thome and Pierre Soury. According to Ragland-Sullivan, "[t]he symptom may be a word, sound, event, detail, or image that acts in a way peculiar to a given subject's history...the enigmatic symptom belongs to the sign or the unconscious signifying chain of language because it is susceptible of being deciphered or decoded" (1990b: 73). We will briefly explain the wherewithal of the symptom, and then indicate its importance for a constitutive theory of law and for the potential of understanding the necessary dynamics of a replacement discourse.

The function of the fourth term is to repair, mend, correct or restore a fault in the knot R.S.I. (Lacan, *Le Synthome,* 16 December 1975; Granon-Lafont, 1990: 141). It's a form of "suture" that Lacan had developed in his earlier seminars. Put in another way, absent a knot, the three Orders experience no consistency: they are, in Lacan's formulation, S(∅). In other words, an inherent lack (-1) exists in the Other. It is with the fourth term that "naming" ("donner-nom") takes place, a response to the lack in the Other, to the failures and breakdowns in the Other (Lacan, S, 22, 11 March and 13

May, 1975; Skriabine, 1989: 21). This naming operation, depicted by "doubling," is what provides relative consistency for the psychic apparatus.

Speech production, for example, constitutes itself in the doubling of the symbolic with the symptom (*le synthome*) (Granon-Lafont, 1990: 147). Put in another way, these three relatively autonomous spheres must be knotted in order that consistency and a sense of permanency prevails. In the Freudian construct, the Oedipus complex performs this function. Absent this, psychosis awaits. In the Lacanian schema, it is the name-of-the-father that acts as the stabilizing structure (Caudill, 1992a, 1992b, 1992c). The name-of-the-father functions to overcome the failures in the Other by realizing the knot, R.S.I. (Skriabine, 1989: 24). Of course it follows that a number of other candidates exist that may function in the capacity of "repairing" the knot as, for example, postmodernist feminists have pointed out. In a phallic Symbolic Order, all is tainted with the phallus. The upper limit of jouissance is phallic (Jφ), and therefore women are left out, *pas-toute* (Lacan, 1985).

More generally, ongoing hierarchically organized political economies need to provide "fillers" in order to overcome this inherent lack-in-being. Absent this, crisis tendencies (legal, economic, political, ideological) may tend toward radical upheavals. Thus, for example, we have imaginary constructions of agency such as the "reasonable man" in law, the rational man/woman in economic planning, and the notion of the private citizen bound within the logic of the rule of law. The advertisement industry, too, provides a plethora of discursive subject positions with which to identify.

Topologically speaking, the fourth term can be continuously deformed, producing numerous "repairings"; it can always stir elsewhere (Granon-Lafont, 1990: 141-2) with specific effects. Thus *le synthome* can "double" the Symbolic, Real, or the Imaginary (ibid.; see figure 5).

We can seen in figure 5, under the doubling of the Symbolic, that the ring representing the Symbolic Order is replaced by a binary, S+Σ,[18] producing a new form of the Symbolic, S" (Skriabine, 1989: 24; Granon-Lafont, 1990: 143-61; Lacan, 1976: 58; Lacan, 1987b: 46-8). In fact, "this binary corresponds to two slopes of the symbolic: the signifier able to couple itself with another in order to make a chain, and the letter [that 'insists']" (Skriabine, 1989: 24, my transl.). Hence, these two are complementary functions, one acting to represent in a chain of signifiers, the other remaining embedded in the symptom and acting as the support. It is this that anchors the discursive chain and provides meaning (*sens*); that is, it reflects the speaking subject's truth even though s/he does not know what it is. It is also this dynamic that produces the *objet petit (a)* and provides a sense of plenitude, an overcoming of -1, experienced as a *jouis-sens* (Lacan, 1987b: 47).

Figure 5. Le Synthome and Doubling

"Doubling" of the:

Symbolic   Or Equivalently: Real

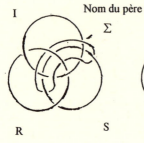 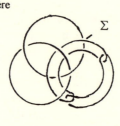 

Imaginary

Let's consider the *discourse of the master*. According to Lacan, "the subject in this state can only represent itself by the signifier indicated as 1, while the signifier indicated as 2 represents itself...by the duplicity of the symbolic and the symptom" (1987b: 47; my trans.). The receiver of the message enacts the S1, producing his/her symptom, and at the most manifest level, a body of knowledge, S2. Lacan goes on to say, "S2, there, is the author [*artisan*], in so much by the conjunction of the two signifiers he is capable of producing the objet (a)..." (Ibid.; my trans.). Thus, in the discourse of the master, S2, knowledge, divides itself into the symbolic and the symptom. The symptom remains the support of S2, knowledge. The sender's S1 activates, or elicits S2, which nevertheless "insists" in producing the *a, le-plus-de-jouir* in the unconscious.[19] Here, something is left out, is not embodied in signifiers. This excess has only potentiality in being given form. The subject is represented by a signifier. For Lacan, the signifier is that which represents the subject for another signifier in a signifying/borromean chain. Knowledge, therefore, is always supported by an underlying *symptom*, is always a function of a fractal space at work. This is why Lacan refers to the "said" as the *dit-mension*.

On the other hand, in the *discourse of the analyst*, the receiving subject divides itself, producing new S1s as a response to the information that the sender is reflecting about her/him. These are new master signifiers that become the basis of an alternative symptom and, consequently, become a basis of an alternative jouissance.[20] Put in another way, this has everything to do with the process of knot-breaking and "repairing." And if we were then to take the discourse of the hysteric and analyst, together, we could see the basis for the revolutionary subject in so much as s/he continuously reconstitutes her/his truth by giving form to alternative master signifiers and body of knowledge. Put in yet another way, a new configuration of borromean knots now anchors being. This could be mapped as the *strange attractor* that chaos theory offers.[21] Of course, this could only operate in a supportive milieu. Thus, again, borrowing from chaos theory, *far-from-equilibrium* conditions would seem the desirable form of a social formation (see also Milovanovic, 1992a: 236-56; Henry and Milovanovic, 1996: 235-41).

For Freud, the doubling of the Real produced the "psychic reality" of each subject; for James Joyce, whose writings Lacan analyzed extensively, the doubling of the Symbolic Order produced "Joyce the Symptom"; and the doubling of the Imaginary Order may produce perversion (ibid.: 149; Juranville, 1984: 423-24). Let us be more concrete. The doubling of the Real can be seen historically as represented, in a more active mode, by "doers," such as Hobbsbawn's "primitive rebel" (Milovanovic and Thomas, 1989), who are without a sophisticated political articulation but nevertheless in touch with the prevailing deprivations. In a more passive mode, we could also include here many repressed and exploited subjects who find inadequate linguistic coordinate systems within which to embody desire and to construct narratives that more accurately define their plight. Surely, the discourse of the master and university will impose its understanding. The doubling of the Symbolic produces a subject who lives his symptom in the form of being totally embedded in discourse itself (Ragland-Sullivan, 1990b: 72); on the one hand, the poet is exemplary, on the other, so too the committed (seduced) lawyer who is convinced of the liberating potentials of the rule of law ideology. For the doubling of the Imaginary, a grossly distorted view of self and others manifests itself; perhaps totally self-engrossed dreamers tend toward this pole.[22]

In each case a temporary join is produced that is a source of jouissance. These joins, however, can break, or, alternatively, the fourth term may manifest itself elsewhere with entirely different effects. This is precisely what Jurgen Habermas was getting at when he spoke of steering mechanisms undergoing change, and the "life-world" being coordinated by purposive rational action in advanced forms of capitalistic modes of production. It becomes the basis of new centers of articulation and thereby of sense, producing in the end, jouissance. This essential instability is both the source for manipulative powers and the basis of a potentially new articulation that better embodies human desires.

LITERARY EXAMPLE OF REPAIRING THE KNOT: JOYCE THE SYNTHOME

An exemplar of the functioning of the *symptom* can be offered from the literary sphere. Skriabine (1989) and Ragland-Sullivan (1990b), following Lacan's extensive analysis of Joyce's prose (1987b), suggest that the fault in R.S.I. had to do with the Imaginary Order not being knotted with the Real and Symbolic, which are knotted (figure 6a).

Figure 6. Le Synthome and Repairing the Knot (James Joyce)

a. A Fault in the Borromean Knot
   (R,S are knotted; I is not)

b. A Repaired Borromean Knot
   (R.S.I. are now knotted)

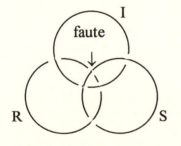
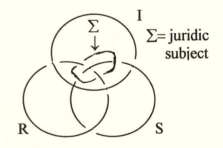

Localizing the *moi* (Lacan's imaginary ego) at the fault (*faute*) can correct this deficiency and thereby connect all three Orders (figure 6b). The imaginary ego is the component of Lacan's quadrilaterally constructed subject that provides illusory but necessary perceptions of unity in order that the subject can function at all. Here, therefore, the ego is *le synthome* (Skriabine,

1989: 25: see also Ragland-Sullivan, 1990b: 70). It is also this resolution that gives peculiarity to Joyce's prose: "Joyce, the symptom," as Lacan would say. "This ego as a symptom [*synthome*], as a supplement, restores two links between the symbolic and the real, and makes the imaginary hold" (Skriabine, 1990: 25: my trans.). Otherwise, of course, the imaginary would continue to glide without anchorage. An initial trace of the original fault, however, remains, and with the Real and Symbolic remaining continuously enlaced, produces the different enigmatic epiphanies in Joyce's work (ibid.), and reproduces his uniquely constituted truth (*savoir*). As Ragland-Sullivan aptly puts it "The prose of *Finnegans Wake* becomes the fantasy of language, knotting together images, words, and traumas to (re)constitute knots into which signifying associative chains from the Real, Symbolic, and Imaginary can hook themselves" (1990b: 77).

CONSTITUTIVE THEORY

Let's return to constitutive theory in law. What Lacan's work on the borromean knots offers is mechanisms by which agency in relationship to social structures could be understood. Legal ideology is transmitted by dominant linguistic coordinate systems, most importantly, the juridic form. This represents the discourse of the master, often dressed as the discourse of the university. What the dominant political economic order offers are "fillers" that provide, on the one hand, illusory conceptions for fulfillment, mastery, understanding, and, on the other, objects of desire [*objet petit (a)*], by which illusory perceptions of the unitary self can be built.

Whether it is the construction and stabilization of the juridic subject, the reasonable man/woman in law (and other forces of rationalization), or the development of new *steering mechanisms* celebrating *purposive rational action* at the expense of symbolic action and communicatively established shared understanding, or the insidious development of ubiquitous and pervasive forms of control such as in Foucault's *disciplinary mechanisms*, or, finally, whether it is the offerings by a manipulative advertising industry providing seductive discursive subject-positions and objects of desire with which to identify —, what are being provided are modal forms of knotting of the three orders. In each instance a pathway is provided for producing *le synthome*, which is the support of jouissance, a safeguard against the fall into an abyss, or alternatively, a way of plugging up the hole-in-being from which all sorts of fragmentary psychic material gushes, threatening to overwhelm the subject.

Subjects both constitute order out of the framing material provided by dominant discourse, and reconstitute the framing material itself. This is most apparent in law where key master signifiers such as due process and formal equality, and juridically constituted joins (*capitonnage*) of signifiers to signifieds, i.e., the legal definitions of "person," "insanity," "duress," "willingly," "maliciously," "negligently," etc., become key material from which hegemonically supported knots are constructed that produce particular forms of the borromean knot and which are reproduced by litigants before the court by their reliance on their framing capabilities. Oppositional groups, too, in so much as they frame their politics within the dominant linguistic coordinate system, will reproduce, be it inadvertently, dominant conceptions and understandings of reality.[23]

Transpraxis, which follows from the combined discourses of the hysteric and analyst, produces the revolutionary subject, one more in line with the views expressed by Nietzsche rather than Hegel. Here, the subject must self-divide, the S1 from the S2, and reconstitute new forms of master signifiers and produce a new knotting in the borromean chain.[24] This can only begin and continue to be, however, in *far-from-equilibrium* conditions. The strange attractor (one wing representing the discourse of the hysteric, the other, the discourse of the analyst) may be a modal form of being; here, self- and societal-transformation will be continuous. The task before us is not only to strive to develop alternative materialistic conditions of existence but also to engage in the development of a cultural criticism in tune with it. And here we are in agreement with Bracher (1993: 192) that the vacuous nature of the latter will certainly be counterproductive to any initiative in the former. Accordingly, the nature of desire, fantasy, objects of desire, and forms of jouissance must be examined. A replacement discourse to the contemporary phallocentric Symbolic Order must develop in which the embodiment of desire finds fuller expression.

NOTES

1. For the *interpellated subject*, see Althusser, 1971; for the *spoken subject* in cinema theory, see Silverman, 1982; for the *good subject*, see Pecheux, 1982.

2. Lacan's four discourses were developed in 1969 and were often referred to well into the 1970s (Lacan, 1991a). The four terms of the discourses include: S1, master signifiers with which the subject strongly identifies; S2, knowledge, which is always embedded in a chain of signifiers; $, the split or divided subject, which means the subject is located on two plains: one is the plane of the subject of speech, the other, the speaking subject; and finally, we have a, here representing *le-plus-de-jouir*, the excess in enjoyment. Lacan tells us that Karl Marx had discovered this in his notion of surplus value. These four terms can take up position in each of four locations:

agent   other
truth   production.

The left-hand side represents the sender of a message, the right-hand side the receiver and enactor of the message. The bottom right represents what is produced in the receiver's unconscious, within his Other. Truth, which is unique to each subject and "insists" nevertheless is never completely known by the subject. The upper left-hand corner represents the initiator of the message. If we take the discourse of the master, we can see that the initiator of the message, here offering master signifiers (the word of God, Democracy, Communism, etc.), S1, interpellates a subject with knowledge, S2, which has the effect of producing, in the unconscious, unembodied knowledge, a left out (i.e, consider colonized subjects). This, in turn, comes to support the truth of the initiator of the message who only offers the word (master signifier) as the solution. Given these mathemes, Lacan goes on to identify four intersubjectively structured discourses:

discourse of the master:

$$\frac{S1}{\$} \rightarrow \frac{S2}{a}$$

discourse of the university:

$$\frac{S2}{S1} \rightarrow \frac{a}{\$}$$

discourse of the hysteric:

$$\frac{\$}{a} \rightarrow \frac{S1}{S2}$$

discourse of the analyst:

$$\frac{a}{S2} \rightarrow \frac{\$}{S1}$$

3. In Seminar 20, published as *Encore* (1975: 108), Lacan said that "mathematical formalization is our goal, our ideal." His many uses of mathemes or ideograms, however, point to a more intuitive mathematics. For example, in the *discourse of the master*, master signifiers, S1, are enacted by the other as a body of knowledge; hence, the other is interpellated, producing and reproducing a given body of pre-established knowledge, S2. However, what is driven below the bar is the *a*, the left out. Consider the colonized forced to speak the language of the conquerors, or activists before the court relegated to the construction of the "what happened?" within the legal linguistic coordinate system, cleansed of politicized sentiments. In other words, the desire of the other (subject) is not being fully embodied in conventional discourse, S2. This process, however, reinforces the split subject, *$*, that remains the support of the sender of the message. On one level, this reflects the strong form of linguistic determinism; on another, we see that desire remains a destabilizing force, ready to be mobilized and embodied in more critical signifiers, which systematized, may lead to potentially subversive replacement discoures.

4. In the discourse of the university, the initiator of the message offers some body of knowledge to the other, who enacts this by reproducing this knowledge. But something is left out, the "a." The subject is driven below the bar and nevertheless provides support to conventional master signifiers, which in turn support the given, prevailing body of knowledge, S2.

5. In the discourse of the hysteric, the hysteric offers her/his unexpressible truth to the other, who merely provides conventional master signifiers as answers to the hysteric's plight. This in turn produces an ongoing conventional body of knowledge, S2, which further maintains the hysteric in her/his resisting mode, for no signifiers are being provided that can embody her/his plight.

6. In the discourse of the analyst, the analyst, embodying the *a*, which is supported by a knowledge (S2) reflected from the alienated subject's master signifiers (S1), induces the alienated subject *($)* to enact entirely new master signifiers (S1), which now come to anchor her/his being.

7. D. Cornell has in fact recently argued for the potential emancipatory imageries of the Imaginary Order as a pathway toward deconstructing the law and as a basis of an "ethical feminism" (1991). This, by itself, overlooks the effects of the other two Orders.

8. Although Lacan's position on desire may seem to imply a homeostatic model consistent with Freud's, our reading is that the discourse of the analyst certainly attests to the polyvalent and open nature of modes of fulfilling desire. The Imaginary Order, too, will militate against any universalism. Our conception of desire is much more in tune with Nietzsche's notion of the "will to power," Freud's notion of Eros and the libido, and Deleuze and Guattari's open-ended nature of desire working its way out along rhizomatic pathways. As Lecercle has it, "desire can also be conceived as a forward movement, a flight towards an object that always eludes our grasp, the attempt, never successful but never frustrating, to reach the unattainable by exploring the paths of the possible" (1985: 196).

9. It also should be noted that "j'ouis" is a pun on "I hear" or "I enjoy," reflecting the conversation between the unconscious and conscious portrayed by the topology of the Mobius Band.

10. Consider, for example, an activist lawyer before the court. In the symbolic construction of reality (the defense's version), the activist is faced with an ongoing tension with her/his own imaginary identifications with a political ideal, and the realities of the court. Juridic sense production has more to do with making use of juridically recognized signifiers and tropes (paradigm/syntagm), rather than those supportive of a politicized sense production.

11. Lacan's conception of the subject was represented in Schema L and Schema R (1977). For Schema L, two axes implicate discursive production: the unconscious axis is the Other-je. Here the "I" (je) is merely a signifier representing the subject for another signifier. The other axis, which is on the imaginary plane, is the moi-other. Here the subject develops imaginary constructions of self through the other. The two axes work together to produce relatively coherent narrative constructions and provide the illusion of a subject in control. Schema R was also offered by Lacan as a topological construction (1977) portraying the desiring subject. It was depicted by projective geometry in the form of the cross-cap (Granon-Lafont, 1985; Milovanovic, 1993b).

12. Lacan makes many usages of *objet petit (a)*. He has instructed his interpreters to understand it in context. Although space limitations preclude an exposition of all the complex terms, overlays, and registers of figure 2, we point out that the *objet petit (a)* is at the confluence of the Symbolic, Imaginary, and Real Orders and at the center of a number of psychic processes (i.e., thought, creation of sense, embodiment of desire in signifiers, etc.). Figure 2 indicates that *sens*—the unique aspect of meaning that is specific to each person—appears at the intersection of the Imaginary and Symbolic Order.

13. At one level, concepts relating to the subject—*sens, jouissance, objet petit (a)*—can be located within this unique structure of the borromean knot. At another level, anxiety, the symptom, and inhibition can be mapped (Juranville, 1984; Granon-Lafont, 1985: 111-47). These represent complex, interpenetrating spheres with specific effects in real-world events. We are in the domain of: fractal spaces; semiotic iterations with nonlinear effects; periodic but effervescent manifestations of lack and its mobilized desire; psychic material seeking expression ("insisting"), gushing to the surface of consciousness, making its zigzag journey (rhizomatic) through the three semiotic axes of condensation-displacement, metaphor-metonymy, and paradigm-syntagm; and the "cork," the *objet petit (a)*, which saves us from our psychosis and potential disappearance into oblivion. In the end, we are provided our illusory sense of control, self-direction, and coherence.

14. Consider, again, the activist lawyer defending activists before the court. It may very well be that s/he desires to introduce a politicized version of the "what happened," but the paradigm-syntagm structure of the Juridic Symbolic Order militates against this version (See, for example, Bannister and Milovanovic, 1990; chapter 7, this book).

15. It was Freud's *Interpretation of Dreams* (1900) that first attempted to explain "dream work." It has been inspirational for those who have sought to develop a psychoanalytic semiotics.

16. Bracher has referred to master signifiers as "identity-bearing words" (1993: 23). The constellation of master signifiers unique to each speaking being becomes the basis of the ego ideal.

17. See also, the following seminars by Lacan: *R.S.I.*, 14 January 1975: 103; *Le Synthome*, 18 November 1975: 44-48; "Conferences et Entretiens dans des Universites Nord-Americanes," 25 November 1975: 39-41; 2 Dec: 56-58. Pierre Soury has also specified possible permutations of *le synthome* (1980: section 18).

18. Where (Σ) represents the Fourth Order.

19. Consider for example, colonizers and their propaganda introduced and imposed on the native population; or, during a break up of a relationship, consider the offering by the other of the signifier, "irreconcilable conflicts"; or consider the role of the psychiatrist in offering signifiers that provide one possible explanation of the hysteric's plight; or, finally, consider the inmate before a "disciplinary hearing" in prison/jail or an inmate seeking advice from a fellow jailhouse lawyer, who is offered only bureaucratic and/or legalistically recognized signifiers as answers to issues of controversy.

20. P. Freire's work (1985) is notable as to how collaborative efforts in generating master signifiers and a body of knowledge can take place.

21. A strange attractor maps phenomena in such a way that two outcome basins develop. The classic example is of two butterfly wings. Here, each wing indicates one space region to which the system tends. We have both global stability (the outside form of the wing) and local variability (within the wing indeterminacy reigns). Hence, there is an orderly disorder.

22. D. Cornell's work on the "imagination and utopian possibility" (1991: 168-96) has provided one element for a transformative politics. However, by itself this falls short (see Milovanovic, 1993b).

23. See, for an application to activist lawyers (Bannister and Milovanovic, 1990); theorizing in criminology (Henry and Milovanovic, 1991; Milovanovic and Henry, 1991); and to jailhouse lawyers (Milovanovic and Thomas, 1989); part 2, this book.

24. Pecheux (1982) has referred to this as "dis-identification"; Cixous, as a "dépensé" (1990).

Constitutive Criminology
The Maturation of Critical Theory

Stuart Henry and Dragan Milovanovic

INTRODUCTION

Critical criminology has recently seen the delineation of several new and competing perspectives (Schwartz, 1989; Thomas and O'Maochatha, 1989). These include left realist criminology, socialist-feminist criminology, peacemaking criminology, and poststructuralist criminology.[1] Each of these perspectives is undergoing internal critique, while variously engaging each of the other perspectives. Such developments might raise the specter of a Kuhnian paradigm crisis, with fragmentation taken as indicative of a failure of the existing critical criminological paradigm to resolve the mounting anomalies with which it is confronted (Greenberg, 1981; Klockars, 1980). Indeed, a not dissimilar crisis has been identified in critical legal studies (Boyle, 1985a; Coombe, 1989; Friedrichs, 1986, 1989; Hunt, 1987; Milovanovic, 1988c).

An alternative interpretation of these transformations might be that the current divergence of perspectives is the foundation of a new critical paradigm, whose character will depend on one of the emerging positions becoming victorious. The problem here is that such divisions might also lead to the all-too-familiar radical factionalism in which internecine wars among critical thinkers sap new life from each other's potential growth. Put simply, the recent developments are subject to the dialectic of enlightenment and constraint. In constructing distinctions between different theoretical positions, criminologists must be cautious not to overlook the connections that exist between them. Thus, rather than address these issues through criticism, we sketch an approach that draws on developments in social construction, left realism, socialist feminism, and poststructuralism. We also borrow heavily from social and critical legal theory, from the rich intellectual history of constitutive thinking, and from discourse analysis.[2]

Our aim here is not to add another shot to the paradigmatic cross fire, but to examine reflexively the paradigmatic umbrella under which these saplings of critical growth can gain strength. It is this umbrella that we term *constitutive criminology* (Henry, 1989a). In the following sections, we address core themes that will lead to the establishment of the necessary and logically ordered elements of a constitutive criminology. These themes are (1) the codetermination of crime and human subjects through crime-control ideology and how this ideology has the capacity to reproduce and to transform; (2) discursive practices as the medium for the structuring of crime and its control institutions; (3) symbolic violence as the hidden ideological dimension of legal domination; and (4) the use, by control agencies, of sense data to construct meaning that claims space and displaces the intersubjective construction of meaning and, through this process, sustains control institutions as relatively autonomous structures.

THE CODETERMINATION OF CRIME AS IDEOLOGY

A core theme of constitutive criminology is its rejection of reductionism. Advocates decline the seduction that either human agents, through choice or predisposition, or structural arrangements at institutional and societal levels, have priority in shaping crime, victims, and control. Rather, following Giddens (1984), they see social structure and its constituent control institutions as the emerging outcome of human interaction that both constrains and enables criminal action and recognizes that those structures are simultaneously shaped by the crime and crime-control talk that is part of their reproduction. Constitutive criminology is not an exercise in polemics, in which human agency is separated from the structures that it makes. Thus, we share Coombe's view (1989: 70) that:

> To characterize structure and subjectivity as two poles of an ineluctable dichotomy is problematical and that . . . we need to radically reconsider our understandings of structure and subjectivity if we are to appreciate the complexity of the relationship between the structures of the socially constructed "languages" like liberal legal discourse and the subjective consciousness of social actors and if we are to avoid reproducing the conceptual poles that characterize liberalism in our efforts to deconstruct it.

THE MAKING OF HUMAN SUBJECTS: TRANSPRAXIS

Constitutive criminology, then, is concerned with identifying the ways in which the interrelationships among human agents constitute crime, victims, and control as realities. Simultaneously, it is concerned with how these emergent realities themselves constitute human agents. It follows from this that the current notion of praxis needs to be replaced. If praxis is taken to be purposive social activity born of human agents' consciousness of their world, mediated through the social groups to which they belong, then this must be supplanted by the richer notion of transpraxis. Transpraxis assumes that critical opposition must be aware of the reconstitutive effects—the reproductions of relations of production—in the very attempts to neutralize or challenge them. The dialectic of control is such that praxis assumes dualistic forms—negation/affirmation, denial/expression. In the process of negation, relations of production are often reconstituted along with the human subjects that are their supports. But often neglected is that with affirmation, relations of production are also deconstructed, along with those same human subjects. Thus, its very dynamic reveals the tenuous nature of the ideological structure on which it is based. Critical theorists have been particularly myopic as to the potential for change afforded by this insight.

Labeling theory tried to cover some of this ground, particularly in its notions of role engulfment and deviancy amplification. But labeling separated meaning from the agents generating it. It posited a dualism between agency and structure rather than a duality (Giddens, 1984). Ignored was any sense of an interconnected whole. Although early symbolic interactionism elaborated the ways that the human actor became that which the audience constructed, it said little about the way audiences—their imageries, symbolic repertoire, and *verstehen*—are constructed, constituted, and undermined by historically situated human agents in the context of a historically specific political economy. The construction process tacitly acknowledged and uncritically accepted that the power relationship flowed one way, monolithically and asymmetrically. While those who were officially designated deviant actively participated in their own identity transformation, little construction was done of the control agents, by themselves. Actors designed as deviant or criminal ultimately became passive acceptors of audiences' degradation, and fulfillers of their prophecies. Audiences made victims. But little was said of the making of audiences during their attempt to construct labels for others; absent was the dialectic of control. Coombe (1989: 117) notes that "one of the most promising areas of research suggested by a practice theory is the consideration of the ways in which legal discourse and practice actively participate in the making of human subjects and thus reproduce social relations of power." The danger here, however, is reifying human subjects by giving priority to their discourse as though discourse somehow operated independently of those using it. Even more problematic is losing sight of the potential for transformation inherent in the reproduction process, since it is precisely here, in the remaking of subjects through the ideology of control, that they are revealed as vulnerable to unmaking.

Constitutive criminology, then, recognizes human agents' power to undermine the structures that confront them and asserts that agents both use and are used in the generation of knowledge and truth about what they do. Agents' ability to undermine and invert structures of control, to episodically render them edifices of subordination, is one of the major missing dimensions of conventional and critical criminology.

Occasional glimpses of the dual nature of this process are exposed in examples of prisoners' power over prison guards through trade in contraband, of police committing or facilitating the commission of property crime, and of police provocation of the very riots they are supposed to prevent (Jefferson, 1990). The notion of "confinement by consent" found in the accounts by Milovanovic (1988a) and Milovanovic and Thomas (1989) of the inmate, turned jailhouse lawyer, who inadvertently maintains legitimation and conventional understandings of capitalist legality, is as constitutive of the hegemony of overarching capitalist relations as is the workplace trade unionist defending employee disciplinary cases in settings of private justice (Henry, 1983). But both are also undermining of that which had previously been constructed. Or consider Goffman's (1961) early work in *Asylums*, in which he showed that some inmates in their "secondary adjustments" internalized and verbalized psychiatric jargon as a way of leveling hierarchical power relations; while negating, they also affirmed, implicitly or explicitly, the very hierarchical structures that they attempted to neutralize. Again, consider the work of Bannister and Milovanovic (1990), in which they showed that the activist lawyer attempting to politicize the trial begins to make use of the constraining categories and legal discourse that are the very supports of the rule-of-law ideology. Indeed, Karl Marx (1984) recognized this duality facing practitioners of radical change when he observed that

> the tradition of countless dead generations is an incubus to the mind of the living. At the very times when they seem to be engaged in revolutionizing themselves and their circumstances, in creating something previously non-existent, at just such epochs of revolutionary crisis they anxiously summon up the spirits of the past to their aid, borrowing from them names, rallying cries, costumes, in order to stage the new world historical drama in this time-honored disguise and borrowed speech (p. 115).

For Marx, the crucial issue for revolutionary change was whether the concepts of the past could be used selectively to enable the liberation of the future. Until the spirit of revolutionary change could be captured and used without reference to the past, automatically and spontaneously, it was but a bourgeois revolution, short lived, soon reaching its climax. No more vivid an illustration of this process exists than Henry's accounts (1985, 1988b, 1989b) of the way those oppositional collectives, cooperatives, and communes, whose commitment was to an alternative socialist order, typically resorted to capitalist control forms and state law in their ironic attempts to defend their own internal order, thereby reproducing the very structures that undermined and overwhelmed them. Similarly, in presenting the polemic between Nietzsche and Hegel, Milovanovic (1991a) has indicated that would-be reformers often react and negate rather than act and affirm positive values. In fact, transpraxis, an oppositional agenda, actively negates and produces, affirmatively, new values. Socialism, for example, as envisioned by Marx, is a transitional phase to the "higher forms." Here there still exists a predominant reactive and negative orientation, and that still reconstitutes the very forms of domination found in capitalism, be it now by the victorious proletariat. The state apparatus becomes but an instrument of the victorious proletariat to be used to repress the former repressors, and thus is the cycle react-negate-reconstitute perpetuated.

TWO SIDES OF TRANSPRAXIS

These contradictions are not temporary aberrations of the structure of control, but fundamental pillars of its constitution. In Bourdieu's terms (1977), they are instances of the way in which the discourse of control in society is in harmony, even when in apparent opposition. This dialectic of control must be addressed. That criminologists and practitioners ignore it is part of the constitutive silence that sustains crime and control as object-like entities. A transpraxis must envision oppositional practices themselves as inadvertently reaffirming instruments of hierarchy and control.

Transpraxis should not, however, ignore the reverse side of this dialectic of control. The affirmative reproduction of social control by human purposeful action also undermines that which is being constituted. For example, it has been shown (Henry, 1988a) that when state agencies seek to control economic relations that fall outside national tax accounting, they attach derogatory labels to such activity and attribute to it motives carrying negative connotations. Terms such as the "black," "hidden," "underground," "shadow," "secret," "subterranean," "submerged" economy are used to suggest that the economic relations of those working "off-the-books" are perpetrated by nefarious creatures of the night who are interested unilaterally in pecuniary rewards incommensurate with effort, who are dishonest, and who cannot be trusted. Although such attempts at control may initially dissuade some from participation, they also show many of those who participate, and others who subsequently do so, that these accounts are inaccurate descriptions of the meaning of their relations. Those whose actual experience of irregular work is enjoyable, communal, and socially nutritious stand in contrast to the cutthroat black-market dealing that control-labeling suggests. Another well-documented example of the same process occurs in drug education in regard to the discredit that can be brought on the "moral, clean-living" messages found in the scare of shock talk of health educators. When directed at young people whose actual experimentation and peer knowledge reveal that drug use does not produce instant addiction, necessary escalation, or death, the effects can be counterproductive.

Thus, the more state agencies elaborate their control talk, and the more people experience the different reality of relations subject to control, the more contempt accrues to the controllers and their control institutions. As a result, people begin to question other distinctions, such as those between theft and the legitimate acquisition of property, between honesty and dishonesty, between street crime and white-collar crime, and between hard and soft drugs. Such questioning, stemming from the attempts of control institutions to control, actually undermines that which the controls were designed to protect: the existing relations of production and the moral and social order.

We now turn to three additional foci (discursive practices, symbolic violence, and sense data and meaning construction) that are integral to the process of codetermination as seen by constitutive criminology.

DISCURSIVE PRACTICES AS THE MEDIUM OF CODETERMINATION

A central issue in constitutive criminology is the role of human agents' discursive practices. The use of particular ways of talking, as in Cohen's (1985) "control talk," Manning's (1988) "organizational talk," or Milovanovic's (1986, 1988a, 1992b) and Thomas's (1988) "law talk," both reflects and constitutes narratives that provide the continuity to reproduce social structures of crime and its control in time and space. As Knorr-Cetina and Cicourel (1981) have argued, human agents transform events that they see or experience as micro-events into summary representations, or mind patterns, by relying on routine practices through which they convince themselves of having achieved the appropriate representation of these events; these are then objectified in coherent narrative constructions.[3] The well-documented media synthesis of harmful incidents into crime waves is allied with Fitzpatrick's notion of the "synoptic process," whereby disparate patterns of regulation are synthesized into formalized law (Fitzpatrick, 1988). But no clearer example exists than the very categorization of the diversity of human conflicts and transgressions into crime, or of the multitude of variously motivated acts of personal injury into violent crime or types of violent crime, such as when various disputes between family members are described under the unifying term "domestic violence" or "spouse abuse."

In the constitutive criminological vision, social structures are the categories used to classify the events that they allegedly represent. As such, they are strengthened by routine construction in everyday life and by activity organized in relation to them, as though they were concrete entities. The principal means through which social structures are constituted is language and discursive practices that make conceptual distinctions through the play of differences (Derrida, 1973, 1981; Lacan, 1977).

At the organizational level of analysis, the complexity of the human condition is given a static, decontextualized meaning to enable controllers to better negotiate routine cases (Cicourel, 1968; Manning, 1988; Sudnow, 1965; Thomas, 1988). Discourse, indeed, is the "disciplinary mechanism" by which "docile bodies" are crested and "bodies of utility" stabilized (Foucault, 1977).

At the societal level of analysis, capital logic and the integrally related processes of rationalization are constitutive of categories that capture essential relations, be it often in fetishistic forms. Not the least are rhetorical structures, figurative expressions, and verbal mannerisms that are used as primary signifiers of meaning. Consider, for example, those signifiers used to give material form to capital logic (e.g., commodities, market forces, producers and consumers, the juridic subject), to technological imageries (e.g., "she's a dynamo," "coiled for action"), and to the phallocentric order itself in which male signifiers occupy a privileged position (e.g., the power "to penetrate," as opposed to the weakness of "seduction"). Hence, at the levels of intersubjective communication, organizational processing, and capital logic, discursive practices are given anchorings, a "pinning down" (Lacan, 1977; Manning, 1988; Milovanovic, 1992b). In other words, discursive practices produce texts (narrative constructions), imaginary constructions, that anchor signifiers to particular signifieds, producing a particular image claiming to be the reality. These texts become the semiotic coordinates of action, which agents recursively use and, in so doing, provide a reconstruction of the original form.

Once social structures are constituted as summary representations, their ongoing existence depends on their continued and often unwitting reconstruction in everyday discourse, a discourse replete with tacit understandings whose basis lies outside the realm of intrinsic intersubjective communication and intersubjectively established meaning. Core meanings are typically preconstructed elsewhere as part of a common "stock of knowledge" (Schutz, 1967; see also, Manning, 1988). Agents in organizational settings tend to reduce feedback that represents contaminating and disruptive "noise." The fluidity of organizational processing in criminal justice contexts demands a high degree of rationality and formalism, which is both the product and the effect of crime-control practices. In part, this is due to the increasing complexity in the social formation, which demands more abstract categorization encompassing more and more variants—a "surplus of possibilities" (Luhmann, 1985)—but which produces, in the process, symbolizations that are steps removed from the "real" (e.g., concrete reality).

For example, process justice is held to require equality of treatment, that is claimed to be enabled by general rules of procedure that reduce people to like individuals, decontextualized of their different cosmologies of meaning, and substituted by a universal individual intent tied to units of material reward. In order to sustain abstractly constructed distinctions, these representations are made applicable to events, despite the contradictory evidence that comes from renewed microinteraction. Contradictory evidence and potential disruptions are engendered by the internal transfer of messages, a basis of instability that is best negotiated by framing it into already understood narrative constructs (Goffman, 1974, 1981; Manning 1988; Thomas, 1988).

It is often not enough, however, simply to repeat distinctions in order that such representations be sustained as apparent realities. Part of the reality-constituting process involves routinely investing faith and interest in them, fighting over them, manipulating them, and above all defending them (Knorr-Cetina and Cicourel, 1981). These morality plays often take place in symbolic form in publicized trials, political and business scandals, "moral panics," and other boundary-policing structures. In more subtle forms, they take place by the use of prevailing discursive practices, even in the use of the oppositional form. As Foucault (1977) and others (e.g., Morrissey, 1985) have reminded us, oppositional discourse is as constitutive of existing reality as is supportive discourse, since each addresses and thereby reproduces the prevailing distinctions while disputing their content rather than deconstructing them or discrediting them through the construction of a new, replacement discourse. For example, Selva and Bohm (1987) have emphasized that in many respects an oppositional legal discourse, which utilizes the existing structure of legal discourse, may prove more productive and liberating than a replacement discourse, but this downplays the significance of the constitutive effects of "liberating" practices in law. A graphic example of this process is the oppositional adolescent reaction to the school by working-class kids. Although they "resist" and reject the system that rejects them, it is their very reaction that subsequently consigns them to the bottom of the very hierarchy they despise (Willis, 1977).

Organizing action to defend representations—framed and objectified in narrative texts—is one of the principal means of defending and conferring object-like reality on them, providing life, form, energy, sustenance, and a high degree of permanence. The institutions of capitalist legality (involving formal police, courts, and prisons) represent the visible manifestation of human agents organized to defend the overarching social form of capitalist society from internal deconstruction. Capital logic is a ubiquitous rationalizing form; the more investment that is made in it, the more difficult it is to sustain that which it is not. This is not to imply conspiracy but to specify formal function, for while defending the wider totality, agents and agencies also compete to defend their own integrity within the framework of capital logic, as Jessop's (1982) work forcibly reminds us.[4] Compare, for example, the mobilization of opposition to racism and sexism that manifested itself, within the legal frame, in the form of affirmative-action programs, formal equality doctrines, and comparable-worth legislation. The latter two essentially maintain capital logic—subjects are still measured by some external standard of equality and are still compared to an abstract criteria that is constitutive of capitalistic social relations. Consider, also, Daly and Chesney-Lynd's (1988) insightful analysis advocating a socialist-feminist perspective and critiquing "first-wave feminism," which often advertently or inadvertently (1) situated itself in legal discourse with its reliance on notions of formal "justice" and "equality" and hence celebrated the fetishistic notion of the juridic subject, (2) used male standards as the criteria of correctness and an ideal end, (3) laid the groundwork for greater and more pervasive forms of state and informal control in women's lives, and (4) grasped too quickly the get-tough approach, thereby rejuvenating deterrence and retributivist theory.

Alternatively, human agents can be envisioned as unique, with a multiplicity of needs, drives, desires, and abilities, and as intersubjectively constituted. Any subsuming of these qualities to some "equal" measure must be read as an imposition, a reification by submission to macroconstituted forms of capital logic, an idealization of relations constitutive of the capitalistic mode of production. Affirmative action, indeed, is the more radical in so far as the use of substantive rational criteria militates against a universalism and points to a recognition of built-in biases of the sociopolitical and legal order. The imagery of affirmative action is system-destabilizing, and it is now evident that the sociopolitical order is being brought around from this recognition (e.g., the mobilization of the ideology of "reverse discrimination"). Socialist feminism, however, is on the cutting edge in redirecting analyses of hierarchical and exploitative relations often objectified in seemingly value-neutral criteria and standards.

From the perspective of constitutive criminology, then, control institutions are the relations among human agents acting to police the conceptual distinctions among discursively constructed social structures. Those relations are mediated by the availability, through intersubjective relations, of a sedimented, differentiated symbolic system, a repository of value-laden signs that are politically anchored. Once constituted, those relations, expressed in symbolic form, themselves become structures, and, as agencies and institutions, appear to have relative autonomy from both wider structure and human agency. In turn, they too are policed by further "private" or internal relations of control. Thus, signifying chains, narrative constructions, and objectified bits and pieces of every day actively float within specific discourses, within which distinctive, discursive subject-positions exist that structure what can be framed, thought, and said. Tacit understanding is rooted in these subterranean semiotic systems that continuously receive support through their use (Manning, 1988).

SYMBOLIC VIOLENCE AS IDEOLOGICAL DOMINATION

According to Bourdieu (1977: 192) "symbolic violence" is a form of domination that is exerted through the very medium in which it is disguised, wherein it is the "gentle, invisible form of violence, which is never recognized as such, and is not so much undergone as chosen, the violence of credit, confidence, obligation, personal loyalty, hospitality, gifts, gratitude, piety...." But criminologists have forgotten this dimension of domination. The silence of the present and the celebration of that aspect that is likened to be law constitute the forms of control that appear as reality. Suppressed by silence, this pervasive domination is itself frozen in the past as "custom" (the informal law of nonindustrial societies), "prelaw," and the "law" of multiplex relations (Black, 1976, 1989), as if multiplex relations can exist without simplex relations or simplex without multiplex! But, in so far as we accept that they exist independently, we are actively, though unreflexively, creating and maintaining the illusion that is the reality of law. The omission of informal, nonstate social control from consideration as part of criminal justice is how "criminal justice" is constituted. Buying into dominant definitions of what counts as law, crime policing, and justice by excluding rules, deviance, informal social control, and private justice is part of the way these concepts, as entities, are made and remade as realities. Take as an example again, a constitutive view of law (Fitzpatrick, 1984; Harrington and Merry, 1988; Hunt, 1987; Klare, 1979). Rather than treating law as an autonomous field of inquiry linked only by external relations to the rest of society, or investigating the way law and society, as concrete entities, influence or affect each other, as is typically done in nonconstitutive approaches, constitutive criminology takes law as its subject of inquiry; but as Hunt (1987) and Harrington and Yngvesson (1990), have argued, constitutive theory pursues the study of law by exploring the interrelations between legal relations and other social relations. As Harrington and Yngvesson (1990) say,

> To speak of the constitutive dimension of ideology is to examine legal ideology as a form of power that also creates a particular kind of world, specifically, a liberal-legal world constituted as separate spheres of "law" and "community," with "practice" or "process" located uneasily between the two. In such a world actors impose ideologies or persuade others to take them on as "voluntary" (p. 143).

From the constitutive perspective, the notion of the "juridic subject" (i.e., the reasonable man/woman in law), for example, can only be understood in its inherent dualistic relation of being both a constitutive element and a recursive outcome of capital logic. As Henry (1983) argues, with such an approach one begins to see the possibility of transcending the view that law is either a product of structure or the outcome of interaction. One begins to see how informal social control is not so much an alternative form of law but a necessary part of the ideological process whereby the crystallized, formalized, object-like qualities of law are created and sustained in an ongoing manner, be it within a different arena. Thus, constitutive criminology directs attention to the way law, crime, and criminal justice are conceptualized and implied as objective realities having real consequences, consequences attributed to their claim.

Seen in this way, institutions of law are the organized acting out of discursively produced "control thoughts," whose very action reflects on the reality of that which they are organized to defend. There are parallels here with John Brigham's research on social movements (1987: 306), in which he found that the social movement was integral with the law that it used, such that "Legal forms are evident in the language, purposes, and strategies of movement activity as practice." As such, legal forms and their control institutions are rooted in control discourse and in their own parent social structures and cannot be divorced from them, but neither can the structures exist without their control forms, since each implies the other.

No better an example of symbolic violence exists than in "fighting crime" rhetoric. In a microcosmic form, undercover work of policing in the 1980s, such as those Gary Marx (1988) and Bob Weiss (1987) so poignantly document, produced the new "maximum-security society." Here, there is an increasing emphasis by control agents on developing dossiers in computerized form; an increasing use of predictive and actuarial instruments that focus on producing statements about persons in particular created categories; and an obsession to find the "predisposed" criminal. This has led to an extreme manipulation of the environment, with the continued acceptance by the courts, to induce the very criminality that is the controller's own creation. It is concluded by Gary Marx that the resultant new transparent society has seen the erosion of traditional notions of privacy such that even the citizenry have been recruited to monitor others as well as themselves for deviance or deviant proclivities (G. Marx, 1988: 219).

At the same time, however, the constitutive nature of the dialectic of control is apparent in its oppositional form. When Gary Marx and others oppose the affront of privacy, they actually take part in perpetuating the elaboration of privatized relations of production, since they unwittingly defend this bastion of capitalist society while discrediting and displacing notions of commonality. Indeed, it is ironic that in seeking to defend people against the invasion of their lives by control agents, critical criminologists have acceded to supporting the ideological protection of privacy while being silent on the theft of that which was traditionally held in common. Protecting privacy is nothing less than ideological legitimation for theft of the common (Einstadter, 1989).

SENSE DATA AND MEANING CONSTRUCTION

All this leads to recognizing the high premium on collecting, filtering, categorizing, and disseminating increasingly complex information framed in coherent narrative constructions (Jackson, 1988; Manning, 1988; Thomas, 1988). The process of constructing meaning intersubjectively is increasingly being both abdicated and usurped by agents of organizations who use these constructions as the criteria by which to survey, control, and act on subjects, particularly those in predicted high-risk categories in the existing social arrangements. Simultaneously, these constructions are inadvertently given ideological support through oppositional attacks on the autonomization of social-control instruments. Oppositional attacks by some critical theorists and reformers take as a given many of the concepts, presuppositions, or working hypotheses of these same agents of control, thereby in the end, reproducing the self-perpetuating machine. We are reminded of how escape from reproduction is constrained, even in the most radical perspectives, by the actions of others who read criticism as simply more of the same; for example, booksellers who categorize works like Cohen's *Against Criminology* (1988) in the section of their bookstore dealing with criminology, and publishers who reject proposals that they are unable to fit into the needs of a preexisting market. Indeed, there is some danger of the "realist" criminological perspective having this tendency toward reproduction, which has been recognized in the private soul-searching of various of its members. The challenge for a transpraxis here is substantial. How does one build an alternative "framing" of narrative texts to the exclusion of system-sustaining elements (e.g., imageries, signifier-signified anchorings, and so on)?

Institutions of social control are framed within the mediating effects of symbolic systems. Symbolic systems are constituted by sign systems, which in turn make use of the dyad of (1) signifiers—acoustic images, psychic imprints, or simply expressions—and (2) the signified—the concept referred to, the content.[5] Organizational agents, including control agents, must produce stable meaning in the very process of controlling deviance. Hence, human agents' semiotic work stabilizes the endless drift of signifieds under those signifiers, giving a particular meaning that is formalistic, rationalistic, and logical, and producing a stable and static semiotic grid that henceforth anchors the multiplicity of forces in movement (Milovanovic, 1992b). Meaning construction based on "purposive rational action," as opposed to shared intersubjectively constituted meaning (Habermas, 1984, 1987), increasingly underlies the constitutive process within the semiotic grid producing narrative coherence. This becomes the narrative structure (text) that conveys images of deviant behavior and simultaneously produces agents that are its supports. Those who, in their nonreflexive practices, oppose images of deviance, more often inadvertently affirm the reality of their existence. Organizational imperatives, which reflect human agents' deference to concepts of rationalization and capital logic, rely on signifying practices by those agents. The agents in turn rely on a tacit understanding in constructing meaning (Manning, 1988).

The outcome of this constitutive work is the organizational supports, deviant cases, correctors, and rebels who unwittingly purify these structural distinctions in their critical attack on its assumed operating principles. Oppositional narratives (texts), for example, are most often replete with the very core imageries, metaphors, and signifiers that are the supports of a hierarchical and dominating apparatus. But activating system-supportive imageries and then attempting to react and negate does not in itself produce alternative imageries of what could be. The "at best"—react and negate—turns often to be "at worst," for the canceling of a negation by a negation in the Hegelian sense does not produce transcendence. At best it produces, instead, destruction on one level, but a reconfirmation of system-generated elements on another.

Social-control agents both produce and sustain deviant categories, and they tacitly frame coherent narratives of "what happened," hence objectifying primordial sense data. These objectifications become increasingly the anchoring points for everyday constructions by those in the social formation, which in turn sustain the organizationally framed narrative. Routine investment of time and energy make this constitutive process recursive and self-referential, cyclically generating a more refined and purified version of the substance of their actions as object.

To refer to control institutions as relatively autonomous, then, is not to say they are separate from the wider social structure since they are part of its constitution. It is to say, rather, that recursivity reinforces conventional notions by giving permanence and stability to them. Nor do control institutions support the wider structure simply because that is their assigned social function. Such a vision is rabidly reifying because it ignores the integral role of human agency in this process. Rather, as Fitzpatrick (1984) reminds us, control institutions support the relations of reproduction within the totality of society because they are some of those relations of reproduction. Therefore, as we have argued elsewhere (Henry, 1985, 1987; Milovanovic, 1992b), these social relations do not exist independently of human agents who repeatedly bring them into being.

Likewise, the "internal" relations that monitor control institutions are some of the relations of the control institutions that they police. A police agency would not be what it is without the relations that police it, informal or otherwise, and those relations would not be what they are without the action of human agents. As a result, any examination of control institutions that analyzes them outside of the structural context that they police, that ignores the internal relations that police them, or that ignores human agents' recursive action, produces a partial account that itself becomes part of the constitutive discourse that sustains their reproduction. Concomitantly, any challenging practices used by agents not sensitive to the reconstituting effects of their very practices, further reproduce, elaborate, and stabilize the existent structural arrangements. Thus, although relations of control are most visible in their institutional form, that should not lead one to neglect their pervasive presence in informal and alternative modes of control or even in Foucault's sense of a dispersed disciplinary technology pervasive throughout our society. Neither should it lead one to gloss over the human agent's renditions and intersubjective creative work that daily make these relations into organizations and structures. So what is to be done? As implied in our preceding argument, there are a number of ways that a constitutive approach to criminology can be transformative. In the concluding section we suggest a direction that this might take but a more elaborated treatment must await further analysis.

CONCLUSION

In short then, constitutive criminology, in the tradition of dialectical theory, is the framework for reconnecting crime and its control with the society from which it is conceptually and institutionally constructed by human agents. Through it criminologists are able to recognize, as a fundamental assumption, that crime is both in and of society. Our position calls for an abandoning of the futile search for causes of crime because that simply elaborates the distinctions that maintain crime as a separate reality, while failing to address how it is that crime is constituted as a part of society. We are concerned, instead, with the ways in which human agents actively coproduce that which they take to be crime. As a signifier, this perspective directs attention to the way that crime is constituted as an expansive and permeating mode of discourse, a continuously growing script—a text, narrative—whose writers are human agents, obsessed with that which we produce, amazed that it is produced, denying that it is created by us, claiming that it grows independently before us, but yet worshipping the very alienating, hierarchical creations that are our own. A direct consequence of such an approach is that any "rehabilitation" from crime requires that criminologists and practitioners alike deconstruct crime as a separate entity, cease recording it, stop dramatizing it, withdraw energy from it, deny its status as an independent entity. Through this vision, we are suggesting that criminologists write a new script, a replacement discourse that connects human agents and our product back to the whole of which we are a part. "Control talk" (Cohen, 1985), "organizational talk" (Manning, 1988), and "law talk" (Milovanovic, 1986, 1988a; Thomas, 1988), must be replaced by a reflexive discourse that allows for change, chance, being, becoming, multiplicity, and irony, and that reflects a sensitivity to the nuances of being human. Criminologists must explore "alternative logics" in criminology, as Nelken calls them. We must cease to invest in the myth that human agents are either individuals with free choices driven by a utilitarian calculus or biologically and psychologically programmed, when all that is known shows that human agents are inextricably social beings whose total script is the medium of birth to our differences and whose differences continuously, but cumulatively, shape our total script.

Control concepts, such as the juridic subject and hierarchically organized dualisms—rational/irrational, subject/object, actor/action, center/periphery, agent/structure, with their privileging of the former term over the latter, and other logocentric, reconstituting discursive practices must give way to an "affirmative action" of discursive practices that privileges the interconnectedness, the interrelatedness, of phenomena in the social formation rather than any privileged hierarchical division. One of the few criminological scholars to recognize the importance of developing an agenda of replacement discourse is Gregg Barak (1988) with his "newsmaking criminology." He says that "in the post-modern era, social problems such as homelessness, sexual assault, or drug abuse are politically constructed, ideologically articulated, and media produced events" (1991: 5). He advocates that criminologists become credible spokespeople and that they make criminological news and participate in the popular construction of images of crime and crime control, that is, produce crime themes "as a means of bringing about social change and social justice" (Barak, 1988: 585; see also, Barak and Bohm, 1989).

Constitutive criminology, then, is a step in the deconstitution of crime, a peacemaking movement (Pepinsky and Quinney, 1991) toward an alternative vision of what is and what might be. Transpraxis must be the guide for those challenging hierarchical structures of domination. Anything less, advertently or inadvertently, contributes to hegemonic practices that sustain human agents' subordination to that which we construct. Accepting this does not mean that criminology should be blind to the human suffering that is the reality of crime for those who are its victims. Indeed, their suffering is not aided by the public celebration of their pain, nor by the glorification, sensationalization, and vilification of their offenders. Constitutive criminology is also peaceful criminology. It recognizes the harm and suffering, and seeks to examine how criminology might reduce it through transforming the totality of relations of which it is a part. It does not imagine that some structural transformation will eventually rescue society from the harm of murder, rape, and corporate fraud. Rather, it seeks to affirm those aspects of intersubjective experience that are capable, if invoked, of displacing the excess crime that comes from giving in to those energizing its continuity. Of course, it is true that even in a society of saints there will be sinners, but the task of constitutive criminology is to suck life from their discursive enterprise.

NOTES

1. On realist criminology, see especially; Jones, MacLean, and Young (1986); Kinsey, Lea, and Young (1986); MacLean, (1991); Matthews (1987); Matthews and Young (1986, 1987); Young (1987, 1988, 1989); and the special issues on left realism of *Contemporary Crises*, vol. 11, (1987), and *The Critical Criminologist*, vol. 2, (Summer, 1990). On socialist-feminist criminology, see Cain (1989); Chesney-Lynd (1986); Currie (1986); Daly (1987); Daly and Chesney-Lynd (1988); Danner (1989); Gelsthorpe and Morris (1988); Harris (1987); Klein (1973); Messerschmidt (1986); Schwendinger and Schwendinger (1983). On peacemaking criminology, see Braswell (1990); Bianchi and van Swaaningen (1986); Christie (1981); Dennis (1989); de Haan (1986); Pepinsky (1986, 1989); Quinney (1988); Pepinsky and Quinney (1991). For poststructuralist criminology, see Manning (1986, 1987, 1988, 1990b); Milovanovic (1988b: 125-40; 1989a, 1991a, 1991b); Pfohl (1985).

2. We are especially indebted to the post-Foucauldian critical legal theory of Boyle (1985a), Coombe (1989), Fitzpatrick (1984), and Hunt (1987); the critical approach to legal ideology found in the work of Brigham (1987), Harrington and Merry (1988), and Klare (1979); Cohen's (1985) vision of social control; Bourdieu's (1977, 1989) sociology of knowledge; Giddens' (1984) structuration theory; and the variations of macro-micro integrative theorizing found in the work of Knorr-Cetina and Cicourel (1981). Key links, we argue, must also begin to integrate discourse analysis as formulated by Baudrillard (1981), Benveniste (1971), Deleuze and Guattari (1987), Derrida (1981), Foucault (1977), Lacan (1977), Lecercle (1985), and others from the more pragmatic orientation, such as Bakhtin (1981) and Volosinov (1986).

3. In other contexts, see also Cressey's (1953) discussion of embezzlers' "verbalizations" and Schwendinger and Schwendinger's (1985: 128-60) discussion of "moral rhetorics" of delinquent youths.

4. We need not unilaterally accept a pure capital logic formulation, for, as critics have shown, it is replete with an economic reductionism. We do, however, acknowledge its continued pervasive and ubiquitous force. It would be reasonable to point out, also, that bureaucratic logic, regardless of the capitalist mode, is just as pervasive and ubiquitous, as Weber has shown.

5. Meaning, as Greimas (1987), Jackson (1988), Jakobson (1971), and Lacan (1977) have pointed out, is constructed at the intersection of the two main axes in semiotics, the paradigmatic and the syntagmatic. (See also chapters 2, 3, this book.)

PART 2

Application
Doing Affirmative Postmodern Analysis in Law, Crime, and Penology

Jailhouse Lawyers and Jailhouse Lawyering

INTRODUCTION

Jailhouse lawyers, inmates who have taught themselves law and practice it, and jailhouse lawyering are two phenomena little understood, and little researched, although both have been formally recognized in the U.S. since 1969. This study will examine this phenomena in an exploratory manner, focusing particularly on the relationship of the jailhouse lawyer to the legal structure. Is the jailhouse lawyer a "primitive rebel," or have many overly romanticized the phenomenon? Does he obtain liberation from the form of law itself? Or, are jailhouse lawyers inadvertent contributors to the production of the rule-of-law ideology? To what extent can change occur within the parameters of the relative autonomy of law? What can be said of the "trade" of jailhouse lawyering?

The indigent inmate's initial encounter with the legal structure and his assigned public defender (or legal aid) is an awakening to the discrepancies and hypocrisies in the rule of law. Initially, the defendant is more a pseudo-juridic subject denied many of the formal, abstract rights in law. With the intervention of the jailhouse lawyer, movement toward a full-fledged juridic subject results. We will examine some prominent themes surrounding this movement. We will focus on becoming a jailhouse lawyer, constructing what happened, case concentration, moral codes and confidentiality, and status and power. We will conclude with a discussion concerning the historical place of jailhouse lawyers as reformers and legal-service providers.

This study, in its concentrated form, took place over a three-year period of participant observation. It was preceded by four years of teaching inmates in a maximum security jail in New York City, during which much time was spent chatting, informally, with jailhouse lawyers (in the law library as well as in their cells). The study focuses on male jailhouse lawyering as seen by one career offender whose name is Sonny. I met Sonny in the law library of a large jail in the Northeast. After he was released, we spent many hours taping in his natural settings. The data were transcribed and categorized in some general themes. Each theme is an element in the phenomena of jailhouse lawyering.

HISTORICAL ROOTS

Jailhouse lawyering in the U.S. probably had its formal start in 1963 with the Supreme Court decision of *Gideon v. Wainwright* (although the groundwork perhaps had already been set by the struggles of incarcerated Muslims). Gideon was a poor Floridean who was charged with breaking and entering a poolroom with intent to commit a misdemeanor. This offense was a felony according to Florida law. Even though Gideon was poor and requested counsel, he was denied because, at the time, Florida law allowed appointed counsel only when a person was charged with a capital offense. Gideon then conducted his own defense, including making an opening statement, cross-examining, presenting witnesses, and questioning the accusatory instrument used by the prosecutor. He was found guilty and sentenced to five years in prison. Gideon appealed via "in forma pauperis" and the U.S. Supreme Court, citing the Fourteenth and Sixth Amendment to the Constitution, overturned the conviction and reaffirmed the right to counsel spelled out in the Sixth Amendment. Gideon was the first jailhouse lawyer to reach notoriety.

Subsequent to Gideon, Martin Sostre, an African American imprisoned on drug charges in New York State in the late 1960s, was the next major jailhouse lawyer. Eventually he was pardoned, mostly because he was adopted by Amnesty International as a prisoner of conscience. Sostre taught himself law while incarcerated and helped other inmates in their cases. He was harassed constantly by the guards, even placed in solitary confinement for a stretch of 18 months— the charge: "having dust on his cell bar."

A series of court cases, beginning with *Johnson v. Avery* in 1969, to *Bounds v. Smith* in 1977, established the principle that unless "adequate" access to the courts and legal facilities exist, the jail/prison officials must establish a law library for inmates' use. Most states, after doing a cost-benefit analysis, realized that setting up a law library was, in the long run, much cheaper than providing further legal assistance (beyond the public defender, or legal-aid attorneys assigned to indigents at the beginning of the prosecution process). Some, no doubt, thought that perhaps it would be a way of keeping the inmates busy.

Socio-historical factors exist for the evolution of prisoner litigation and the rise of jailhouse lawyers. Ever since 1871, in *Ruffin v. Commonwealth*, the courts practiced a "hands-off" policy toward jail and prison administration: the inmate was seen as a "slave of the state." Citing separation of powers, lack of judicial expertise, and concern for "meddling" in an already volatile situation found in prisons, the courts did not actively entertain prisoner writs until the late 1960s. Partly as a result of black civil-rights' movements, student rebellions against the war and other activist movements, a "spillover effect" took place — the courts in the late 1960s and early 1970s became more active in entertaining prisoner litigation.

Three specific congressional acts were applied. First, the Fourteenth Amendment to the U.S. Constitution, passed in 1868, which states, in part, that "no state shall make or enforce any law which shall abridge the privileges or immunities of citizens of the United States; nor shall any state deprive any person of life, liberty, or property, without due process of law; nor deny to any person within its jurisdiction the equal protection of the laws." Second, the so-called "Ku Klux Klan Act" of 1871, surviving today as 42 U.S.C. Section 1983, provided civil remedies enforceable in federal courts for the deprivation of constitutional rights. Finally, several civil rights acts during the 1960s were passed by Congress, protecting rights from arbitrary or capricious infringement. The new outlook toward prisoner rights was that s/he "retains all the rights of an ordinary citizen except those expressly or by necessary implication, taken from him by law" (*Coffin v. Reichard*, 1945). This was reinforced with the U.S. Supreme Court decision *Wolff v. McDonnell* (1974). There it was said that "though his rights may be diminished by the needs and exigencies of the institutional environment, a prisoner is not wholly stripped of constitutional protections when he is imprisoned for crime. There is no iron curtain drawn between the Constitution and prisons of this country."

The prison reform movement culminating in the early 1970s almost disappeared by the mid 1970s. Radicalized inmate revolutionary leaders such as George Jackson, Malcolm X, Eldridge Cleaver, and Angela Davis disappeared. Several reasons can be given. (Some have contended that George Jackson was executed by the state.) The decline of student movements, particularly against the Vietnam War, led to the erosion of their cohesion and solidarity. Students became more concerned about their immediate interests, particularly in jobs. Many political activists who were involved in the prison movement turned to other concerns. Much of the developing oppositional ideology of the early 1970s, too, died a premature death. The prison movement was mostly abandoned to religious and professional organizations and to those on the far Left as well as to the romanticists (Wald, 1980). Whereas in the late 1960s and early 1970s many coalitions developed in support of the prisoners, in the late 1970s disunity was the norm. The early vision of the prisoner as a "primitive rebel," however, was retained by many, epitomized now by the jailhouse lawyer. With *Johnson v. Avery* and *Younger v. Gilmore* in 1969 and 1971, respectively, appeared also a rise in individual reactions to the repression in the prison, litigation facilitated by U.S.C. 1983. In 1970 there were 2,030 civil-rights petitions by inmates; in 1980 it grew to 12,397 (reported in Thomas, 1984: 153). Many—and it is hard to know the exact figure—no doubt were either initiated or influenced by jailhouse lawyers. It was not difficult then to conclude, romantically, that these were indeed revolutionary figures.

Anyone who visits a law library in a jail or prison will find it teeming with activity. Typically, the library is no larger than perhaps 30 feet by 30 feet. Basic law books, dictionaries, a typewriter or two, sometimes a Xerox machine, chairs, desks, and a guard in charge make up the setting. (In some prisons, however, due to jailhouse lawyers' active litigation, the law library can rival some of the best law offices.) Usually a small group of inmates, chosen because of their expertise in law, work in the law library, assisting other inmates. These are the jailhouse lawyers. To this day, however, those in the formal legal profession refuse to address them as jailhouse lawyers, rather, the old notion of "writ writers" is preferred. After all, the professional lawyer has spent three years of very difficult times in law school, investing much time, energy, and money in his/her future career, and here, inmates have often managed to equal their level of expertise.

Jailhouse lawyers have already been recognized—again, not by that name, but as "substitute aid"—in court decisions as far back as *Wolff v. McDonnell*. There it was a case of procedural due process rights of prisoners subject to loss of "good time" credit, or placement in solitary confinement. The Court, apart from other rulings, also stated that in disciplinary hearings, where an "illiterate" inmate is involved, he may seek the aid of a fellow inmate, or "substitute aid" (note: not a jailhouse lawyer).

Further, in 1975, in *Faretta v. California*, the Supreme Court established the right of a *pro se* defense. The defendant himself/herself can act as his/her own counsel if s/he willingly decides to do so and is competent to do so.

BECOMING A JAILHOUSE LAWYER

One just doesn't wake up one day and become a jailhouse lawyer. There is a process involved, a drift. And, if we are permitted to use the analogy, the drift is not random but follows a current already existing because of the contingencies of receiving adequate legal services. Obviously, one of the constitutive factors of the current is the lack of adequate legal services for inmates. This is partly due not only to the lack of professionals seeking the public defender's office, but is also partly a function of the legal institution and its educational training, and its service delivery to the indigent.

The jailhouse lawyer, and we will use a broad definition—an inmate who renders some legal service to follow inmates with some degree of competence— drifts into jailhouse lawyering. Given the lack of adequate legal services, the inmate seeks an alternative. Typically, an inmate not involved with the law library, housed in the cellblock area (spending much time thinking about his case and contemplating when he will be seeing his legal-aid lawyer), is nevertheless in touch with the jailhouse rumors that abound. Occasionally someone "wins" his case on some point of law. A jailhouse lawyer is implicated. The inmate begins his search for a jailhouse lawyer. He puts in a "slip" to go to the library for the first time, oblivious to what may be in store there. At the law library he is referred to one of the jailhouse lawyers. Sonny: "Guy'd come down and say, 'Yo, uh, I hear that the second circuit or whatever, overturned, uh, blah, blah, blah.'" Or an inmate typically would come to the law library and say "Give me something on burglary." Sonny: "So I show him the penal code under burglary..." This begins an interaction process in which the jailhouse lawyer points out the relevant penal codes, the use of a law dictionary, the legal meaning of a particular crime, the necessary elements needed to be proven, the steps that must be followed in prosecution, etc. For the less literate:

> . . . you work with them a lot . . . uh, collaboration, as just an example. They can't grasp what it means, to collaborate. So you give them a law dictionary . . . you can give them any dictionary, that's what I used to do, I'd given them a regular dictionary and then a law dictionary to see what it means legal-wise, so when you see that word again you know what it means, and, uh, you see some of them with the law, with the Black's last dictionary, right...with words and phrases...indexes, right...and a case and five books, you know. And they'd be flipping back and forth. 'Cause if they can read, they'll get it together. . .if they can read.

For the uninitiated, reading law material can be a frightening and frustrating experience. Jailhouse lawyers even push those who are initially frustrated. Sonny: "I know it's turning off guys who don't read . . . very well, uh, to come down there and they are interested . . . then they can't read the shit, uh, they can't read . . ." Continuing, "you see the guys laying around the hallways, and you know they got a case they could . . . work their way out of... with a better deal." And extolling: ". . . hey man, I ain't seen you down in the library, get your ass down there . . . you want to get the fuck out of here?"

Becoming acquainted with the law library and jailhouse lawyers thus, for the neophyte, entails a process of drift. Partly because of inadequate legal services, partly because of the apprehensions of the pending case with no control over the situation, partly because of wanting to re-establish control over his destiny, the inmate exposed to the jailhouse rumor mill, particularly to stories of some inmates "winning" their cases, is very susceptible to being attracted to the law library and to jailhouse lawyers. The initial step often leads to a succession of steps where, with each, the inmate becomes more involved and usually more competent regarding his own particular case and the relevant legal issues. Being in the milieu of a law library also places him in a situation where a hierarchy of competence exists—from nonacquainted to fully acquainted jailhouse lawyers. Advice, second opinions, appropriate procedures all are available to the developing jailhouse lawyer. Inmates, then, subject to the "pains of imprisonment" can, through involvement and legal research on their own cases, re-establish some control and meaning to their existential plight. Those who venture forth and feel overwhelmed by the legal sophistication that exists, who are turned off by their inability to read and write and frustrated because they are aware that this is an avenue for bettering their legal situation, withdraw to the cell-block area and what it has to offer. Sonny: "they'd rather play baseball or basketball, go to the yard and bullshit..." This group is left to the vagaries and whims within the institution. Their frustration no doubt will escalate.

CONSTRUCTING WHAT HAPPENED

Constructing "what happened" is a function of interactive and communicative work. The defendant initially finds himself in a dyad. With the intervention of the jailhouse lawyer, often unobtrusively, the situation is changed into a triad. Initially, the defendant finds himself in a situation of power inequality vis-à-vis the legal aid attorney. In addition, he is often bewildered, anxious, confused, and legally naive, with little control over the situation he finds himself in. As has been shown elsewhere (Scheff, 1968; Sudnow, 1965; Daniels, 1970; Kahne and Schwartz, 1978; Balint, 1957; Bennet and Feldman, 1981; Hosticka, 1979), the professional "helper" must establish the definition of the situation. The defendant, too, attempts to portray what happened and competes with the helper in establishing the definition of the situation. The definition of the situation includes (1) a description of the defendant's existential dilemma, (2) an evaluation about how to go about correcting it, and (3) an explanation of what will take place next against the defendant given the former (see, also, Rubington and Weinberg, 1968: 5-7; Hosticka, 1979: 599).

As has been argued by others, managing uncertainty entails reducing the complexities found in an immediate case. The professional lawyer does this by making use of empirically normalized categorizations (see, also, Sudnow, 1965; Hosticka, 1979: 609). Control is reestablished for easy processing. Hosticka: "This control is exercised in the direction of stereotyping descriptions of client's problems so that routinized courses of action will seem appropriate and be facilitated...lawyers seem to force the definition into precast molds by using the devices of control . . ." (1979: 607) . The result is that the professional lawyer more often will be concerned about the good deal he could render given the legal situation the defendant finds himself in (or, is defined to be in). The defendant, more appropriately, at this point in a dyad, can be seen as a pseudo-juridic subject.

The intervention of the jailhouse lawyer changes the situation into a triad. With his suggestions, advice, clarification, evaluation, and instigation in writing petitions, the defendant finds himself in a situation of more power equality with the professional. Also, there is a movement to a full-fledged juridic subject with formal, abstract rights respected in law. The professional soon realizes he is no longer dealing with a naive, helpless, anxious inmate, but rather one with some degree of legal sophistication and one who can also make things uncomfortable by merely filing the appropriate petition to several juridic parties. The defendant finds himself in a new situation. Power differentials have been offset somewhat. He exercises more control in contributing to the definition of the situation. More formal justice will be rendered. In sum, the three elements of the definition of the situation mentioned above will be answered more favorably for the defendant. For example, take a bail-reduction petition (we shall have more to say about it later). The jailhouse lawyer will be able to create some movement in the defendant's position in social space toward a position of more respectability. This in turn may have an impact on whether he gets lower bail. It is a well-known fact that bail, indeed, is a predictor variable: it not only predicts convictions but also the quality and quantity of sentencing (see, Swigert and Farrell, 1976: 75-84). The jailhouse lawyer can also point out missing elements in the formal charge, or he may suggest that damaging evidence was illegally obtained and should be suppressed. All this shows that there has indeed been a movement in the defendant's position from a pseudo-juridic subject to a juridic subject with formal rights. At the minimum, the defendant can present better stories about what happened; important legal elements and linguistic codifications will now be included in the story presented.

On another level, does this represent the ultimate attainment of justice? Even if the defendant should have all formal rights of a juridic subject respected, does this mean that "genuine" justice has been served? We think not. On the one hand, it is true that the defendant, because of the jailhouse lawyer's involvement as an invisible third in the triad, now approximates a juridic subject. The description of the situation, the evaluation of what should be done, and the stipulation of what will happen next are all rendered problematic, and hence open to negotiation. The defendant, on a formal level, will have more justice rendered; at the same time overcoming, somewhat, his initial existential situation of dependency, anxiety, bewilderment, naiveté, powerlessness, and confusion. On the other hand, the jailhouse lawyer has aided in linguistic and legal exploitation.

From the rich mosaic of social life the singularity of the event (alleged crime) is abstracted from context and recontextualized within legal linguistic coordinates. The jailhouse lawyer finds himself in two worlds, in two linguistic communicative markets. On the one hand is the legal linguistic communicative market. Such things as the law dictionary and case law codify reality in a specific way—cause, intent, duress, responsibility, attempt, negligence, self-defense, accomplice, conspiracy, etc., for example, have specific delineated meanings; others are rendered non-justiciable—on the other hand, the inmate's world is made up of linguistic coordinates that reflect that existential reality (even though not well articulated, that is, neither well accented nor well codified). Explaining what happened, legally, as opposed to explaining it in street language, will vary as to the necessary elements needed to make a story believable (see, also, Bennet and Feldman, 1981). Given this dilemma, the jailhouse lawyer opts for the pragmatic. What needs to be done is to transpose "what happened" as codified in the street to what will be seen as believable in a courtroom setting. What is denied in the process are political-economic factors—questions of race, class, sex, alienation, unemployment, repression, exploitation, etc. This recontextualization into legal linguistic categories assures that the political-economic structure will be safe from attack, even from codification (inmates often argue against the system in the third person, as "they"), and more.

This tension between the two types of linguistic coordinates is more apparent during the preconviction phase. "Meaning," here, is in a state of dynamic flux; it is being politically negotiated and constructed. The convicted offender, on the other hand, finds himself within a more static configuration of legal linguistic coordinates.

The jailhouse lawyer inadvertently aids in not only blocking possible emerging oppositional linguistic forms, but also in maintaining the "rule-of-law" ideology. The legal form itself is not challenged; rather, it is seen as a neutral instrument in resolving problems. In many ways, perceiving the jailhouse lawyer as a "primitive rebel" must be tempered. Whereas it is true that the pseudo-juridic subject begins to reap the rewards of his new position as a juridic subject, even, occasionally, making quasi-radical challenges to the political and economic structure via class-action suits and civil-rights litigation, he does not progress radical causes or challenges by, for example, developing the notion of a class not only in itself but for itself, a class consciousness. The closest he comes to this is when the "indigent defendant" or a race category is being employed; but very rarely, if ever, will the category "social class" be applied. Nor, on the other hand, will the judicial structure be willing to accept this as a "suspect category" worthy of a day in court. It is nonjusticiable.

CASE SPECIALIZATION
Within a jail setting, three broad areas of litigation are the focus: bail reduction, case dismissal and/or reduction of charges, and suppression

hearings (with the attendant Fourth Amendment questions, particularly those revolving around constitutionally permissible searches and seizures).

Being able to make bail is obviously an important step in criminal defense. Those who can manage bail (ostensibly set to assure the defendant's appearance in court, although many argue that it is a form of preventive detention) are free on the streets to assist in the gathering of evidence, in consulting with their attorneys, and not least in maintaining their jobs and supporting their families. Part of the duty of legal representation is to assure reasonable bail. Unfortunately, the legal-aid lawyer does not often put in a "bail-reduction petition." Why? Sonny: "They don't want to be bothered. I'll level with you, they just don't want to be bothered . . . because the lawyer can't spend three hours with you . . . he don't spend three hours with you." Typically, in this court, bail is set at arraignment. And, typically, the defendant first gets a legal-aid lawyer at this point. According to Sonny, the assigned counsel then stands up in court and says: "I don't know nothing about this case your honor, uh, I haven't had a chance to talk with my client, all right . . . bail such and such, all right ... swoosh, you're gone. You're never gonna see that guy again..." (In this county, a different lawyer is assigned at different stages). After a series of formal appearances, requests and denials of bail reduction (Sonny: "the D.A. pops up, your honor, we don't have his full record, rap sheet; your honor, we don't know if this man is going to appear or not appear, we recommend five thousand, all right"), the defendant finds himself back in jail with the original bail. Meanwhile, postponement after postponement lengthens the process even more. Frustration builds up. At some point some of these defendants come to the law library and ask what they can do about bail.

Sonny boasts of over a 70% success rate in doing bail reductions. Other jailhouse lawyers claim a 90% or greater success rate. Sonny: "I type the whole thing up [two pages], make three copies, have it notarized, send a note to the attorney, one to the court and you get a hearing scheduled in twenty-one days." To alleviate any apprehensions on the part of the client, the jailhouse lawyer would typically, according to Sonny, "show him the whole thing on bail [penal code] . . . read it. This is what you're entitled to. This is the bail you're entitled to, all right. I pull out my old cases. This is what we did for this guy; that is what we did for that guy ... All gone. They're out on bail." At this point, the jailhouse lawyer coordinates getting letters from friends, community members (doctors, landlords, grocery-store owners, employers, etc.). The petition is then sent to his lawyer, the judge, and sometimes a third party. All petitions are notarized.

Clearly, legal-aid lawyers are not stupid, lazy, nor capricious individuals. Workloads are so great that a few hours spent with one client would mean less adequate legal services for others. The legal-aid lawyer attempts to minimize losses and maximize energy by focusing on "real" lawyering, not filling out forms and tracking down witnesses. His focus is on resolving cases; if he can work out a good deal, so be it, justice has been rendered. The inmate, on the other hand, is caught in this maze of shuffling to one sector of the courthouse, then to another, and finally back to his cell. Then a pause. And then a return to shuffling around. This maze continues with no end. The jailhouse lawyer, often for a price, (cigarettes, drugs, future favors, information, food, etc.) consults with the troubled client, giving advice and suggesting directions to be pursued. A bail reduction from $2,000 (or more) to $1,000 is not unusual, and many clients do in fact make it. Doing bail-reduction petitions, then, is one of the most active duties of the jailhouse lawyers. On paper, however, it appears as the work of the client and the legal-aid attorney.

Getting charges reduced is another area where the jailhouse lawyer provides his services. A defendant, charged with burglary, comes to the law library and asks: "What do you have on burglary?" The jailhouse lawyer pulls out the penal code and notes the elements of the crime of burglary. Sonny: "I show him the penal code under burglary. I read it to him . . . to enter or remain inside a dwelling without permission thereof, with the intent to commit a crime therein, that's burglary." If intent is not proven, he continues, then it's trespassing. Consultation thus continues. Does the defendant have copies of the charges? No, then a letter is written to his lawyer. Does he understand the charge? No, then the jailhouse lawyer carefully goes over the charge compared to what, in the defendant's mind, happened. Reducing charges is the goal. Sonny: "What I'm trying to say is that the lawyer, or the public defender in this particular instance, had lied to the kid and told him he was charged with burglary, all right...that's a D felony. . .could get, uh. . .two to four, three and a half to seven all right. . .he's trying to make a cop-out for him, all right. . .from one and a half to three, all right. . . .Give him an E felony...when in fact he had exactly an A misdemeanor, trespass at best." The jailhouse lawyer then encourages the defendant to file a motion contending that he was illegally charged and cites the relevant statutes. At all times, correspondence is notarized and sent to the legal-aid representative and the judge.

The third area where a jailhouse lawyer is very active in a jail setting concerns "suppression hearings" and, generally, Fourth Amendment questions, those oriented around permissible "searches and seizures." Anyone who has ever dealt with these issues realizes how difficult this terrain is. Probable cause, reasonable suspicion, search warrants, arrest warrants, searches incidental to an arrest, Miranda warnings, coercion, waivers (willingly and knowingly made), all these and more become contested issues. The jailhouse lawyer, in consultation with the defendant, points to areas where suppression hearings should take place.

Critical for a good defense is that the defendant truthfully relate what took place. As the defendant relays the story, the jailhouse lawyer is noting where evidence should be suppressed because it was illegally obtained. Case law is being cited. Further research by the jailhouse lawyer often follows. Other jailhouse lawyers are asked for their expertise. Inmates often sign waivers in haste because of the exigencies and hustle and bustle of a jail and court setting. Often they have done so "unwillingly and unknowingly." These, too, are challenged. Again, these points/petitions/motions are brought to the attention of the legal-aid attorney. The burden is then on him to explain why he failed to pursue these points (if he had, in fact, failed to have done so). In the absence of a reasonable explanation, a case of incompetency can be built. What it boils down to is that the defendant is directing the legal-aid lawyer to areas where he may not normally investigate, file petitions, request hearings, challenge waivers, etc.

As the jailhouse lawyer consults and researches a case for each client, he is building up more expertise. He becomes more competent. The client also establishes some mastery over the unfolding events. Nowhere is there more satisfaction than when the client and jailhouse lawyer get "action" and "win" on a legal point. I might note, in passing, that the kinds of cases that one focuses on in prisons, as opposed to jails, differ.

CONFIDENTIALITY AND MORAL CODES

Two somewhat connected issues concern the moral/ethical codes of jailhouse lawyers as well as the issue of confidentiality in the client-attorney relationship. The nature of the jail environment dictates that both codes be upheld, not because of some written mandate as in the ABA code of ethics.

First, as to confidentiality in the client-jailhouse-lawyer relationship: "Ratting codes" already exist in any jail or prison and it is but a short step to equate giving out confidential information to others with ratting, particularly because some inmates are already looking for some information that they might use to get a better deal by the prosecutor. On the more positive side, jailhouse lawyers insist that their clients be completely truthful about their case. Only in this way, they tell their clients, will they be able to help them. In all probability, more "truth" comes out between these two than in the dialogue between a defendant and a lawyer of the bar.

Some cases pose a problem. Take, for example, an alleged child-molester. He is seen by his fellow inmates as one of the most despicable individuals. Jailhouse lawyers will avoid providing services for him. Why? Not only because of his soiled character, but also because the institution of confidentiality will be strained. Other inmates will want to know, first, if the inmate is a child molester, and, second, why he is being "helped." According to Sonny, for example, "someone says, 'Yo . . . what the fuck is he in here for?'. . .[and Sonny replies]. . .Uh, that's his business. . . 'Why are you protecting this guy? You protecting a fuckin' child molester!' No man, uh...I don't need that." Two points are brought out here. First, the idea of confidentiality is taken very seriously. Second, jailhouse lawyers, unlike attorneys of the bar, will pick and choose who they will do legal services for. Sonny: "There's some guys you just don't give a fuck for. They ain't worth a fuck, and you know it . . . you don't want to get lucky and get this fucker out."

In sum, contingencies within the prison walls themselves dictate that confidentiality be respected and that some cases shouldn't be defended. The latter may vary, however, according to personal conceptualizations of individuals who are too soiled to be defended. Citing confidentiality when other inmates ask questions about a particular client, and knowing this will be respected, assures that the jailhouse lawyer will also get fairly accurate information from his client. Finally, some cases, as with a child molester, are so "hot" that the notion of confidentiality may not survive.

Jailhouse lawyers are exposed to three major moral codes: the inmate code, the code of the legal bar, and personal codes. Unlike lawyers of the bar, jailhouse lawyers are not entirely bound by the ABA code of ethics. The delivery of legal services is then a function of the interaction of these three codes. The inmate code supports any activity for getting an inmate out, or that makes his stay less onerous. The code of the legal bar prohibits fabrications of stories in order to get someone out. Typically, the jailhouse lawyer will listen to the story presented by the client and will screen it for consistency. And, much like the professional lawyer, the jailhouse lawyer will abide by the bar's ethics and keep what is said completely confidential. Sonny typically would say "I don't care what you did, it don't make no shit to me." Here the jailhouse lawyer's code parallels the bar's. At the point the jailhouse lawyer detects an inconsistency he would point out the consequences: ". . .it's up to the jury. . . you got to get a little facts in there."

Does it make any difference, in regard to how much help the client will get if deliberate distortions are perceived? Sonny: "No, in fact, if he could win I'd tell him to lie till the fuckin' cows come down . . . . If I think I could win, you know, you got to do whatever it takes to live." Further, the jailhouse lawyer relies on the pragmatics of the situation: "If you tell your lawyer some bullshit story . . . next thing you know you're on your way to the joint. . .'cause. . . somebody'll get up on the stand and say things . . . ." Thus, the jailhouse lawyer, more so than the public defender, is in a conspiracy of sorts to help the client "win." The justification for this is quite simple. Street-sense, as well as court-sense, indicates that many police, in order to prevent illegally obtained evidence being thrown out, will lie. Examples are plentiful. Such things as the "plain-view doctrine" stipulate that if police, in the normal investigation of a crime, come across other crimes, they may investigate or seize contraband if it is in plain view. Many times illegal searches take place, but are later "dressed up" in constitutionally permissible language (See, also, Gilsinan, 1982: 43-4, 49, 61, 78-84, 96-107). The same is true regarding issues of "probable cause" to arrest. An ex post facto contextualization of the original situation develops, justifying the intervention constitutionally. People in the streets know this only too well.

Jailhouse lawyers, in anticipation of this, will also coach their clients, or point to the necessary legal elements needed to comply with a constitutionally prescribed mandate. In brief, the original situation is transposed to a new co ordinate and referent system. The new coordinates are legal linguistic reference points. Rendering justice has more to do with the effectiveness of taking some "facts" from a street incident and dressing them up in legally acceptable categories—linguistic recontextualizations. Perhaps the public defender may not want to participate in this linguistic conspiracy; the jailhouse lawyer, abiding by personal and inmate codes, will not hesitate. Law-finding is but a show performed by well-coached actors. Actors have already rehearsed the script. Rarely, if ever, will the contextualization of the actual crime be replicated in story form in courtroom settings.

What has taken place is a transposition of linguistic coordinates. The legal categories now dictate the content. Inadvertently (and we shall return to this point later), however, the jailhouse lawyer, bound by the pragmatic and expedient, denies one world, while giving legitimacy to another—the world coordinated by legal linguistic categories. Such legal conceptualizations as approximate cause, duress, intent, responsibility, negligence, self-defense, attempt, liability, conspiracy, etc., become fetishes, in fact attain "exchange value." The linguistic coordinates become part of a juridic actor's background horizons. Effectively blunted is any accentuation, any codification of such things as motivation for action in the street world—a world in which the poor attempt to scratch out a living and find a place in the sun.

STATUS AND POWER: "INFLUENCE"

The status and power of a jailhouse lawyer—"influence" in the argot of prisoner subcultures—comes directly from the ability to get things done, or from how much legal "action" can be mobilized. Sonny:

> You got to get action. A lot of guys could write a writ, that would be denied....Poorly prepared...too many technical errors...the idea is when you have action coming, when all the guys you're doing writs for. . .they're getting called up and going back to court. They have action coming. You got 'em back to court, you raised a good point, you raised it right, you cited precedent. 'Cause a lot of guys can write a writ, or an appeal. You fill out a form. . . .So the fact you got

action. . .the more action you get or the more people you do writs for getting action, getting results too.

A jailhouse lawyer's status, then, can be immediately measured, objectively, by how much "action" takes place. In addition, the inmate rumor mill spreads the word quickly. Typically, an inmate would approach a perceived reputable jailhouse lawyer and say "maybe you can help me.... I hear you're pretty good . . . you got three or four guys out already." The interaction process then unfolds, culminating in a particular petition or action.

The other side of the coin of status is power, or in the inmate's argot, "juice" or "influence." Inmates are constantly spreading rumors, and some concern technical points of law that are difficult to understand. The jailhouse lawyer steps forth in these interactions where legal issues are discussed, and presents, in the other inmates' eyes, the definitive word as to their meaning. Status is achieved because the jailhouse lawyer is seen as a person who really knows what is going on.

Power is also derived from the jailhouse lawyer's knowledge of the intimate details of many incarcerated defendants' cases (many of whom have "heavy" cases). Having information that can corroborate rumors concerning a client's identity and alleged infraction, as well as knowing new laws, adds up to tremendous power. Sonny: "So no one wants to fuck with you. No one wants to give you a hard time, 'cause you know a lot of guys. You know a lot of guys that are in there for some terrible things . . ." And on the positive side, "you get well known....Everybody wants to be...friendly with you...you never know, maybe you can help a guy at one time or another." Recall that the jailhouse lawyer, unlike a paid state lawyer, exercises much discretion as to which case he will take on. Even guards pay respect, since they can be an object of a writ. These are not idle saber rattlings. Making a particular guard "visible" by way of a writ, or even its potential, is enough to keep guards off the jailhouse lawyer's back. Other inmates also observe this, which in turn gives the jailhouse lawyer more power. An escalating mechanism takes off.

Jailhouse lawyers, too, are in a position to tap into the inmate informational flow. Although much segregation exists within the jail or prison walls, all inmates are entitled, by law, to visit the law library. Consequently, the jailhouse lawyer is in a unique position to know what is going on within the institution's walls. They can even manipulate the request forms for the law library so that accomplices to a crime can meet and discuss strategy.

Other power structures exist. Sonny: ". . .the other power is in your Chicano gangs, your black gangs, your Muslim leaders, all right. They have power also but they have to come to you...to get certain things done, all right...." A jailhouse lawyer's power then cuts across many pockets of power, even transcends many of them. Sonny: ". . .but, what they have is bartering power because they're heavy into drugs..." The well-understood service that the jailhouse lawyer has to offer is quite simple: the potential always exists for release based on some point of law; the jailhouse lawyer is the key, in the inmates' eyes, to getting out—this is power. He always has this card in reserve. Every day there are cases where inmates "win," reinforcing the conception that the jailhouse lawyer offers one of the few hopes of getting out. Other powerful inmates, by whatever means, must respect the jailhouse lawyer. Guards, inmates generally and the more powerful inmates in particular, accommodate the jailhouse lawyer, allowing him the time to work on cases. The result is getting "action," the objective, visible source of power.

Other inmates will gain little in making an enemy out of him. He offers not only legal services but is at the center of the informational flow. And scarce commodities and services within the jail/prison walls become readily attainable for him through barter. He is, indeed, a person with much status and power.

A hierarchy of competent jailhouse lawyers, too, is quickly established. Competence can quickly be measured by the quantity and quality of "action" generated. Within a desert, little oases flourish, providing a profession, an identity, diverse rewards, and a meaning—a purpose of being.

DISCUSSION

Our investigation of jailhouse lawyers and jailhouse lawyering, in the sections concerning becoming a jailhouse lawyer with status and power, has led us to conclude that for some, because of the very structure of jails and prisons, there is an attractive force to stay in or return to prison. A sense of self, status, and power, ironically, is assured and reinforced for the jailhouse lawyer within the walls, but is missing outside the walls. The jailhouse lawyer will return with his previously acquired skills for further refinement. He, too, has had his hostilities channeled; he will play by the rules of the game, even becoming the moving force for some piecemeal change. Other inmates are given an alternative model to outright rebellion. He is an example of a productive inmate. Could it then be that because of the jailhouse lawyer's activities in providing alternative channels for redressing grievances that more uprisings have not occurred? The jail and prison authorities will, no doubt, play out two responses: on the one hand, accusing the jailhouse lawyer of being a trouble maker and a writer of frivolous writs; on the other hand, covertly supporting his activities, particularly for channeling much dissent within the rule of law.

And here lies the radical's predicament. If, on the one hand, insurrection or rebellion is chosen, some concessions by Leviathan will be made— conditions of confinement will become less onerous. (However, long-range assurance sanctioned by law will not necessarily exist.) Because of the focus on collective action, the raising of consciousness, the development of group solidarity, and the movement toward political goals would be better realized. On the other hand, by abiding by the "rule of law" and engaging in legal reforms, some concessions will be made along with the establishment of case law and the long-range assurance that the state will come through on its end of the bargain. But the "rule-of-law" ideology is upheld. Legitimacy tied to a political economic structure based on exploitation is assured. The law will be seen as a neutral instrument for change. Its inherent repressive and ideological function will not be discovered, nor challenged. And little class solidarity and consciousness will develop. Each inmate pursues his own immediate interest to "beat" the system, or at the minimum, to establish some relief from the repressive conditions within the prison walls. A cruel, but effective trick.

Would-be humanistically oriented activists are faced with the same dilemma as the activist jailhouse lawyer—the political jailhouse lawyer. Change can occur by legal reform or by rebellion. Just as the student entering law school begins to incorporate a new way of reasoning, so, too, the jailhouse lawyer. Both become imprisoned within the linguistic coordinates of legal formalism. Both, to be proficient at their trade, must semiotically recode the world—good lawyering is the ability to apply the forms of law, as given, to "factual" situations. To "run" a good "equal protection" or "due process" argument (centered on the Fourteenth Amendment) is to render reality as it existed a new linguistic codification, a new accentuation. To the degree that "reality" is recontextualized within legal linguistic categories and coordinates, and argued thus, is to do good lawyering. The more proficient, the less able to transcend the limitations imposed by this very form of thought. Tinkering with the system, fine-tuning, and speeding up the assembly line is the best that can be done.

A juridical linguistic filter system exists at two levels, screening out certain primordial sense data found within the existential field of the "crime." First, the jailhouse lawyer finds himself within two linguistic coordinates— one oriented toward the street world, the other, the juridic sphere—opts, because of pragmatic exigencies, for transposing "what happened" into legal linguistic coordinates. He actively, if inadvertently, participates in the process of linguistic repression by failing to codify much of "reality" as it appears for the lower economic class lawbreaker. In exchange, missing legal elements are given content, stories become more believable. The taken-for-granted frame is the given juridic linguistic communicative market within which juridically constructed linguistic forms circulate. To be heard and understood within this discourse is to use the given linguistic forms found there (Milovanovic, 1988b: 125-38; 1989b: 141-62).

The initial dyad (defendant/public defender) is not an "ideal speech situation" (Habermas, 1984). However, with the intervention of the jailhouse lawyer (now making the situation a triad), more power equality results, with the defendant's claims now having greater efficacy—the contents of the legal form ("validity claims") are more efficacious in the construction of the definition of the situation favorable to the defendant's interests. But the legal form is accepted as nonproblematic; the content, the substance, is merely given a better legal accentuation within given legal boundaries. Accepting the legal form and accepting the rule-of-law ideology contributes to maintaining legitimation. Hegemony—the active acceptance of the given form and social political order by those most oppressed—too, is being maintained, ironically, by those most brutalized by a mode of production and the inadvertent support of the legal form (formal rationality), supportive of and synchronized with the internal needs of the capitalist mode of production.

To expand our analysis of the dynamics of linguistic repression, generally, we first note that codification of primordial sense data (prelinguistic raw material of the social world) may take place along three core linguistic tracks. The *oppositional linguistic track* renders the social world a critical accentuation, demystifying and undermining socioeconomic relations supportive of a given capitalist mode of production. The *pluralistic linguistic track* reflects the diversity of forms found in a pluralistic society. This includes the codifications of dominant groups, although a dominant form is pervasive and overdetermining. The *juridic linguistic track* consists of the juridic sphere and its codified forms. It is characterized by a Cartesian paradigm that dichotomizes reality into simple yes-no, two-dimensional Euclidean space. It is a world of Boolean logic of "either...or," abstracted from the complexities found in the social world, decontextualized and recontextualized into discrete, static, and reified structures and forms. The form of legal thought and reasoning here is formal, logical, and rational.

During codification of the social world (the sphere of linguistic production) and during justice-rendering (law-finding), tension exists among these three schemas. In lower courts—trial courts—this tension is at its most severe between the pluralist and juridic linguistic track. (Defense lawyers, even activist ones, usually relegate the oppositional track to hallway or post-mortem discussions). For instance, although the question of "motive" is not supposed to be introduced during the law-finding phase, some codified material does enter into this stage, in fact, even if it is subject to "objections" or to the judge telling the jury to "disregard what was said." Another example could be given with the recently completed trials of the religious activist groups in Tucson, Arizona (U.S.A.), giving support to refugees from Central America (see Golden and McConnell, 1986). Even though the judge specifically instructed the defense not to bring in issues of the conditions of Central America, some were brought in anyway. Another example can be given in the recent trial of two self-avowed revolutionaries defended by William Kunstler in a Somerville, New Jersey, court. The judge cited

Kunstler in contempt of court for refusing to rise when he entered the courtroom. Kunstler's response was that it was a statement about his solidarity for his clients (*New York Times*, 17 January, 1987, p. 18). Finally, activist groups in the U.S. have recently discovered the "necessity defense," which allows defendants to argue that their "criminal" act was justified in order to prevent a greater imminent harm. During trial proceedings, alternative and oppositional accentuations take place; indeed, the form of argument is substantive rational. For the latter three examples, some oppositional linguistic forms are being articulated reaching maximal codification in trials focusing on the necessity defense (see Bannister and Milovanovic, 1990).

The tensions are played out and resolved, to a considerable degree, during the law-finding phase; resolutions tend toward a juridic codification. The higher courts do linguistic work with "purer" (sterilized, static, decontextualized) forms and principles of formal rationality. Here contextualization remains several steps removed from the social world. One can rest assured that what is presented at the beginning of a written opinion as the "facts" of the case has little to do with what actually happened on the streets.

Juridic actors, including the jailhouse lawyers, through their everyday encounters within the legal arena, have their "life worlds" "colonized" by this alien structure, which is, in turn, synchronized with the internal needs of the capitalist mode of production (see Habermas, 1984; Milovanovic, 1986). Emerging oppositional linguistic forms are repressed. One has only to recall the previous example of the church groups being prosecuted. Whereas the state prosecutor attempted to render the smuggling of Central American refugees a judicial accentuation by using given juridic linguistic forms, calling the priests and nuns "chief executive officers or generals" of a "criminal enterprise," the defendants attempted to render the activity a political and moral accentuation. The judge disallowed any arguments by the defendants based on religion and conditions in Central America. To show how convoluted the state's argument is, and how asymmetrical the rule of law is, one only has to cite the case of the U.N. World's Court ruling in the case of the suit brought by Nicaragua in 1986 against the U.S. The Reagan Administration declared the court as incompetent to hear the case, that it lacked jurisdiction, and that the issue should be resolved within a political forum. In both situations, the rule-of-law is proven to be a big lie.

In the case of jailhouse lawyers initiating appeals, habeas corpus, and U.S.C. 1983 petitions while in prisons, we note that legal argumentation will be centered directly in the juridic linguistic track. We add that after conviction, the "what happened," too, has been stabilized within a static linguistic coordinate system. In fact, the whole negotiation process in constructing "what happened" evolves, from the initial arrest stage where primordial sense data has not yet been completely captured within a linguistic coordinate system (rather is lodged within competing ones), through the trial stage where tensions among the three competing linguistic tracks is maximal, to its terminal phase (conviction), whereby, increasingly, primordial sense data is captured and centered by a politically determined "reflective glance of attention" within this static linguistic coordinate system. Doing "good" law has everything to do with operating within the parameters of this reference system, although, for the *pro se* defendant, a few alternative accentuations are tolerated by the courts. In sum, the intrusion into the life world by legal linguistic structures assures the political-economic system's continued existence by providing well-programmed juridic automatons to run the machinery, and by rendering emerging, potentially challenging, oppositional linguistic forms an early death.

The second juridic linguistic filter operates within the higher courts, notably state supreme courts, federal appeals courts, and the U.S. Supreme Court. First, the higher courts are active in recontextualizing "what happened" in cleansed, sterile, static, legal categories; in the process they stabilize dominant understandings and deny any alternative readings (including pluralistic and emerging oppositional forms) by redefining contradictory elements, assimilating incongruous lower-court rulings, specifying correct readings of juridic concepts, and positing what the "correct" relationship among diverse legal forms are, thus situating them within an acceptable linguistic coordinate system.

Second, the higher courts, in deciding what constitutes a "liberty" or "property" interest protected by the constitution, namely by the Fourteenth Amendment, have increasingly made use of a "balancing test" by which they balance the interest of the state in maintaining, for example, an orderly prison, with those of the inmates in arriving not only at what "rights" exist but also what process is due before their infringement. In determining inmates' interests, the courts must actively codify, or engage in, signification. Some events are not signified, some are. The latter become "facts," legitimate interests, the former, judicially speaking, non-events (see also, Milovanovic, 1987). If the inmate chooses to bring up wider issues and questions of motive, unemployment, alienating and brutalizing workplaces, slum conditions, racism, classicism, etc., he is assured that none will be signified, none will be given redress in the courts—time and effort would be better spent, in the short term, supplying content to given formal, legal, linguistic categories favorable for the inmate's immediate interest. The form of law lives on; repression and denial of emerging oppositional forms is the result. Less-accented lower economic class primordial sense data means that these inmates will be resigned to falling back on the amorphous "they" when trying to criticize who their oppressors are. The courts fill the graves but find many willing helpers.

Third, the higher courts, by accepting the "finding of fact" by lower trial courts, legitimate one understanding of causal determinants of phenomena in the social formation to the detriment of a broader critical understanding. Fourth, the higher courts stabilize constituted signifier-signified relationships established in lower trial-court proceedings within the juridic, spatiotemporal linguistic coordinate system; put another way, parameters to appropriate legal discourse are established, and legal forms are infused with specific content. Linguistic forms are given precise legal meaning, as if words, from common everyday speech, rather than having a dynamic, contextual meaning situated in the use made of them (as Wittgenstein has informed us), have fixed borders and are devoid of contextual meaning. All told, to practice law is to work within this circumscribed, static sphere where codifications lack multidimensional, mutually interpenetrating connectedness and effects— atoms and molecules exist, but no conscious, creative, self-actualizing, interacting human beings inserted within a social formation marked by hierarchy, domination, and exploitation. The jailhouse lawyer is, then, the unfortunate user of an apparatus that simultaneously assures that hegemony will be maintained while presenting the promise of the possibility of radical change.

Although the form of law is repressive in the capitalist mode of production, some emancipatory potential exists because of relative autonomy. Social struggle or social praxis can transform those who are objects of law into subjects with formal rights and privileges, who may exercise some limited amount of control over the jailers (Thomas, 1984). Who would argue that much beneficial litigation and piecemeal reform has not developed? Genuine radical praxis, however, one that challenges the very core of the political-economic structure, is not engaged in by either the jailhouse lawyer or members of the bar. The rule of law lives!

CONCLUSION

Jailhouse lawyers and jailhouse lawyering have, and will continue to have, a tremendous impact in reforming the jails and prisons. The political legal structure has well accommodated the phenomena. The challenge for humanistically oriented critical reformers to demystify the law while at the same time practicing it to attain some measure of redress or relief will be a dialectic difficulty to reconcile. Romanticizing the jailhouse lawyer in the form of the primitive rebel must he avoided. However, some instances of genuine leadership and radical inmate praxis will arise and must be placed in the proper perspective for assessing beneficial overall system change.

CHAPTER 6
Overcoming the Absurd
Prisoner Litigation as Primitive Rebellion

Dragan Milovanovic and Jim Thomas

INTRODUCTION

A theme central to the literature of existentialism is that when the conditions of life seem to preclude meaningful and efficacious action, one must find meaning and humanity in resistance, in effect, in saying "no" (Camus, 1956: 13). To acquiesce to the deadening contradictions and meaninglessness of an absurd existence is to mirror the tragedy of Joseph K. in Kafka's (1972) *The Trial*: a victim unable to act yet unable to say "no." In this paper, we draw on these existentialist themes to examine the circumstances and actions of one category of prisoners who use the law as a weapon against the absurdity of their lives in prison. Based on our past research on these "jailhouse lawyers" (JHLs; see Milovanovic, 1987; Thomas, 1988, 1989), we argue that although not revolutionaries who bring fundamental social change, these prisoners are like Hobsbawm's (1969) primitive rebels who, through their resistance, confront and help to hold at bay their own and other prisoners' complete oppression. Our discussion proceeds from the premise that social existence can be read like any other text and that the concept of "the absurd" provides one useful exegetic tool for interpretation.

Our data and observations come from our experiences in prison research and from work with prisoner litigants since 1980. These data include several thousand pages of interviews with prisoners, jailhouse lawyers, and other litigants; data from court records and case summaries; and documents from prisoners, corrections institutions, and courts. For a detailed summary of our perspective, methods of data collection, and background, see Milovanovic (1987) and Thomas (1988). All quotes of prisoners are verbatim, taken from transcribed interviews in Illinois maximum-security prisons between 1982 and 1987.

ABSURDITY, EXISTENCE, AND PRISONS

The characterization of modern life as "absurd" is found throughout a body of literature produced and/or influenced by existentialist philosophy. Among the most well-known and often cited works are Brecht's *Galy Gay (A Man's a Man*, 1964), Kafka's *The Trial* (1972), Sartre's *No Exit* (1955), and the general corpus of Albee, Adamov, Beckett, Ionesco, Jarry, and others who have written in what is broadly called the "theater of the absurd" (see Esslin, 1961). Borrowing from Esslin (1961: xix), by absurd we mean a condition of existence out of harmony with reason, a set of circumstances devoid of ostensible purpose that makes behavioral choices futile. An absurd existence is one in which we are unable to discover the meaning and significance of our social world. Activity rooted in reflexivity, self-affirmation, collective development, and social praxis (or world transformative activity), are, as consequence, impossible.

Existentialist literature depicts the individual as faced with the dilemma of choosing between acquiescence and constraint on the one hand, and resistance and freedom on the other. By acquiescing, however, one embraces and promotes one's own further domination. Resistance, choosing to act while offering an avenue of escape from absurdity, comes at the price of embracing the understanding that, in Goodwin's words (1971: 832), such *"action will resolve nothing"* (emphasis in original). The unhappy irony, of course, is that only through such action can one live with more rather than less freedom. Yet, when individuals confront absurdity through resistance, they may give meaning both to their existence and their actions by creating dissonance (Goodwin, 1971: 843), regardless of whether they are successful in ultimately altering their conditions.

Following Goodwin (1971), we suggest that confronting absurd institutional conditions also may be a way of rejecting the status quo and altering existing definitions of power and authority. Our research has made us deeply familiar with one such absurd institutional setting, the prison. As Fairchild (1977) observed:

> The inmate is faced with certain dilemmas in his relation with those in positions of authority over him. He continues to exist in an atmosphere of subjection, at best paternalistic, at worst repressive and arbitrary. The best way for him to achieve his goal of getting out as soon as possible remains conformity and passiveness on his part toward the prison system. He is expected, however, to stress self-determination and individual responsibility as a rehabilitative goal. (p. 313)

Prison life may be seen as an allegorical analogue to other forms of social existence in which the potential to act is obstructed, and social actors remain powerless relative to their potential to engage and transcend their circumstances. Choices suppressed or pacified lead only to organizationally determined identities; one becomes what the environment dictates. The debilitating conditions that reduce autonomy and personal freedom, coupled with a hostile and often violent ambiance, do not provide significant opportunity for self-expressions that deviate from the desired norms of staff or other prisoners. Prisons illustrate an absurd environment that smothers the psyche and the will to act meaningfully, by conventional standards.

RESISTANCE, PRISONER LITIGATION, AND THE JAILHOUSE LAWYER

Within the prison environment, however, there exist some ways to mediate absurdity with reason. Using threats and/or violence is one way, but such a strategy seems, inevitably, to bring punishment and greater oppression and dehumanization. Another way, litigation, seems to offer an occasionally effective way of acting meaningfully and rationally in what is experienced as a chaotic environment. One prisoner who had pursued litigation expressed the appreciation of not using violence due to its consequence:

> We don't want to be locked up [placed in lockdown status]. We don't want everybody locked up. We don't want them shutting down the schools. We don't want them stoppin' us from going getting a couple hours of fresh air, we don't want to be left in our cells when it's 90 or 100 degrees in our cells. We don't want that. So guys will come and sit and talk about those types of problems. (interview, JHL)

When the problems cannot be readily resolved through interpersonal means or institutional channels, and if it appears that a constitutional issue is at stake, then the law or threat of its use may be invoked. From our observations of and interviews with prisoners who have turned to JHLs with their problems, law is viewed as a resource to act against various conditions of their and other prisoners' lives. This provides one way prisoners can attempt to overcome the powerlessness of their position to challenge behaviors and policies that make little sense to them and seem capricious and unjust.

In the past two decades, state prisoners have increasingly turned to federal courts in attempts to resolve private troubles in public forums. This is called prisoner litigation. Critics of prisoner litigation contend that prisoners sue primarily because they are either unwilling to accept their conviction or because they wish only to hassle their keepers by "abusing the law" (Thomas et al., 1988). However, prisoners who challenge policies or conditions to which they object do so for a variety of reasons, many of them certainly as honorable as those of their litigious civilian counterparts.

There seem to be two types of prisoner litigants (see Milovanovic, 1988a). First are those who file a single suit during their entire incarceration and who generally require the assistance of others to do it. Between 1980 and 1986, Thomas (1989) found in his study of 3,350 prisoner petitions filed in Illinois that nearly three quarters (71%) of all litigants filed only one suit, but accounted for only half (49%) of all litigation. Second are those who make a prison career out of law. We call these specialists "jailhouse lawyers."

We are here concerned with the more common kind of prisoner litigants who use the law not only on their own behalf but, more commonly, also to help others decide whether a complaint is adjudicable, identify the relevant legal and substantive issues, and shape the case narratives into what are judged to be the most persuasive stories. The most talented JHLs attempt to link a particular issue that affects only a single inmate to one that may ultimately affect broader prison policies. These JHLs also serve as gatekeepers between prisoners and the federal courts by weeding out suits that do not possess legal merit from those that do.

The jailhouse lawyer of interest here, then, is a prisoner knowledgeable in law who helps other prisoners shape or translate the personal troubles and problems of prison life into legal issues and claims. These legal claims are diverse, and can include preincarceration problems with landlords or employers, family problems involving divorce and child custody, or postconviction complaints. However, JHLs most often assist inmates with grievances against the keepers.

MODELS OF UNDERSTANDING LITIGATION IN THE PRISON
Explanations of behavior within a prison culture typically proceed from one of three general models. Conventional researchers have tended to examine prisoner behavior as the consequence of either a set of norms or values imported into the prison from the streets (the "importation" model). Irwin (1970), for example, has argued that prisoner's roles are largely a re-creation of roles brought in from the streets. Still others theorize that prisoners possess a Marxian "revolutionary consciousness" that guides their conduct in prison.

THE IMPORTATION MODEL
We find the importation model unsatisfactory to help us understand the relationship between prison culture and litigation because the tendency to litigate seems to emerge independent of previous experiences or behaviors on the streets, and we see behavioral variation among JHLs differing by educational levels, racial composition, political sophistication, crime

committed, and world outlook. Further, neither the legal skills nor the predilection to litigate are characteristics, skills, or values learned in the streets. Our data indicate that legal expertise and enthusiasm for the law are simply not traits imported from the outside. We can identify only one instance of an active JHL importing formal legal skills into an institution and using those skills to oppose conditions. This person, however, knowing that incarceration was inevitable, delayed trial long enough to obtain a law degree in order to pursue litigation while in prison. Other lawyers have been incarcerated, but these, to our knowledge, did little to challenge prison conditions and they used their skills, if at all, to fight their own convictions or to exchange services with other inmates in cases unrelated to civil-rights actions.

THE DEPRIVATION MODEL

The deprivation model seems equally unsatisfactory (see Irwin, 1970) in that even though litigation may be seen as a response to debilitating conditions (Thomas, 1988), and new forms of debilitation may arise as old ones are eliminated, the choice to litigate instead of pursuing other—often less productive—courses of action cannot be explained by deprivation alone. There are numerous alternatives to litigation as a response to deprivation: fighting, predatory behavior, drug use, gang activity, withdrawal to fantasy or incessant television viewing, obsessive confrontation with guards, body-building, avaricious reading, or other activities— some highly productive, others not.

Why some prisoners become JHLs instead of engaging in other forms of behavior is difficult to determine. Although there is equal structural access to courts, not all prisoners possess the requisite skills or temperament. However, two characteristics seem shared by all JHLs: an aggressive intellectual capacity, and a desire to "fight back." One JHL described how he became involved in litigation work:

> I was forced into it. But everybody who's got a lot of time isn't forced into it. Some people die, some people shrink from it, because if it's a burden, and you come out of the ghetto or you come out of the suburbs—it don't make no difference—it's difficult to get off into those law books, mountains of law books, read all them mountains of cases, and see all day the insanity and madness there, it's difficult. It's overwhelming. It'll burn you up. And it burns up some of the best lawyers. I was forced to fight. I've been pushed into a corner. (interview, JHL)

It would seem, then, that deprivation alone is not sufficient to trigger the impetus to resist. The deprivation view also glosses over the complexity of the prison culture by attributing more homogeneity to it than is actually found. While we recognize the role deprivation plays in shaping prison culture, we do not find it a particularly helpful concept in illuminating the meaning of litigation as a form of accommodation to prison existence.

REVOLUTIONARY CONSCIOUSNESS

Finally, the Marxian "revolutionary" view also seems inadequate because there is no evidence that JHLs, in the main, possess a "revolutionary consciousness." In fact, most suits are neither initially motivated by nor developed with any consistent or explicit political agenda (Thomas, 1988: 117-19; Milovanovic, 1988a). The past decade has clearly belied the belief that prisoner activists have become a "class for itself." This view does little more than romanticize prisoners without adding to our understanding of either the nature or meaning of litigation.

Contrary to some of the radical writings by both academics and prisoners in the 1960s and early 1970s, prisons, with rare exceptions, are simply not fertile breeding grounds for raising political consciousness. As Pallas and Barber (1980), Fitzgerald (1977), G. Jackson (1970), Wald (1980), and numerous others have argued, however, there was, among some prisoners in the 1970s, an inchoate revolutionary consciousness. Yet despite their visibility and theoretical sophistication, radical prisoners were a minority, and it is unclear how widespread their support was among the general prison populace. For a less sanguine and thoughtful variant of this position, see Fairchild (1977), who attempts to empirically examine the politicizing processes inside prisons. The rhetoric, and even a rudimentary understanding, of a radical analysis may exist, but this does not translate into a "class for itself." Although some individual JHLs may possess considerable legal and theoretical sophistication, en masse most are oriented toward resolving the mundane problems of the prison world.

AN EXISTENTIAL VIEW

In many ways, prisoner litigants resemble the protagonists in existential literature—both the winners and losers—in that they are surrounded by mysterious forces that threaten to overwhelm them, yet they do not readily acquiesce. In this light, prisoner litigation may be seen as a form of overcoming, of actively dealing with irrationality, of attempting to make sense of senselessness, and of yearning to be human in an inhumane environment. One JHL described the typical frustration that led him to the law as a means of resisting. After describing and documenting a series of perceived no-win situations created by staff, he concluded:

This leads to total madness. It's like being put into a cage and having them poke at you constantly. You don't have to do nothing, just because you're in that position, in that cage, they throw your water at you and throw your meat at you, and sit back and laugh at you, and constantly watch you, and poke sticks at you. And you have no recourse. You can't run nowhere, you can't hide nowhere, you can't even beg the guards . . . .(interview, JHL)

It seems, then, that it is not so much the function of prisons as "houses of punishment" that impels resistance, but the way staff, through interaction with prisoners, generate animosity:

And [staff behaviors are] wrong. Because you can't do this to human beings and expect them to accept it and lay down and play dead, because 80 percent of the people in this institution are here because they're violent. The other 20 percent shouldn't be here. (interview, JHL)

One universally perceived method of harassing prisoners is through disciplinary proceedings in which privileges may be lost and the length of time incarcerated increased by loss of "good time":

An officer can make it virtually impossible for you not to go to G-house to segregation. An officer, male or female, can come in here and make it so difficult for you to vent your hostility, because they treat you as though you are the lowest form of life on earth. (interview, JHL)

In fact, disciplinary proceedings against prisoners reveal many of the absurd characteristics of prison life, and disciplinary hearings constitute about 11 percent of prisoners' civil-rights suits in the federal courts (Thomas et al., 1988). For example, a guard may command an inmate to obey an order that seems to have no legitimate basis in existing rules, such as standing in a given spot waiting for the officer to return. The inmate asks, "Why?" The guard replies, "Because I said so!" After an hour, the inmate leaves to perform assigned tasks and is later disciplined for not remaining. "Why was I disciplined?" asks the inmate. The guard replies, "Because you violated the rules." Or the inmate may wait, and when the guard returns after nearly an hour, he disciplines the inmate for not reporting to a work assignment. The guard reasons that, considering the delay, the inmate should have realized that the guard would not return as planned.

These examples, drawn from prison disciplinary documents and from our disciplinary-hearings observations, illustrate the catch-22 situation of rule-following. To obey the rule and remain risks punishment for not being on, for example, a work assignment. To leave and avoid possible punishment for other rule violations risks punishment for "disobeying a direct order," which is a rule violation. Thomas et al. (1988) provide other examples of the double-binding dilemmas that prison rules often present.

This escalating merry-go-round of absurdity has one clear end: The inmate is given a disciplinary ticket and later unsuccessfully attempts to explain this absurdity to a disciplinary committee. The explanation ("I was told to stay, but the guard never came back") ultimately indicates guilt, and punishment for "rule infraction" follows. The absurdity of both the situation and the consequences remains. For the JHL, however, the matter does not end here.

USING THE LAW TO MEDIATE ABSURDITY

Despite arguments to the contrary (Landau, 1984), the evidence suggests that law is quite effective in challenging the prisons' absurdities (Mika and Thomas, 1988). This, however, must be tempered with several caveats. First, one must be chary of romanticizing the legal practitioner, lest litigation behavior be falsely elevated to the status of political activism. Law, despite its utility, does not engender dramatic structural changes.[1] Hence, changes in prison conditions brought about by litigation are, at best, modest. Second, some critics correctly suggest that even reform occurring through litigation may increase coercive control by strengthening legitimate prior practices or by masking existing illicit ones under the "color of law" (Brakel, 1987). Examples include legal reforms of sentencing that have shifted discretionary power of release from the judicial to the correctional realm (Bigman, 1979; Jacobs, 1983a) and the irony of legal reform of disciplinary proceedings that seem to have enhanced, rather than curtailed, staff's coercive power (Thomas et al., 1988). Finally, the dual character of law as both emancipatory and repressive means that, even if changes occur, the authority of prison administrators is preserved, albeit in a different form or by a new discourse.

However, one set of truths does not obviate others. Recognizing litigation as an act of existential rebellion allows us to understand litigation as a dialectical process that creates and mediates the contradictions of prison power, culture, existence, and transcendence. Litigation may mediate absurdity in several ways.

LITIGATION AS SELF-HELP

There is some evidence that prisoner litigation may be a form of what Irwin (1980: 16) has called gleaning, or using the prison experience and resources for self-improvement. In a related context, Black (1983) has suggested that crime may be conceptualized as "grievance expression." In an ironic twist, those who formerly expressed a grievance in ways defined as socially unacceptable now have learned new and acceptable means by which to express dissatisfaction. One JHL attempted to withdraw from a street gang as a way of avoiding problems, but was soon faced with other problems that drove him to law:

> I knew I couldn't be in this gang, because it was hurting me [physically] and I'm not into pain under any circumstances whatsoever. So, I started going over to the library a lot, playing around with the typewriters that was for the public population usage; also, I started having small conflicts with the correctional officer. I didn't like the way they treated me, so I started writing complaints on them concerning their action towards me. (interview, JHL)

The transition from a passive recipient to whom things "just happen" to a more conscious actor attempting to take control over the immediate life-world can take many forms, and entry into the world of law is just one. In this way, litigation can become a newly learned skill for exerting a growing "personhood." Moreover, these skills and ways of thinking increase the probability and the facility of saying no. Once the utility of law is recognized as a force in solving personal disputes, its role in helping others is also soon perceived. For example, JHLs seem to pass through a "save the world" phase in which they begin to feel that law is a means of changing prison conditions (Thomas, 1988: 210-11).

In sum, JHLs identify the primal emotions of desperation, anger, and the will to resist as the reasons to explain their attraction to law (Thomas, 1988: 201). For them, law becomes a form of self-help to overcome the problems they face in prison when there are no alternative means to secure relief. For some, these emotions may have emerged during their trials, where they perceived themselves to be judicial victims—not in the determination of guilt, but in the pretrial or sentencing process. For others, treatment by staff prompted a desire for retaliation. For all, the acquisition of literacy and analytic skills, coupled with functional knowledge of judicial processes and practices, became a path to personal salvation.

LITIGATION AS EFFICACIOUS

There is a view among critics of litigation that it is frivolous, and only the exceptional suit entails any grievance of substance (Anderson, 1986; Burt,

1985; Federal Judicial Center, 1980; Reed, 1980). Hence, litigation is seen not as rebellion, but as abuse of the courts by those already "proven" to be antisocial. "Frivolousness," however, is embedded in a variety of social meanings and is not value-neutral. As a legal term, it means lacking in judicial merit. But, the legal use is often translated into the lay meaning of "worthless," and a suit that is not then becomes, in the lay view, one that totally lacks substance. There is considerable evidence that prisoners, in the main, file neither excessively nor frivolously (Thomas, 1989). Even if there is no adjudicable remedy or relief, there is usually a substantive problem over which the plaintiff sues. The problem may seem trivial (deprivation of toilet paper) or severe (held a year past formal release date) but, to the prisoner, it is not frivolous.

DiJulio (1987) has provided a powerful argument that there is no "prison crisis," but rather an "administration crisis." In DiJulio's view, problems impelling litigation, violence, fiscal crisis, recidivism, and other factors commonly associated with a "failing system" can be traced directly back to incompetent administrators, which he sees as the norm, not the exception. Although we believe that prison problems can not be fully understood without analysis of broader social relations, we find much of merit in DiJulio's argument. Prisoners sue to redress a wrong, and these wrongs tend to exist because of the actions of staff or administrators. The act of challenging a decision, policy, or condition defined as unacceptable thus becomes an act of rebellion in that it resists the "what is" and attempts, through action, to change it into something more to the prisoner's liking. Examples of such changes can include reducing staff harassment, increasing security of vulnerable inmates from predatory attacks by other inmates, increased access to showers, health care, or prison programs, reducing overcrowding, changing "catch-22" rules, or making minor, but more humane, changes in facilities (for example, improved lighting, sanitation, or general ambiance).

LITIGATION AS NEGATION

Litigation, or even its threat, can often curtail perceived staff abuse of power. A suit signifies that a monologic or asymmetrical power relation is momentarily replaced by a dialogic and more symmetrical state of affairs, albeit a formal one (see Blum, 1974; Bakhtin, 1981).

Whether a suit is substantively won or lost, the act of filing the suit *requires* a formal response from prison officials. Presumably, even abusive staff and insensitive administrators would prefer to avoid additional paper work, visibility, and hassle, especially at the behest of prisoners. By challenging the expression of power, the conditions it engenders, and its extreme uses by power holders, such litigation can negate at least some of the deleterious conditions of the prison conditions (see Palmer, 1985).

LITIGATION AS THE SUBVERSION OF HIERARCHY

Critics correctly claim that prisoner litigation does little to change the structure of hierarchical power arrangements. However, it does not follow that there has been no impact of litigation on the exercise of power in prisons (Jacobs, 1983a: 54-60). An act of rebellion begins with a refusal to accept the existing structure of power. Prisoners' suits challenge the prison staff's power. When, for example, the administration of Cook County jail refused to allow inmates to possess hardcover books because they were potential weapons, a suit overturned the policy (*Jackson v. Elrod et al.*, 86-C-1817, N.D. Ill. 1986). When the isolation, lack of health care, and living conditions in Menard's condemned unit became unbearable, a federal decision alleviated at least some of the problems (*Lightfoot et al v. Walker et al.*, 486 F. Supp. 504, 1980). When staff refused to properly deliver an inmate's legitimate mail, a law suit corrected the problem for that inmate (*Woods v. Aldworth*, 84-C-7745, N.D. Ill. 1984).

These examples seem relatively trivial, but they typify inmate civil-rights complaints. They also symbolize acts of resistance and refusal to cooperate with and reaffirm the power of officials to control existence. In such cases, law mediates domination by staff power, and although it does little to rearrange or redistribute power, litigation imposes constraints on the ability of staff to exercise it. Resistance, then, may not necessarily change the power hierarchy, but it can rearrange the use of power within it (although, see *Holt v. Sarver*, 300 F.Supp. 825 [E.D. Ark. 1969]; *Ruiz v. Estelle*, 650 F.2d 555 [Fifth Cir. 1981] in Arkansas and Texas).

LITIGATION AS "VICTORY"

If the popular view that prisoners rarely win their cases is true, it would seem to follow that prisoners are not effective rebels. But we do not accept the argument that to be a legitimate rebel one must "win." Nor do we find convincing evidence that prisoners rarely win. Of course, what counts as a victory for one person may be perceived as a defeat by another. The conventional method of scorekeeping simply calculates the number of cases won and lost by prisoners, a method that, for several reasons, we find unsatisfactory.

First, the measure of success must be determined, at least in part, by whether the suit curtailed or corrected the objectionable behavior. A prisoner who sues staff for $1 million for an improper conviction in a disciplinary hearing may have the case dismissed without any formal judicial action taken, but may nonetheless have the improper conviction expunged from the record and any lost good time restored. A prisoner who is injured because of staff's recklessness may opt to settle for remedial action or token damage awards out of court. Official records record these as "victories" for state defendants

(Thomas, 1989), even though the prisoner's challenge has resulted in a consequential form of resistance.

Second, although prisoners are rarely awarded all that they request in a suit, we reject the general conclusion that they lose in the legal forum. In a study of 2,900 cases in Illinois's northern federal district, Mika and Thomas (1988) found that while about 38 percent of prisoners' complaints are dismissed on pleading, about 62 percent of those surviving result in a "victory" of some kind. The outcomes, usually settled out of court, may result in token damage awards, but more often they are in the form of rectification of the original problem, modification of prison policies, or discouragement of objectionable staff behavior toward the plaintiff. We must caution that unless a complaint challenges a policy or specific conditions that affect others, the impact of most suits is limited to a single individual.

Third, as one experienced JHL argued, "Just the doin' of it, we win!" In this view, litigation can provide a symbolic victory to the extent that, even if the case is lost, it makes staff aware that they may be accountable for future actions. Milovanovic (1988a) suggests that one objective indicator of the effectiveness of JHLs might be how much legal "action" has been mobilized (see also Black, 1976). In this view, an inmate returning to court for redress, appeal, suppression hearings, or other action, can be seen as attaining some symbolic gain to the extent that they continue to keep their issue before the courts. Similarly, in civil-rights cases, litigants usually gain at least temporary respite from the objectionable action even prior to case termination.

THE POLITICAL VALUE OF JAILHOUSE LAW

What then is the political value of jailhouse law and the action of the JHLs? The answer to this question lies in how one views the role of law in social change (Milovanovic, 1988a). While conceding the lack of a consistent collective political consciousness, we see prisoners' litigation as social praxis, specifically, in affirming the act of saying no. Even while reinforcing the ideology of the rule of law, prisoners simultaneously subvert the expression, if not the structure, of certain existing power arrangements in the prison. The problem is not that law is ineffective, but that the effectiveness of law is misdirected. As Klare (1979) has written in defending "law-making as praxis,"

> My argument is that we can conceive law-making as, *in theory*, a form of expressive social practice in which the community participates in shaping the moral, allocative, and adjudicatory texture of social life, but that in class society, this process is alienated. In history, law-making becomes a mode of domination.

not freedom, because of its *repressive* function. (emphasis in the original, p. 132)

The utility of jailhouse law as social praxis, then, is not unqualified. Both its content and its form of expression re-create and sustain the broader class and other power arrangements that lead to unnecessary social domination. As Klare (1979: 135) has suggested, the exercise tends to promote the instrumental pursuit of client or self-interest at the expense of "political lawyering."

But objections to viewing the JHL as a rebel, although sometimes cogent, tend to neglect the subtleties of the meaning of litigation as both a means of change and as a form of existential negation. Rebellion defines the relationship of an act to its context, not its consequence nor its motive. Rebellion begins when one moves from passive acquiescence to active resistance against forces that threaten to dominate or overwhelm. Sometimes resistance is carefully planned and implemented, as occurs in social movements or in such individual acts of defiance as refusal to pay taxes or terrorism. Other times, rebellion is more subtle, as occurs when people reject the authority of the state by exceeding the speed limit or refusing to wear seat belts. A prison rebel is not a revolutionary:

> "Revolutionary" action is defiant action that seeks to change the prison structure or its relation to the external environment in a fundamental way. The most important factor associated with revolutionary action is identification with defiant counter communities. (Useem and Kimball, 1987: 106)

A primitive rebel, then, is one who has learned to say "no" and intentionally resists authority, but has not yet developed a consciousness capable of translating action into a consistent critical theory or systematic, ideologically informed assault. While there are, of course, exceptions, those few JHLs who possess exceptional skills in political analysis and attempt to link their legal actions to broader issues are not the norm.

The litigation of the JHL may be viewed as an existential response to repression. Where most conventional social theory tends to look for "laws" or "processes," and too often ignores the meanings by which the concepts underlying research are shaped and defined, existential literature evokes a theoretical imagery of action-taking in which individuals confront their environment, even if the confrontation appears futile.

We do not impute to JHLs an explicit existential consciousness, and do not suggest that they are necessarily striving toward authenticity as a coherent philosophical or political act. We are concerned with the more general issue of understanding resistance as a way of creating meaning through social action. In the case of litigation, self-awareness is connected to social formation to the extent that "saying no" symbolizes a rejection of the status quo. When negation is coupled with social action (in this case, legal struggle), there occurs the potential for an accommodation between the resisters and those resisted. It is this dialectical tension between those who impose meanings and those who challenge them that imbues prisoner litigation with its capacity for existential rebellion.

DISCUSSION

By conceptualizing litigation as more an existential than a political act, one that may be viewed as a continuum ranging from extreme individualism to sophisticated political action, we have attempted to reframe the meaning of activist law and applied our analysis to one category of litigant. At one end are those who acquiesce. At the other stand those who resist. In prisons, these are jailhouse lawyers. But the JHL is a "doer," not an ideologist; a reformer, not an articulator of system-generated repression. He is a person who has come to understand how to respond to absurdity with existing tools, but has not developed the broader political or social understanding to use those tools to address the meaning and embeddedness of existence. The efforts of the JHL lie somewhere between conscious and reflective behavior and what Kosik (1976) has called procuring, or mundane social activity:

> The individual moves about in a *ready made system of devices and implements*, procures them as they in turn procure him, and has long ago "lost" any awareness of this world being a product of man.... Procuring is praxis in its *phenomenally alienated* form which does not point to the *genesis* of the human world (the world of people and of human culture, of a culture that humanizes nature) but rather expresses the praxis of everyday manipulation, with man employed in a system of *ready made* "things," i.e., implements. In this system of implements, man himself becomes an object of manipulation. (emphasis in original, p. 39)

The JHL has gone beyond simple procuring but does not yet act in a way consistent with a fully aware political consciousness. The action remains at the intermediate level of resisting institutional absurdity, but does not yet, and perhaps cannot, transcend it.

If Lukacs (1971: 199) was correct in his assertion that "Whether an action is functionally right or wrong is decided ultimately by the evolution of proletarian class consciousness," then prisoner litigation may be "politically incorrect." But this seems too uncharitable, because social change, as a historical process, occurs in many cases with successive acts of saying no. Precisely when an act becomes transformed from mundane practice to rebellious praxis is an empirical question, and the effects of an act may not be visible until some future date.[2]

Of itself, this may not lead to fundamental social change but, in the dialectic of social struggle, neither do fundamental changes occur through the efforts of any single social group. Social change arises from social action, and a group "in itself" can contribute to the creation of circumstances that can help it congeal in a group "for itself," as has occurred with such groups as feminists, blacks, and gays. Obviously, reforms are only a partial victory, but they function to exacerbate other conditions, and the dialectic of struggle continues.

Our argument suggests several questions for research. First it suggests the need to reconceptualize the meaning of JHL activity in particular and the role of legal activists in general. Rather than view legal struggle by examining its consequences, we should also examine the meanings of the use of law in the context of "saying no." Second, existentially oriented research gives attention to institutional and other social arrangements that constrain both behavior and consciousness. Especially in total institutions, the often contradictory structure promotes double-bind, no-win situations, and inconsistent practices that must be continually negotiated and managed. Third, consistent with Marxian and conflict theory, this research reminds us, as Goodwin (1971) has cogently argued, that people may seek dissonance as much as consonance. Dissonance offers not only an instrumental means of potential resistance, but provides as well a source of meaning to an otherwise meaningless existence. Fourth, given our contention that JHLs are primitive rebels, one crucial research task requires, as Fairchild (1977) suggests, identifying the relationship between the correctional experience and social and political empowerment. More simply, what factors impel some prisoners to resist while others acquiesce? Under what conditions does simple rebellion become transformed into explicit political action? Finally, this research shifts attention from the alleged "pathological" or abusive motives of litigants to the meanings litigation has for those who pursue it for themselves and others who share their situation. This suggests that litigation should be interpreted diagnostically as reflecting the pathology of the deeper institutional structures that impel resistance while simultaneously offering the means for challenge.

These symbolic meanings of this prison litigation lead us to view the JHL as a primitive rebel. By refocusing attention on the existential conditions of resistance, we cautiously temper the contentions of some, such as Foucault (1977), who impute excessive unilateral power to those in charge of discipline. A position informed by the existentialist tradition recognizes the mediating, yet often ironic and futile, capacity of human beings:

It is essentially a struggle against great odds to allow the individual to realize his *existential freedom* and to feel his capacity to influence his future and to participate in the decisions which affect him (Fairchild, 1977: 316; emphasis in original).

NOTES

1. A helpful reader suggested that we underestimate the impact of law in generating structural change. We agree that civil-rights law especially has had a profound social impact; we are less convinced that law was the primary independent variable in these changes. The point is well taken, however, and it is not our intent to devalue the role of law in social change but, instead, to be cautious in the extent to which it, in and of itself, creates fundamental structural change.

2. An example of an apparently spontaneous act that symbolized a resistance movement occurred when Rosa Parks, a black woman, refused to give up her bus seat to a white male in Montgomery, Alabama. Some have identified her refusal as the birth of the civil-rights movement.

POSTSCRIPT, 1 JUNE, 1996, DRAGAN MILOVANOVIC

Since the initial publication of the two included articles on jailhouse lawyers, no prominent theoretical work on the subject has appeared in the literature. Jim Thomas and I are planning a new article on the subject, "Re-Visiting Jailhouse Lawyers." A response to the accusation by various state attorneys general that inmates submit "frivolous lawsuits," by the National Prison Project and the Coalition Against STOP has recently appeared on the World Wide Web (http://www.wco.com/`aerick/ten.htm). The "Top Ten Non-Frivolous Lawsuits Filed By Prisoners" included:

1. Prison guards routinely sexually assault female prisoners. One officer sexually fondles a prisoner who is receiving medical care in the infirmary, forces her to perform oral sex, then rapes her. Another officer forces a prisoner to perform oral sex while she empties trash as part of a work detail. *Women Prisoners v. District of Columbia*, D.C. (1994) (post-trial order).

2. Prisoners restrained in handcuffs and shackles have their heads bashed into walls and floors by prison guards, their bodies repeatedly kicked and hit with batons, their teeth knocked out, their jaws fractured, their limbs broken, and their bodies burned with scalding water. *Madrid v. Gomes*, Cal. (1995) (post-trial order).

3. Confined youth are routinely beaten by facility staff, staff trafficking in illegal drugs is rampant, and sexual relations between staff and confined youth is commonplace. *D.B. v. Commonwealth*, Penn. (1993) (consent decree).

4. Dozens of women, some as young as 16, are forced to have sex with prison guards, maintenance workers, and a prison chaplain. Many become pregnant and are coerced by prison staff to have abortions. *Cason v. Seckinger*, Ga. (1994) (consent decree).

5. A 17-year-old boy, in jail for failing to pay $73 in traffic fines, is tortured for 14 hours and finally murdered in his cell by other prisoners. Another teenager had been beaten unconscious by the same prisoners several days earlier. *Yellen v. Ada County*, Idaho (1985) (consent decree).

6. Prison officials ignore warnings by the Commissioner of Health and fail to implement basic tuberculosis detection and control procedures. Over 400 prisoners are infected in a single prison. *Austin v. Dept. of Corrections*, Penn. (1992) (post-hearing order).

7. Prison staff engage in sexual relations with female prisoners and allow male inmates to enter the prisons to engage in forcible intercourse with the women prisoners. *Hamilton v. Morial*, La. (1995) (consent decree pending court approval).

8. Several suicidal children are transferred to the state mental hospital where they are placed, naked or in paper gowns, in four-point restraints, hands and feet bound to the four corners of their beds, and then forcibly injected with psychotropic drugs as part of "aversive therapy." *Robert K. v. Bell*. S.C. (1984) (consent decree).

9. A prisoner gives birth on the floor of the jail without medical assistance three hours after informing prison staff that she was in active labor. Other prisoners have deformed or stillborn babies as a result of receiving almost no pregnancy-related medical care. *Yeager v. Smith* and *Harris v. McCarthy*, Cal. (1989) (consent decree).

10. Single-person cells house four or five prisoners with mattresses on the floor soaked by overflowing toilets, the drinking water is contaminated with sewage, and prisoners' cells are infested with rats. *Carty v. Farrelly*, U.S.V. Is. (1994) (consent decree).

The Necessity Defense, Substantive Justice, and Oppositional Linguistic Practice

Shelley Bannister and Dragan Milovanovic

INTRODUCTION

Doing critical law has raised the radical's dilemma. Do we work within the framework of formal legalism to eradicate oppressive practices generated by the system, and by so doing, inadvertently give legitimacy to the rule-of-law ideology, or should we seek an alternative praxis outside of the narrow dictates of formal legal rationality?

In posing the dilemma in this way, we need not be constrained by the theoretical construct concerning the question of the degree of autonomy of the legal order. Law is neither pure reflection of an assumed elite, nor does it work independently from a particular mode of production. However, the *form* of law and prevailing *form* of legal thought do attain an "objective" existence transcending the pressures exerted by interest groups and a particular mode of production. It is within this sedimented framework that *doing law* is recognized. Elsewhere it has been argued that a particular circumscribed legal discourse develops resulting in juridical linguistic repression (Milovanovic, 1986, 1988a). Here we shall explore the liberating potential of one legal form, the "necessity defense."

Weber pointed out that a form of law that is "logically formal rationality" militates against presenting substantive issues in lawfinding (1978: 729-30). The range of possible responses by rebels before the court could extend from arguing only within the given categories of law: e.g., entrapment (citing agent provocateurs), duress, insanity, Title 42 of U.S.C. Section 1983 (denial of civil rights), exclusionary rule (evidence illegally obtained), to reluctant recognition of the jurisdiction and expertise of the courts (users of the necessity defense), to outright rejection of its jurisdictional claims and prophesied claims to competence and expertise (i.e., by not participating in formal legalistic procedures). Acceptable argumentation in law is bounded by the rules of evidence, precedence, and myriad procedural stipulations. Doing acceptable law, then, means working within linguistic codes that express sense data in a one-dimensional way. The "facts" of a case, for example, are stripped of their contextual nuances and are given a narrow meaning. Lawfinding tends to the singularizing of the event.

Balbus (1977: 13), analyzing the rebellions of the late 1960s in Detroit, Chicago, and Los Angeles, has noted that "to sanction participants in collective violence by means of the ordinary administration of justice is to divert attention from the singularity of the event and its causes in favor of an exclusive focus on the mere 'facts' and their relationship to general categories of formally proscribed acts."

Thus, in arguing issues that are extracted from the ebb and flow in a social formation, a decontextualizing, a cleansing, a sterilizing of the "facts" takes place. Consider, for example, Bennet and Feldman's point (1981):

> Trial justice consists of one symbolic universe (that of language and rhetoric) laid upon another (that of symbolic representations of action in story form). The physical or "object" world enters the production of justice only at several steps removed from the terms on which judgments are ultimately based. In this fluid symbol system the real world and the symbolic representation of it in the courtroom are in tension. (p. 142)

Linguistic codification is both arbitrary and politically selective. The particular legal codification of reality, then, can be seen as a political-economic decision. This sterilization of the "facts" can be found nowhere better than in political trials.

We may take for example the prosecution and conviction of the church group involved in the underground railroad of El Salvadoran and Guatemalan refugees in Tuscon, Arizona (Golden and McConnell, 1986; Haas, 1986). The district attorney attempted to argue within the formal categories of law, defining the church group as a conspiratorial criminal enterprise. The members of the church group, however, attempted, in most cases unsuccessfully, to bring out political argumentation centering on the U.S. policies in Central America. The conflict was over the form of law and legal thought. The state argued within the categories of formal law; the defense attempted to move the locus to substantive rational argumentations.[1]

In this article, we will argue that the radical's dilemma, which is apparent and real, can be at least partially reconciled in one important and perhaps unique application of formal law: the "necessity defense." However, as we will show, there are limits to the long-term effectiveness of this strategy. The dialectics of doing critical law indicate trade-offs that perhaps are part of the "insoluble conflict" posed by Max Weber.

The necessity defense is one of the few legal forms that crosses the boundary of formal legalism—logical formal rationality—into substantive rational principles. It enables the defense to attempt to show that, yes, indeed the defendants have broken the law, but for a higher purpose, to prevent a greater imminent harm. It therefore permits as part of the legal argument a much wider codification of reality to take place. Political, economic, ethical, and moral arguments may be given a hearing, a situation quite out of accord with principles of formal logical rationality. It is here that a Trojan horse is being created. Progressive and revolutionary groups have yet to realize its liberating potential. And for the defending, politically oriented lawyer, in using the necessity defense s/he no longer has to be concerned with the radical's dilemma; it is resolved in the form of critical legal praxis.

On another level, the expanded use of the necessity defense, whether it be by civil-rights, anti-war, prisoner, environmental, feminist or antinuclear groups leads to an expanded alternative legal discourse, an oppositional discourse, with contextually codified sense data. The singularization of the event is rent asunder. And the rule-of-law ideology, inadvertently given legitimacy by many honorable and well-intentioned oppositional groups and lawyers working within the traditional legal categories, is demystified.

In the following sections we will briefly explain: the legal basis and the evolution of the necessity defense in U.S. law (paying particular attention to its application in prisoner cases, civil-rights cases, and civil protests against apartheid, intervention in Central America by the U.S., and the nuclear weapons build-up); the dialectical nature of liberating practice; the potential of developing a liberating oppositional linguistic praxis; and some implications and strategies for a critical legal praxis and social reform.

THE EVOLUTION OF THE NECESSITY DEFENSE

The necessity defense is often termed the "justification" or "choice-of-evil" defense. The American Law Institute Model Penal Code (hereafter ALI MPC; the ALI is a legal group that develops laws to serve as standards for legislators' use in the drafting of state and federal law) defines justification as follows:

Section 3.02. Justification Generally: Choice of Evils
(1) Conduct which the actor believes to be necessary to avoid a harm or evil to himself or to another is justifiable, provided that
    (a) the harm or evil sought to be avoided by such conduct is greater than that sought to be prevented by the law defining the offense charged; and
    (b) neither the Code nor other law defining the offense provides
exceptions or defenses dealing with the specific situation involved; and

(c) a legislative purpose to exclude the justification claimed does not otherwise plainly appear.

(2) When the actor was reckless or negligent in bringing about the situation requiring a choice of harms or evils or in appraising the necessity for this conduct, the justification afforded by this Section is unavailable in a prosecution for any offense for which recklessness or negligence, as the case may be, suffices to establish culpability.

As the ALI explains in its "Comment," the principle of necessity allows a general justification for conduct that otherwise would constitute a crime (1985: 9). Such a principle is "essential to the rationality and justice of the criminal law..." (ALI, 1985: 9)

The ALI gives the following examples for application of the defense: the destruction of property to prevent the spread of fire, an ambulance going through a red light, lost mountain climbers appropriating shelter and provisions, violation of a curfew to reach an air raid shelter, and a pharmacist dispensing a drug in a grave emergency without a prescription (ALI, 1985: 9-10).

This is a balancing, or choice-of-evils defense; the implication of this is that someone must make a determination of where the evils lie and which is the greater evil: that sought to be prevented or that committed. The ALI stated that this is to be determined by the court or the jury, whoever acts at trial as the fact-finder (ALI, 1985: 13).

Historically, the necessity defense has been applied in cases in which the choice between and among evils is triggered by a natural physical force (Gardner, 1976: 119; Perkins, 1969: 956; Gold, 1979: 1186). The ALI, however, notes that a "claim of justification is possible when an actor responds to human threats of harm" (ALI, 1985: 16). The necessity defensive derives from common law (ALI, 1985: 6, note 1). "The principle of necessity is one of general validity. It is widely accepted in the law of torts and there is even greater need for its acceptance in the law of crime." (ALI, 1985: 14.)

Gardner terms the balancing test of a resolution a "conflict of values" (1976: 117) . The defendant's position in a necessity defense case is that her or his conduct was necessary for the public good even though it violated a criminal law. "The success of the justification defense will turn on the court's evaluation of the utility produced by the act against the disutility of not acting and thus enduring the harm which violating the law could reasonably have avoided" (Gardner, 1976: 117). If the court finds that social utility is maximized by the defendant's actions, the *actus reus* requirement of criminal law is negated and the defendant is acquitted. Obviously, the defendant will be acquitted only if the courts agree with the defendant's value choice.

The courts are concerned with the presidential effect of such an acquittal; in the protester cases discussed below, appellate courts have been loath to extend this defense to any situations other than those that have historically utilized the defense. Gardner explains that "a judicial opinion in a justification context creates a new rule of law instructing future actors, faced with the same conflict of values, how to act" (Gardner, 1976: 117).

Hall explains that necessity designates a situation in which innocent parties are injured by actors who are under "extraordinary pressure" (1960: 415-16).

> These terms [necessity and the legal concept of duress] were derived and took their meaning in the perennial struggles of a frail being against a powerful, sometimes overpowering, force . . . . The doctrines of "necessity" and "coercion" are a tacit admission of man's impotence against some of the greatest evils that assail him, as well as a measure of his moral obligations even *in extremis* (Hall, 1960: 416).

One of the early United States cases involving the successful use of the necessity defense was *United States v. Ashton* (1834). A mutiny by a ship's crew was held to be necessary and justified because of the crew's reasonable belief that the ship was unseaworthy. In another early case, in 1853, a California official was held not responsible for the destruction of homes that he ordered during a large conflagration (*Surocco v. Geary*, 1853).

Since the promulgation in 1962 of the Model Penal Code section cited above, over 20 states in the United States have included in their statutes a section allowing the necessity defense in certain specified instances (ALI, 1985; 18, note 21). There are two basic forms of the necessity defense in statutes: the MPC's rendition cited above and New York State's variation, which differs from the MPC in the following respects: it requires that the action taken be an "emergency measure to avoid an imminent" harm (N.Y. section 35.05); it states that the desirability of the actor's choice must "clearly outweigh" the anticipated harm if the actor chose not to act; and it requires that the need for action cannot be attributable to any fault of the actor.

PRISON CASES

The necessity defense has been argued, with some successes and failures, in a number of cases involving escapes from prison when the prisoner was faced with violence or oppressive conditions.

The United States Supreme Court in 1980 sustained prison-escape convictions for four men who had been unable to explain to the Court's satisfaction that they had attempted to turn themselves in to authorities immediately upon their escape. The four escaped from jail and were arrested one to three months later on the streets (*United States v. Bailey*, 1980).

Based in part on the *Bailey* decision, in 1982, the Second Circuit Court of Appeals affirmed the district-court conviction of a defendant charged with escape from the New York Metropolitan Correctional Center, a federal detention center. In so affirming, the court adopted four elements that must be present before a defendant can rely on the necessity defense in prison-escape cases: (1) the defendant is faced with a specific, immediate threat of death or substantial bodily injury; (2) there is no time for the defendant to complain to authorities or complaints made in the past have been futile; (3) force or violence is not used against prison officials or other innocent persons in the escape attempt, and (4) the defendant intends to report immediately to the proper authorities when he is safe from immediate threat (*United States v. Wyler*, 1981).

While the federal courts require a prompt report to law-enforcement officials by the escapee, many state courts have not included this as a necessary prerequisite for the application of the necessity defense. The state courts and legislatures are not bound by federal standards such as these. The issues in the state court cases generally focus on the immediacy and seriousness of the threatened harm. Some states do require prompt reporting, but others have determined that element to be merely a factor to consider when assessing the defendant's credibility regarding her/his true motivation for the escape.

For example, in 1978, the Oregon Appellate Court held that poor conditions of confinement do not generally justify an escape; for the defense of necessity to be applicable there must be a showing that the harm to the escapee which s/he was attempting to avoid was "present, imminent and impending" (*State v. Whisman*, 1978: 1005, 1007). Oregon does not require immediate surrender as an element of the defense.

Similarly, Illinois requires that a defendant charged with escape present some evidence that her/his safety was threatened imminently within the prison (*People v. Unger*, 1977: 333). This defense derives from the language of the Illinois necessity statute, which states that it is a defense to the charges if the defendant did not cause the problem to arise and s/he reasonably believed that the conduct was necessary to avoid a greater injury. The statute does not include imminence as a requirement in its language (see, Ch. 38, 111. Rev. Stat. section 7-13). The defendant in *Unger* alleged that he had been threatened with a homosexual attack by other inmates and he chose to escape the prison to avoid the attack. The Illinois Supreme Court held that this evidence raised the defense sufficiently for a jury's determination.

The California courts were among the first to take the position later affirmed by the United States Supreme Court in *Bailey*. In *People v.*

Lovercamp (1974: 43), a much-cited case, two female prisoners escaped fearing threatened sexual attacks from other female prisoners. The trial court refused to allow the testimony regarding the reasons for their escape. The appeals court reversed, stating a five-part test to determine whether the necessity defense would be allowed. Those five elements are as follows:

(1) the prisoner is faced with a specific threat of death, forcible sexual attack or substantial bodily injury in the immediate future;
(2) there is no time for a complaint to the authorities or there exists a history of futile complaints which make any result from such complaints illusory;
(3) there is no time or opportunity to resort to the courts;
(4) there is no evidence of force or violence used towards prison personnel or other "innocent" persons in the escape; and
(5) the prisoner immediately reports to the proper authorities when he has attained a position of safety from the immediate threat (43 Cal. P. 3d at 831-832,118 Cal. Rptr. at 115).

In contrast with these standards as established by California, the ALI does not require that the threat be immediate. "Such a requirement unduly emphasizes one ingredient in the judgment that is called for at the expense of others just as important" (ALI, 1985: 16-17). While necessity depends on the absence of reasonable alternatives to the chosen prohibited conduct, "it is a mistake to erect imminence as an absolute requirement, since there may be situations in which an otherwise illegal act is necessary to avoid an evil that may occur in the future" (ALI, 1985: 17). The ALI offers the following example: if Smith and Jones travel in Smith's car to a remote mountain spot for a month's vacation and Jones learns that Smith plans on killing him at the end of the month, Jones would be justified in taking Smith's car after just one week, even though the injury would not occur for three weeks (ALI, 1985: 17).

Many states require immediacy of the harm, notwithstanding this analysis by the ALI. A Michigan court held, though, that "imminency is . . . to be decided by the jury taking into consideration all of the surrounding circumstances, including the defendant's opportunity and ability to avoid the feared harm" (*People v. Harmon*, 1974: 212, 214).

The California *Lovercamp* standard also requires that no violence or force be used against innocent persons. The ALI recognized, however, that one may reasonably invoke the defense of necessity in cases of bodily injury and even in homicide cases if the facts and the choices support the defense. Human lives must be weighed equally. If one death can save the lives of two other people, then causing that death may be justified and excused (ALI, 1985: 7-8). The ALI does note that there may be crimes such as rape, in which it is difficult to support the claim that the crime being committed causes less harm than that which is being avoided; this is "a matter that is safely left to the determination and elaboration of the courts" (ALI, 1985: 8).

There has been an attempt to apply the necessity defense to other prisoner-committed offenses. In a 1979 prison uprising at Stateville Correctional Center in Illinois, twelve prisoners were charged with the offense of "enforcement of discipline," forcible detention, unlawful restraint, and armed violence, a class X felony (Illinois' most serious level of felony, excepting murder). The defendants admitted committing the offenses, which included the taking and holding of hostages while several of the prisoners negotiated with wardens and other correctional employees. The defendants presented evidence at trial of the "deplorable conditions which the prisoners had previously complained of, including bugs and vermin, broken windows, cold food, lack of access to the law library, and yard time and showers only once a week" (*People v. Whitson*, 1984: 999, 1004). Defendant Whitson was tried by the court simultaneously with a trial by jury for the other defendants. The trial court refused to instruct the jury on the defense of necessity because the defendants were not in imminent danger of bodily harm, and because their conduct could have resulted in greater injury than that they were trying to avoid (because of their use of dangerous weapons during the takeover). Even though the defendants were prevented from arguing necessity to the jury as a statutory defense, the evidence of their conditions spoke for itself and resulted in "not guilty" verdicts for all defendants on all but the least serious offense.

The Stateville case is a prime example of a situation in which the necessity defense should have been justifiable, especially in light of the jury's verdict. The most logical interpretation of the verdict reveals that evidence proving substandard prison conditions may be considered a sufficient justification in jurors' minds for the commission of offenses within the walls of a prison.

CIVIL RESISTANCE/PROTEST CASES
Until recently, the necessity defense has been allowed only in the type of cases described above. More recently, however, the necessity defense has been relied upon, in most part successfully, by persons challenging this country's political choices: its support of South Africa's system of apartheid, intervention in Central America, and the increasing expansion of nuclear weapons and nuclear power. In so relying, the protesters, who are typically arrested for trespass or disorderly conduct, become criminal defendants who assert that any harm that they have caused is necessitated as an attempt to prevent the greater harms caused by these United States policies. They attempt to educate other Americans about the injustice of these policies and the loss of lives that these policies cause.

In the past several years, the defense has been extended by trial courts to cover several different groups of protesters.[2] In 1977, an Oregon jury acquitted a group of defendants who had blocked a nuclear power plant. Those defendants, relying on a necessity defense, presented evidence that the harm that they were attempting to prevent was the harm of nuclear power (*State v. Mouer*, 1977). Twenty citizens were similarly acquitted in Illinois in 1978 under the same circumstances (*People v. Brown*, 1979).

The necessity defense has also been used successfully in defending charges of mob action and resisting arrest in blocking the gates of a Navy base. Those defendants charged that their offense was a lesser harm than that committed daily by the U.S. Navy in Central America (*People v. Jarka*, 1985). Additionally, the defense was used successfully to fight charges of trespass by eight community leaders who were demonstrating against apartheid in South Africa (*People v. Streeter*, 1985).

In the *Jarka* case, the defendants called a number of expert witnesses to testify in addition to presenting their own testimony. Under the Illinois statute described above in the context of prison-escape cases, the defendants had to explain the reasonableness of their conduct. They accomplished this by calling witnesses to testify about the effect of American support for the *Contras* in Nicaragua and the effect of the daily American aid to the Duarte government in El Salvador. These witnesses included human-rights workers in these countries as well as victims of El Salvodoran government-sponsored Death Squads. The witnesses recounted the horrors of *Contra* attacks on their villages and cooperatives. An American nun who had lived in Central America for over seven years testified about her life there and the daily fear of American [sponsored] bombings of civilians and their villages.

Two American Catholic priests testified; one concerning his history in the nonviolent peace demonstrations and the efforts to confront and expose racism in America over the years. His testimony supported the defendants' contention that demonstrations and arrests help change peoples' opinions and public policy. The second priest testified about the nuclear capabilities of the Navy ships that had been deployed in the Central American region. He graphically depicted the tonnage of those nuclear armaments and the extent of the damage that they could inflict.

Lastly, several defendants testified that they felt compelled by the dictates of international law to protest against and take all possible measures to prevent the continuation of these American policies. An international-law expert testified regarding generally accepted principles of international law, buttressing the defendants' beliefs that their reliance on this body of law was not misplaced. The expert cited several United Nations documents that the United States violates consistently in its interventionist practices: notably, the U.N. Charter itself, the Universal Declaration of Human Rights (1948), the

Convention on the Prevention and Punishment of the Crime of Genocide, the International Covenant on Civil and Political Rights and on Economic, Social and Cultural Rights, and the 1949 Protocol to the Geneva Conventions, *inter alia*.

The object of these defendants' actions were hundreds, sometimes thousands of miles away. Yet these trial courts recognized the harm as imminent and greater than the injury committed by the defendants' actions. In relying on the necessity defense, these defendants have been able to circumvent the typical criminal process that would punish them for their political statements and actions taken. The trial becomes politicized. Alternative codifications of "reality" enter the lawfinding practices. An alternative, oppositional discourse enters into the determination of justice. Substantive justice makes a rare appearance.

In the following sections we will first identify the dilemma faced in doing traditional law by describing the alienating process involved, and then we will point out how an oppositional linguistic praxis is involved in the use of the necessity defense.

DIALECTICS OF DOING CRITICAL LAW

Doing critical legal praxis poses many obstacles. Frustrations often occur when the well-intentioned activist lawyer attempts to bring issues before the court only to have them rendered "irrelevant" and nonjusticiable. What s/he often finds is that the only way to defend an oppositional group or a politically motivated lawbreaker is to argue within the formal categories of law.[3] During law-finding, then, little alternative linguistic codification takes place, particularly oppositional codification. These arbitrarily restrictive parameters have effects on at least four levels: the consciousness of lawyers, including activist lawyers; the consciousness of the politically motivated defendant; the semiotic codification of reality; and potential liberating praxis for social change.

On the first level in the dialectics of doing critical law—the development of critical consciousness—traditional lawyers, and to an extent, activist lawyers, are often forced to become alienated and estranged from the products of their work, from themselves, and from their clients. Marx, long ago, has shown this pattern generally: "The *alienation* of the worker in his product means not only that his labor becomes an object, an external existence, but that it exists *outside him*, independently, as something alien to him, and that it becomes a power on its own confronting him" (1964: 108, emphasis in the original). The practicing lawyer, no different from the worker described by Marx, attempts to externalize what is internal; the product of work is an affirmation, is a statement of existence, essential being, and identity. The product of work subsequently comes to act reflexively on the author of the work. Marx's ideal communist woman/man would find true fulfillment by being the genuine author of her/his product. But in capitalism, the worker is reduced to a "crippled monstrosity"; the disembodied self merely follows the fractionalized input in the commodity produced. Similarly, practicing lawyers, and to a certain degree, activist lawyers, undergo the same alienating and estranging process. This is especially so where, for whatever reason, the defendant/client chooses a strategy that entails arguing within accepted legal categories. Thus Bankowski and Mungham, comparing the Chicago conspiracy trial (Abbie Hoffman, et al.) to Reverend Daniel Berrigan's trial (in 1969 he was charged with destroying draft files as a statement against U.S. involvement in Vietnam), have stated that in the former, a political praxis was applied during courtroom proceedings. Berrigan, however, chose to play the role of the traditional criminal defendant. ". . . [B]y his conventional behavior in the courtroom he lent legitimacy to the very thing that he opposed. In other words, he left his politics outside of the court, electing instead to play the part of the traditional criminal defendant while in court" (Bankowski and Mungham, 1976: 135). Similarly, the authors note, John Jenkins, a leader of MAC (Movement for Protecting Wales) in England, accused of blowing up waterpipe lines, chose to play the role of the conventional defendant. "This meant in effect, that Jenkins abandoned any political stance accepting, whether he realized it or not, the legitimacy of the court . . . . In this way, the defendant's behavior comes to lose its meaning, other, of course than any legal significance lawyers may care to attribute to it" (Bankowski and Mungham, 1976: 135).

Consider for a moment a sensitive, politically astute lawyer defending a politically motivated lawbreaker. The product of work, here the development of a portrait (the linguistic creation of "what happened"), will, at the same time, be both her/his creation and denial. The lawyer, to do acceptable lawyering, must take what the rebel has said happened and translate it into the appropriate legal categories. Often, in the process, the reality as a whole— what actually took place in the streets—is cleansed, sterilized, and decontextualized. The specialized language that must be used in the courtroom may also place distance between the defendant and the defending lawyer. No doubt the sensitive activist lawyer is aware of this process. But what can be done? To continuously argue for an alternative reading, an alternative explanation, for why something took place, and to have this information continuously rendered nonjusticiable is to jeopardize the rebel's potential for acquittal. Resources must be better used for winning the case. In the process, the lawyer distances her/himself from truly identifying with what the rebel has said. Solidarity, as a consequence, is minimized; so, too, substantive issues are splintered into many sterile, inanimate legal categories, unconnected with a holistic vision of society and social action.

The lawyer becomes increasingly alienated from her/his product. Winning or losing becomes central. Rather than becoming truly one with the struggle, the lawyer has participated in fetishizing the process: winning is worshipped as an end. After all, the argument is that it is better to win and have the rebel return to the barricades than have the rebel incarcerated and hence neutralized.

In addition, Balbus, in criticism of civil-rights leaders during the uprisings he studied in the 1960s, has said "no major civil-rights leader of the period challenged the very effort to "criminalize" the revolts; no significant voices were raised challenging the legitimacy of the effort of American political elites to treat the revolts as if they were 'ordinary crimes'" (1977: 258). The focus, instead, was on equality before the law for the rebels.

Winning within the terms of the rule of law means only winning based on artificial categories and limited linguistic input. This, too, the activist lawyer understands well. The end product, a favorable decision, is not infused with political meaning, with any symbolic worth. Winning means only that the lawyer has been able to outduel the opponent with the given weapons both have at their disposal. For example, a group of defendants are charged with blocking a public building after being given notice to desist. At their trial, the prosecutor fails to prove beyond a reasonable doubt that notice was given. The activist lawyer moves for a "directed verdict," a traditional legal step taken in every trial. It is granted by the court and the defendants are discharged. The product, the linguistic creation of "what happened," in the end, stands symbolically as both a fulfillment and a denial. The bond, the connectedness, between striving to externalize one's creative potentials and its external expression, its symbolic representation, has been torn asunder. The product, a juridico-linguistic creation of "what happened," does not represent congruency between the activist lawyers' yearnings in identifying with politically activist lawbreakers and what has been created—a depoliticized, decontextualized rendering of what happened.

This alienating and estranging process now extends to the relationship toward self. The product is no longer an affirmation of the political ideals and values for which the lawyer fights. The person quickly realizes that, much like Marx's worker in a factory, the product of work that s/he has put everything into now stands as something apart and above her/him. On one level, a sense of accomplishment can be felt that the case was won and the activist can now return to the barricades. But what about the intrinsic rewards, including the symbolic value in the production of the case itself? The lawyer has confined her/himself to a juridico-linguistic coordinate system that reifies one worldview while simultaneously denying another. Hence, the lawyer becomes increasingly alienated from her/himself.[4] During self-reflection, the activist lawyer must ask, what did s/he win? Just as the product does not express fulfillment, rather a denial, the reflexively examined self is denied the very nourishment necessary for its creative development. Increasingly s/he has internalized the given legal structure, categories, and acceptable linguistic codifications; and proportionally with this increasing competence, more cases are won. But during the law-finding process, s/he realizes that s/he has been an active agent in a performance that denies questions of motivation, politics, economics, and so forth. In sum, substantive justice is denied. Gramsci (1971) has long ago shown how hegemony is often actively procured by the willing participation by those oppressed. For the well-intentioned lawyer, the attempt at doing radical law often results in hegemony and self-estrangement.

Finally, this alienation/estrangement from the product, extending as it does to alienation and estrangement from self, is now extended to the relationship with the politically active lawbreaker that s/he is defending. The reinforcement of solidarity, mutuality of interests, friendly communication (i.e., speaking the same language), the development and solidification of a shared oppositional discourse—all this is undermined. The politically relevant issues that the protester has so nobly fought for are not given codification in the courtroom; rather, as we have said, a new creation comes into being, a creation that must be centered within the acceptable juridico-linguistic coordinate system. Because of these exigencies, the lawyer's relation, with her/his client undergoes the same estranging process.

On the second level in the dialectics of doing critical law—the development of consciousness of the politically motivated defendant—the rebel also undergoes a similar alienation process: from the lawyer, product of work, and self. The rebel soon realizes that the game that must be played during law-finding has much to do with applying the appropriate legal linguistic codification.

To win, s/he must attempt to put "what happened" into acceptable legal categories. In the process, there is a clash of two communicative markets—the oppositional discourse of the rebel and the acceptable discourse in the courtroom. During the change in the locus from the former to the latter, the rebel becomes alienated from the lawyer inasmuch as the lawyer begins to speak a foreign language, a language that really is not sensitive to, or reflective of, political factors the rebel is attempting to introduce. The rebel will question whether in fact her/his lawyer really understands the political issues; whether in fact s/he is really working for her/him. As in the example above where the lawyer moved for the directed verdict, the protesters also are disappointed by the reliance on a legal maneuver. The protesters, for example, knew that they should depart from the premises. They had notice as required. They blocked the building to express their political beliefs. These never entered into the court's mind, they were never explained to a jury.

The defendant, too, is alienated from her/his product. In winning the case, s/he, being bounded by the linguistic legal coordinates, denies her/himself by not presenting the substantive issues concerning broader motivational political and economic arguments. After all, these are being rendered by the judges as nonjusticiable. Authorship—constituting as it does an act of self-affirmation, a statement of being, an expression of actively and successfully negotiating and transcending the dictates of one's environment—is continuously undermined, everywhere replaced by impersonal forces that seem to have a life of their own.

Finally, the defendant is alienated from self. S/he, during law-finding, realizes very quickly that the game to be played is to consciously create the appropriate abstract juridic subject in her/his consciousness and then to try and present this image to the jury, hopefully for a favorable verdict. Substantive questions, then, can be quickly replaced by questions of expediency (see, Balbus, 1977: 12, 258-59).[5]

The third level in the dialectics of doing critical law concerns the juridico-linguistic discourse in use and its effects. The continued use of given linguistic legal codes not only gives legitimacy to them but also denies alternative readings of reality. A potential oppositional linguistic codification reflecting the objective conditions of a mode of production and exploitive, repressive practices is denied; hence few linguistic tools for critical and potentially destabilizing analysis develop, and where they do, they are not rooted in a stable oppositional discourse. Hence, would-be rebels must make use of verbalizations and codifications already in existence with their attendant rootedness in dominant discourse and their embedded system-sustaining values. Those entering the domain of the acceptable legal-linguistic coordinates are bounded by both an arbitrary and politically motivated way of seeing and understanding the complexities and system-generated repression in existence. Even where the activist lawyer undergoes internal struggle, trying to reconcile a commitment to radical ideals versus a realistic awareness of what can and cannot be presented in the courtroom, the conclusion often becomes self-evident: winning has priority, regardless of what specific given and acceptable legal category is being used.

Oppositional struggles that are brought before the court, then, are denied full redress. Thus at the fourth level in the dialectics of doing critical law—the potential development of liberating praxis for social change—system injustices, repression, hierarchies, national policies that contribute to the massive suffering of human beings in other countries, and other forms of domination, are not genuinely addressed in the courts. A stabilized, sedimented, oppositional linguistic discourse, too, does not develop. Language, being value-laden, then, does not incorporate an alternative reading, an alternative accentuation; nor is it, therefore, of use in encouraging liberating insights. For oppositional groups, linguistic tools for critical inquiry are repressed by procedural justice of the courts.

Because of the increasing constitutionalization of the social formation, that is, its subjection to juridico-semiotic codification, an importation of narrowly circumscribed legal modes of codification and thought increasingly replace linguistic structures and alternative modes of thought within subjects' "life worlds" (Habermas, 1984) within the social formation. Holistic-oriented discourses, then, are increasingly replaced by modes of legal thought that are issue-oriented, that are abstractly derived, and are, consequently, sterile, lifeless, and decontextualized. The "rational person" is the one who can abstractly construct issues from myriad facts; to speak holistically, on the other hand, is to be dissonant, is to be unable to "stick to the issue at hand."

OPPOSITIONAL LINGUISTIC PRAXIS

This can be changed in some circumstances where the contradictions within the law open up the possibility of an alternative discourse, as with the use of the necessity defense. First, the alienating and estranging process of the rebel and the activist lawyer is eliminated, replaced by genuine dialogue, mutual support and identification, solidarity, heightened clarification of system injustices, and an affirmation of a collective struggle against oppressive practices. The bond to the product, to the self, and to the other is reestablished. Second, allowing the necessity defense encourages a form of law and thought consistent with substantive rational principles to enter law-finding. This recontextualizing of "what happened" liberates the rebel and the activist lawyer from the oppressive dictates of formal legalism and contributes to the increased development of an alternative oppositional discourse. Third, this alternative oppositional discourse, in turn, becomes sedimented, becomes a reference point (linguistic coordinates) for understanding, for "consciencization" (Freire, 1985: 67-91; in a Central American context, see Golden and McConnell, 1986: 125-57). Future oppositional groups, then, have an expanded inventory of linguistic tools for use, all value-laden with oppositional-liberating meaning.

Fourth, the rule-of-law ideology is demystified. Subjects in the social formation are liberated from legal fetishes, legal obfuscations, and abstractions. Jurors, for example, are presented scripts with which they can identify: struggles with bureaucratic agencies; the effects of repressive and alienating work-places; unresponsive hierarchies; existing racism and sexism; potential nuclear catastrophes; injustices and violence inflicted on peoples of the world in the name of "democracy"; institutions that degrade, mortify, and thwart the development of human potentials; and so forth.

In sum, the necessity defense, relying on substantive rationality, offers a great potential for liberating legal praxis. It allows for the redress of substantive issues. The alleviation of misery does not have to wait for the revolution. Issues of prisoners' rights, U.S. involvement in Central America, refugees attempting to escape death squads in El Salvador, protesters being arrested for civil actions against the nuclear arms buildup, and so forth—all, by the use of the necessity defense, are given a judicial hearing entailing a wider linguistic inquiry, an alternative oppositional reading. Additionally, the alienating and estranging practice in doing traditional law is transcended, and is replaced by a genuine critical legal praxis. And, finally, because the conflict between formal and substantive rationality attains a high degree of intensity and visibility, demystification of the rule of law can proceed.

IMPLICATIONS AND STRATEGIES FOR CRITICAL LEGAL PRAXIS AND SOCIAL REFORM

We do not suggest that the necessity defense will alleviate all forms of alienation suffered by progressive lawyers and defendants. In fact, the success of the defense might indicate that it will be dismantled as soon as possible, and the radical bar will have to once again search for another palliative for the constant struggle with the system. The defense does serve, however, as a vehicle for expressing the political and social motivations that cause some defendants to act in a "criminal" fashion.[6]

Usually, the defendants in necessity cases make clear their desire to involve the principle of justification through their pretrial, in-court statements and/or in their propaganda concerning their case. This usually spurs the prosecution into filing with the court a motion *in limine* requesting that the court bar the defendants from relying on the necessity defense. It is at this stage that the trial may be won or lost, even though these are pretrial stages. Unless there is another more typical legal defense position to assert, the trial judge's ruling on the prosecution's motion will be critical to the defendants' likelihood of success in court. Obviously, then, the judge must be convinced of the correctness of the defense's invocation of necessity.

The defense should respond in writing to the government's motion. There is much to be said in support of the necessity defense and the sheer weight of the responsive motion may favorably impress the trial judge. Included in the response should be the history of the defense as explained above and common law applications thereof. The defense should specify state statutes that are applicable (if any) and cite cases that interpret them. Additionally, the defense should identify the principles of international law that the defendants relied upon in committing their acts of resistance. These must be explained in detail as most trial level judges have no familiarity with international law, especially that law pertaining to human-rights violations. This is less an indictment of the individual judges than it is of the American law-school process, which does not include human-rights laws among its standard curriculum. Lastly, the defense should include the governmental policies or actions the defendants were protesting. This section should be brief if the defense wishes to avoid antagonizing the trial judge.

While governmental court officials are often alienated, themselves, from the protesters who appear before them, concentrating on the legal applicability of the defense during in-court arguments may be less offensive to them. Of course, this suggestion clearly points out the pervasiveness of the oppression that progressive lawyers and defendants face. Most lawyers, however, who want to win their cases in the least objectionable fashion will recognize, perhaps sadly, the merit in the suggestion. And the thrill of actually putting the defense into use before a jury of citizens is unparalleled in the court system. Winning is usually cause for celebration, but winning and educating the jury, court personnel, the media and others through the media results in an even stronger feeling of success.

While the necessity defense offers a ray of hope to the progressive person who attempts to identify and counter the oppressive nature of the justice system and the government as a whole, it should not be taken as evidence that the law allows people to undertake attacks on the law or to actually achieve change in our society.

The necessity defense may be viewed as an indicator of the "insoluble conflict" (Weber, 1978) between formal and substantive rationality and justice. We suppose it may be argued that the very fact the defense is allowable speaks for the "flexibility" of law. And, too, users of the defense, it might be argued, are hence contributing to the rule-of-law ideology. We think that both arguments can be dismissed for, first, the defense is not automatic— the judge may simply refuse to allow it—and, second, this "crack" in the legal edifice is but one of the clearest expressions of the tenuous resolutions of the tension between substantive and formal rationality; and consequently, given this "crack," and to the degree that trials become politicized, an oppositional juridic praxis is being mobilized which concretely contributes to overcoming oppressive state policies and system-generated practices. The Trojan horse has entered the fortress!

To the degree that the courts countenance the defense, they do so only as part of the government's general recognition that a safety valve sometimes serves as a useful tool in furthering and intensifying oppression. Citizens are allowed to dissent, but only to a degree.

Hitherto many in the U.S. have been quite quick and pleased to argue that contrary to many existing oppressive governments of the world, we do not have political prisoners in our prisons. All of our prisoners are said to be common criminals.[7] Clearly, however, it is the legal process itself that defines the parameters of the discourse in use. It is within these parameters that "criminal" identities and motivations are being created.

We pause and wonder about how many activists, who had argued traditional legal defenses and who had stayed within the narrow procedural confines of legal formalism, who were subsequently convicted and sentenced to prison, now reflect on their encounter with legal formalism, wondering why they did not try to politicize the trial, even to the extent of not cooperating and even in disrupting trial proceedings and having contempt charges piled high in the process. At least during subsequent proceedings a political statement could have been made. But what of the costs? To win is to lose, and to lose is to win. Again, the necessity defense, where it is available, and where the judge in her/his infinite *noblesse oblige* has granted its use, allows the activist and her/his legal-defense team to transcend the narrow confines of legal formalism.

CONCLUSION

Doing critical law, we have argued, poses a dilemma for the critical, practicing lawyer. Does s/he argue within the traditional framework of legal formalism in hopes of allowing her/his defendant a chance to return to the barricades, knowing full well that by doing so the rule-of-law ideology is being upheld, or does s/he attempt to actively politicize the trial knowing full well that the full weight of state power will be brought to bear at every step in the attempt at politicization. After all, three ideological messages must be saved by the State at all costs: first, the legitimacy of the existing socioeconomic and political arrangements, second, the sanctity of the rule of law, and third, that lawbreaking behavior is simply an expression of criminality devoid of contextuality.

Activists and politically informed legal-defense workers should not overestimate the long-range usefulness of the defense. Indeed, it is a more liberating praxis. However, seeing the defense as the savior, the end, is to engage in simplistic romanticizing. The State and its enforcers will surely not remain idle, and just as surely will respond to its effects creatively.

NOTES

1. For a successful use of this type of defense see cases cited and discussed below. For one highly publicized case, see the Amy Carter case (*New York Times*, 16 April 1987: 17); see, also, Boyle, 1985a, 1987.

2. Shelley Bannister has been an attorney on several legal-defense teams that have successfully made use of the necessity defense.

3. The lawyer's alienation can perhaps best be pictured as following the course of the traditional "bell-shaped curve" revered by social scientists. Following a newly graduated lawyer's admittance to the Bar, s/he feels a new sense of power and a total commitment to and zeal for the law. The law becomes her or his lover, so to speak. The lawyer then appears in the criminal courts, experiencing first-hand a lying police officer, and then another (and yet another; this continues without end). S/he confronts prosecutors who forgot, if they ever

knew, that the prosecutor's first duty is to justice not to winning. S/he is appalled by judges who sleep during bench trials. The amount of alienation climbs higher and higher, day after day, or by months and years. The peak of alienation is reached. Some might sustain this peak for some amount of time, however, most human beings, even lawyers, cannot continue to live at these levels of dissonance with their sense of self. Some lawyers quit and pick up a new career, perhaps that of a college professor. Most, however, slide down the other side of the curve and adapt to and accept the injustice of the system.

4. "When man confronts himself, he confronts the other man. What applies to a man's relation to his work, to the product of his labor and to himself, also holds of a man's relation to the other man . . ." (Marx, 1964: 114).

5. Balbus is quite poignant here: "repression by formal rationality, insofar as it attempts to affix the label of 'crime' on the behavior of the participants, is likely to help convince participants that their violent acts represent nothing more than massive outbreaks of common 'criminality'" (1977: 12).

6. A different analysis is necessitated for doing critical law at the common, everyday court proceedings (i.e., tenant cases, divorces, contract breaches, etc.). We recognize that they, too, have political dimensions that result in the alienation we described above. Demands for a critical practice here are substantial. Consider, for example, the lawyer-regulars in the local court-houses. They interact daily with the same small group of legal actors and officials. To antagonize these actors continuously can only mean that the ability to do anything approaching a good defense will be substantially compromised. Indeed, it is here that a vision for a critical legal praxis is sorely needed.

7. But see, *Can't Jail the Spirit: Political Prisoners in the U.S.—A Collection of Biographies* by the Committee to End the Marion Lockdown (1988). See, also, Oscar Lopez-Rivera's insightful essay, "Political Prisoners in the U.S." (1989).

POSTSCRIPT, 1 JUNE, 1996, DRAGAN MILOVANOVIC

The necessity defense, we have indicated, is one rare occasion where extra-legal factors may be used in narrative constructions of the "what happened" in law. Increasingly, legal cases on battered women are being litigated (see Dore, 1995; Bartlett and Kennedy, 1991a). Various defenses have been employed in the "battered-woman syndrome." "Self-defense" and "duress" are often employed. "Diminished capacity" could also be used. Some of the themes of the dialectics of struggle are also brought here. For example, making use of the better-known and recognized defense of "diminished capacity" often disempowers the victim, and lends little to larger societal change. Necessity, duress, and self-defense lead to greater empowering dynamics and offer greater potential for societal change. This is so because it may have an "educative" function on the public about the nature of "domestic" violence. But, as Bartlett and Kennedy (1991a: 3) point out, this defense "may contradict the safer 'diminished-capacity' defense that the client may otherwise be able to establish." By society's increasing acceptance of the "battered-woman syndrome" what also appears is the greater opportunity to create and stabilize an alternative linguistic coordinate system that better conceptualizes this form of violence. The dialectics seems to be tending toward a more humanistic resolve.

CHAPTER 8

Constitutive Penology

Dragan Milovanovic and Stuart Henry

INTRODUCTION

We begin our perspective on penology from the assumption that human agents, acting in a socio-political context, are the active producers of penal policy and penal practice. That the conceptual and institutional apparatus of society appears to continuously stand above us, disciplining us in accord with political economy (Foucault, 1977), results from our elevation of it through a continual process of engagement and disengagement of our own agency, from an infidelity of submission to that which we produce. This reificatory process is part of the constitutive work engaged in when human agents objectify their social relations through discursive practices.

Penology provides some of the constitutive work that gives form, sustenance, and permanence to the subordination of human agency to its product. Debates over being in and out of prison, over building more or fewer prisons, about prison overcrowding and prison overspending, about alternatives to prison and challenges to those defending prison, all essentialize *prison* and neglect the continuous and reconstituting nature of the historically structured disciplinary discourse whose building blocks we construct around our selves. Theorists, critical or otherwise, penal policy-makers and practitioners, as well as those criminally harming others, coproduce a discourse that gives form and permanence to the very entity that they and we collectively despise. Therein we are all imprisoned.

It is our contention that the verbalized goals and policies at the manifest level of "corrections," the discursively structured routine of prison life, and the meaning of being in prison, must be understood in relation to various and oftentimes contradictory discursive practices that sustain, oppose, and attempt to replace them. In turn, these discursive practices constitute the framework that shapes and conveys structures of meaning. But as concentrations of discursively structured meaning, prisons can only be adequately discussed in the context of other developments in a political economy. As Box (1987) has shown, being in prison is not so much related to the vagaries of the business cycle, or to unemployment per se, but to judges' *perceptions* of the threat of political and economic instability from the "dangerous classes."

In this article we critically analyze the discursive practices whose invocation constitutes both penology and the reality of prison life. We explore the extent to which we are our own jailers, sentenced by our sentences, imprisoned by our words. This is not linguistic determinism, since we do not give priority to discourse, but argue that meaning is *both* preconstituted by historically situated structural processes, and shaped by human agents in their recursive use of discourse in everyday interaction. We outline what an alternative direction might look like, one providing an opportunity for the development of a new "replacement discourse." So far we are merely opening doors in the ongoing development of our work toward a constitutive criminology grounded in semiotic analysis (Henry and Milovanovic, 1991). At this stage it would be premature to present a blueprint for a constitutively framed alternative penology, since to do so would preclude the very freedom glimpsed by our approach. It would further imprison the very human agency whose active recognition of its constitutive contribution to the making of structures of control must be ever-present in order to transcend the tethers of its present alienated and detached oppression. Replacement discourse, as we conceive it, is not merely another package of ways to talk and make sense of the world, but a language of "transpraxis" (Henry and Milovanovic, 1991). It is a nonreificatory connecting of the way we speak with our social relations and institutions, such that through its use we are continuously aware of the interrelatedness of our agency and the structures it reproduces through the constitutively productive work of our talking, perceiving, conceptualizing and theorizing. Let us begin our perspective with an example of how we conceive of penal policy in contrast to how it is conventionally understood. From here we will turn to a semiotically grounded approach to penal policy, followed by an analysis of the discursive production of meaning structures in relation to prison life and practice.

PENAL POLICY AS THE SOCIAL CONSTRUCTION OF JUSTIFICATIONS

Our view of penal policy is that it is less the outcome of implementing new ideas, than of a discursive process through which aspects of existing practice are selected, emphasized, refined, and formally discussed, while other aspects are ignored, subordinated, dispersed, and relegated to the informal. Consider, as illustrative, the debate over what to do with adjudicated offenders. Penologists generally distinguish between six general policies:

(1) punishment/retribution/just deserts;

(2) incapacitation/social defense;

(3) deterrence;

(4) rehabilitation/treatment;

(5) prevention; and

(6) restitution/reparation.

This distinction is artificial, since doing something with an adjudicated offender can be claimed to be, and indeed is justified as serving, one or more of these proclaimed penal-policy goals, depending upon the historical moment and the particular interests being played out through existing organizational structures. The reality of the policy is born largely of the proclamation. But what is done to offenders in the name of policy ranges far wider than what is claimed for it at any historical moment. Suppose we probe incapacitation or containment as one example of how these penal policies are caricatured. The penal-policy goal of incapacitation is taking the offender "out of circulation." It is based upon the assumption that a disproportionate amount of crime is committed by a relatively small number of offenders (Wolfgang, Figlio, and Sellin, 1972). Incapacitation policy asserts that by putting these people "in prison" they are stopped from practicing criminal behaviors and the "outside world" is correspondingly safer, albeit temporarily.

From the perspective of constitutive penology, this policy is reifying in that it falsely separates what goes on internally and further implies a separation of what goes on externally. Being in prison is being in society, since prison is physically, sociostructurally, and symbolically integral to our experience. There exist no true "walls of imprisonment," rather continuity between "in" and "out." The incarcerated are not incapacitated, since they do more and worse forms of offensive behavior in their new architectural space.[1] These new architectural spaces are a reifying medium for the generation of reactive behavior and for the amplification of previously constituted articulations of the excesses of power in street (or suite) contexts. The kept are not just doing worse harm to each other, but they are doing it to us, to those of us "in corrections." Prison officers are corrupted in their stressed lives to escape *their* imprisonment through a conspiratorial dance with the inmate, which both mocks us and oppresses them. We pay the economical cost of prison programs instead of the economical cost of property crime. Moreover, the incapacitation notion has its dialectical enabling in the false security of social order and the "safer with them behind bars" mentality, but the paradox is that for each constitutive brick of incapacitation we release another swirl of freedom for those "accident makers" (Bopal), "liberators" (Iran-*Contra*), "job creators" (GM's Jeffrey Smith) and "risk takers" (Boesky, Milken). How then does incapacitation make for a safer society? All it does is make for the illusion of a safer society. A similar analysis could be applied to each of the so-called penal policies.

Nor is this constitutive dialectics restricted to penal policy-makers. The analytical discourse of penologists makes its own contribution through their ideal typical classifications and abstractions (See for example, Duffee, 1980; Black, 1976). These constitute order-making discursive work, inviting us to make sense of a disarray of correctional practices and to "explain" why disorder occurs. Adopting such schemas one inadvertently connives at the constitutive work done by the policy-makers and penologists of a particular era.

Omitted in such analyses is the way in which policy-makers, practitioners, targeted agents, and theorists de-emphasize some aspects of the reality of prison practice as aberrant, unofficial, informal, or untypical, in order to make claims about its operational identity. By distinguishing between formally espoused penal-policy goals and informal practices such as plea-bargaining, discretion, prison discipline, and oppositional cultural adaptations, we add to the edifice that constitutes prison policy. Instead we should be showing how the recursive definition of these practices as aberrations sustains the reality that is penal policy.

Omitted in such theorizing is the use made of a constitutive refining of diversity into patterns, the phenomenological twist that leaves us making order out of disorder, which can even seduce us into beginning to construct models of these models. As Baudrillard (1988) might argue, to do so reifies the process to the extent that the hyperreality of prison policy contained in such analytical schema feigns a reality in the actual operation of prison life that is no more than a mirage of itself.[2]

Conventional penology fails to recognize the fact that the earlier models were themselves abstractions. It fails to analyze the process whereby invoking certain discourse constitutes the medium of the debate and through it, policy as a reality in practice. Penologists and academic scholars, critical and otherwise, who research this literature can readily find themselves both imprisoned within a particular discourse when explaining phenomena, and disciplined by the pervasive nature of the constitutive mode of discursive construction, inadvertently contributing to the grand prison-concept building program that transcends all need for state funds!

Even the identification of distinctive styles of social control, or the separation of types of prison policy based on the prevalence of a unique vocabulary that is claimed to reflect its manifest goals and working philosophy is suspect, because it portends an alternative truth claim without analyzing the constitution of the reality that is its product. In order to avoid engaging in such constitutive prison work while analyzing the manifestation of penal policy, it is necessary to use a semiotic approach.

SEMIOTIC ANALYSIS AND PENAL POLICY

From the perspective of semiotics, models of penal policy can be conceptualized in terms of a particular discourse.[3] Part of the constitutive process is not only to invoke and innovate discourse but also to construct categories, make distinctions, and draw contrasts (Henry and Milovanovic, 1991). One such debate within the discursive models mentioned above is based on the distinction between "what works" and, by implication, "what does not" (Andrews et al 1990; Whitehead and Lab, 1989; Lab and Whitehead, 1990; Martinson, 1974; Palmer, 1975). Neglected in these debates is any consideration of the way in which prison as an entity is being reconstituted by its liberal and radical critics who, instead of deconstructing the form, take for granted its reality and reassert its presence through their claims about different approaches to corrections.

Whereas traditional penologists discuss the importance of the respective models, a constitutive penological perspective suggests that we begin by suspending belief in the reality of the social constructions that are taken to underlay the model. We start by suspending the claims of models that make distinctions between types of structure and their various discourses. Instead we analyze the discursive practices as they are employed in debates that continue the construction of the phenomenon that is subject to analysis.

By segmenting this process, penologists have merely sustained a view that neglects the active work of agents as theorists in the production of criminality and corrections (see also Gilsinan, 1982). We offer, on the contrary, a view that situates agents who actively and discursively construct their reality, and who carry through their actions along contradictory background relevancies. As Mastrofski and Parks (1990: 499) have argued in the police context, "there is a well-established desire for people to construct empirical and moral meaning about their actions *ex post facto* to reduce disparity among cognition, action, and longstanding beliefs" and that police officers "consider their actions beforehand and rationalize them afterward in ways that affect future actions" (ibid.: 477). Gilsinan's examination of police behavior describes how police attempt to constitutionally "dress up" otherwise illegally obtained evidence or illegal practices for prosecutory purposes. A similar process has been recognized by legal realists and critical legal studies theorists in their examination of the *ex post facto* legal-narrative constructions by judges who, on a formal level, articulate their decisions in deductive logic, syllogistic reasoning, and narratively coherent form, belied, however, by an underlying decision based more on hunch, feel, temperament, or fleeting and transitory thoughts and stereotypes of the moment (see Jackson, 1985, 1988; Milovanovic, 1988c). In the case of prisoner litigation, as Thomas (1988: 169) aptly states, "the law often becomes a motive to justify a decision at least as much as it determines the decision." While public as well as private rhetoric (discourse) used in constructing "reality" may often be contradictory, we seek to expose the process whereby the distinction is used to sustain a sense of the orderliness of disorder.[4]

We see prison policy as one among a number of reality-claiming discursive practices whose use forms part of the constitutive work that sustains prison as a reality. In order to examine that constitutive work we rely on a theory of discursive production that focuses on the recursive development of relatively stable meaning constructions in which the self-referential character of particular discourses in use and the existence of linguistic mechanisms that order disorder are acknowledged.[5]

THE DISCURSIVE PRODUCTION OF MEANING STRUCTURES

Beyond C.W. Mills' pioneering discussion of language use as the motives for action (1940), three rudimentary approaches to discourse analysis can be found in the criminological literature that shed insight on the development of a constitutive penology. Cressey (1953: 94), in discussing the verbalizations of convicted embezzlers, sees a direct causal link between the agent's selected use of discourse and action with his notion that "the rationalization is his motivation" and has said, elsewhere, "the words that the potential embezzler uses in his conversations with himself are actually the most important elements in the process that gets him into trouble" (Cressey, 1970: 111). A crucial issue here is the timing of the use of signifiers. For Cressey, the signifiers become important after the agent has first contemplated the illegal act discursively (e.g., a nonshareable financial problem has been articulated). In the manner of Mills, words and phrases are used to invoke a signified meaning that would project future honoring of an account of the behavior as acceptable, through the use of an excuse or justification.[6] This presupposes, of course, an existing historically situated discourse replete with words and phrases that in the context of the existing sociopolitical configuration serve as meaningful rationalizations, i.e., "it is only borrowing money," "it'll be paid back at next paycheck," "nothing will be missed," "underpaid workers are entitled to perks of the job," etc. Accordingly, the absence of such meaningful discussions will act as a social control on action.

For Matza, no such Machiavellian motive was necessary. It was enough that the signifiers were invoked in a particular context. Because of the preexisting meaning, i.e., that which is signified, the probability of behavior being acceptable is assured since: "The criminal law, more than any other system of norms, acknowledges and states the principled grounds under which an actor can claim exception" (Matza, 1964: 61). The implications of this analysis were often lost by readers of techniques of neutralization (but see Taylor, 1972). It meant that language use, the invocation of particular signifieds, and not necessarily by the actor, was enough to render an action as morally acceptable *prior* to its contemplation.

In an extension of this idea, Henry (1976, 1978) showed how sellers of stolen goods framed their relational discourse to potential buyers in such a way that any moral questioning was preempted. They typically framed a sale with signifiers that invoked the legitimate reasons why, in a capitalist consumer society, a product might be sold as a "bargain." The item might be "damaged stock," the result of "bulk purchase," a "manufacturer's overrun," or even "perks of the job." The seller need not make this claim, but simply cue it, relying on the buyers to invoke the appropriate account and *inadvertently* and *unwittingly* render themselves morally free to conclude an illegal sale.

The Schwendingers (1985: 128) also see discourse as a critical causal link that must be placed in the context of political economy. They argue that different cultures can be characterized by their different styles of "moral rhetoric." These styles of moral rhetoric can change with different contexts and may even be conceptualized in terms of smooth transitions between public and private rhetoric. They further identify an "egoistic rhetoric" (ibid.: 133) and an "instrumental rhetoric" (ibid.: 136). The former, the dominant form in a capitalist mode of production, expresses market thinking — individualism, utilitarianism, and hedonism. The latter, as a variant of the former, "seems to apply egoistic operating principles to a particular set of conditions, but it disregards egoistic standards of fairness" (ibid.: 136). More specifically, this

> guiding principle...assumes people to be engaged in a vast power struggle, with the weak and the powerless as legitimate victims. In this view of reality, the images of humans are virtually stripped of meaningful moral qualities, and individuals are seen primarily as instruments for egoistic ends. Often, moral qualities are not even present in the consciousness of the criminal or in the criminal's selection or definition of the victim (ibid.: 137).

The delinquent has learned the appropriate vocabulary that justifies the infliction of pain or suffering on the victim (Schwendinger and Schwendinger, 1985: 147-8; see also Katz, 1988; Athens, 1989). This discourse is often incorporated in "pragmatic experience[s] in market relationships" (Schwendinger and Schwendinger, 1985: 275-76). A constitutive penology would extend this kind of analysis.

SEMIOTIC ANALYSIS AND CONSTITUTIVE PENOLOGY

Applying semiotic analysis to penological thinking helps us gain a critical understanding of developments in which a particular form of prison is a central feature of our capitalist structure. To understand how this is so, consider the issue of the growth of prison populations, which under conventional analysis is explained in relationship to growing crime rates, themselves related to unemployment and the business cycle. From our perspective such simplistic causal logic fails to capture the process of how prison populations increase. Research by Box (Box and Hale, 1986; Box, 1987) shows that increases in prison population have more to do with the meaning of capitalist recession as perceived by the judiciary, and with their discursively hypothesized connection between crime and unemployment, than to do with actual changes in levels of crime. Box and Hale (1986) argue that during a prolonged period of economic crisis when the "problem" population of unemployed is growing, the state cannot maintain living standards and welfare services, without adversely affecting the interests of capital. As the economic crisis deepens, the judiciary become increasingly anxious about the possible threat to social order posed by unemployed young males, particularly black males, and "it responds to this perception by increasing the use of custodial sentences, particularly against property offenders, in the belief that such a response will deter, incapacitate, and thus diffuse the threat" (Box and Hale, 1986: 86). Box and Hale's statistical analysis broadly supports the view that sentences to immediate imprisonment (but not unemployment rates) are covariant with annual unemployment levels. Moreover, they conclude that the reason little is done to solve the prison overcrowding problem is because overcrowding is a useful ideological device to legitimate an anxious state's real policy of expanding prison capacity where "social order is threatened by the current economic crisis undermining consent amongst those suffering the worst ravages" (Box and Hale, 1986: 94). In other words, prison populations are constructed by the meaning structures of the powerful members of capitalist society and serve to placate fears born of that system, rather than in response to real changes in levels of crime.

The same capitalist political economy from which judges construct the meaning that frames their sentencing policy also provides a discursive resource for adjudicated lawbreakers, who prior to prison experience already have incorporated some elements of an instrumental rhetoric. This rhetoric is *imported* into the prison as a system of background linguistic relevancies. Matza's theory (1964; 1969), and an adaptation and specification by Athens (1989), argues that becoming a committed lawbreaker entails stages of development.   Athens, for example, in his explanation of becoming a "dangerous violent criminal," sees four stages. In the brutalization stage an actor experiences violent behavior. In the belligerency stage, a "state of emotional turmoil and confusion" is experienced, leading to the neutralization of the otherwise moral bind of norms. A third stage is the violent performance, which involves the actual carrying out of a violent act. Finally, there is the stage of virulency, which is a feeling of omnipotence and a subsequent willingness to violently act out, even in minor provocation situations (Athens, 1989). At every stage a narrative construction is developed, each in turn preparing the actor for a more fully developed response pattern, replete with self-justifying moral principles.

Prison experience itself, with the pains of imprisonments and absurdities faced (Milovanovic and Thomas, 1989; Korn, 1988; Zwerman, 1988; Mika and Thomas, 1988; Laurence, 1988) offers various discourses and hence explanatory constructs (Lacan, 1977, *objets petit a*) for use in constructing narratively coherent explanations of "what happened." Both the formal legalist structure (Milovanovic, 1986, 1988a) as well as the bureaucratic structure (Manning, 1988; Thomas, 1988) offer a highly rationalized discourse. Ironically, jailhouse lawyers often legitimize a hegemonic law-and-order discourse by translating everyday contextualized inmate understandings into legalistic versions cleansed of interconnectedness and potential articulations of system-centered injustices. However, informal discourses also circulate. Characteristically, some inmates oppose, some acquiesce, some become fatalistic; but, in each case, a discourse already abounds providing meaningful resources from which "reality" can be constructed, albeit with its own unique turn, which simultaneously and substantially remakes the discursive form. We can identify these discourses as: conforming, alienated, instrumental, and oppositional discourses.

During the imprisonment phase of what can be termed the "IDA (importation-deprivation-amplification) thesis," an instrumental discourse provides a survival and self-justifying device that is well-suited to preprison experiences. We suspect that amplification of this rhetoric will take place in prison architectural space. Subsequently released prisoners, then, are further constituted through their use of a discourse that, in certain contexts, assures their receptivity to further predatory behavior, which is facilitated by rendering certain potential victims as appropriate targets (in the context of juveniles targeting potential victims, see especially Schwendinger and Schwendinger, 1985) In this sense, then, prison provides a vocabulary, structured utterances, and contextual-releases of emotive-instrumental behavior that minimizes questions of moral worth of their targets. Victims are constituted as devoid of moral virtue, (Matza's "denial of victim") and, in fact, are seen as a cause of their own demise — "they deserved it."

However, even where more oppositional discourses develop during the phase of imprisonment, they are also often more constitutive than liberating. Consider, for example, Thomas' (1988) insightful analysis of prisoner litigation, particularly his idea of prisoner cases by jailhouse lawyers (inmates who have taught themselves law and subsequently initiate legal suits against prison conditions) as narrative constructions. What emerges as truth behind prison practices and prisoner rebellions is problematic. When petitions to the courts, or to other tribunals are initiated by prisoners, the legally constructed "reality" of "what happened" is not as "oppositional" as it might at first seem. Rather, it has to do with a "gate-keeping" dynamic whereby the invisibility of the screening of legal cases submitted, assures that considerable discretion as well as extralegal factors are used to determine decision-making. Moreover, due to a multiplicity of decision-making levels and the inherent discretion that exists, a case can be denied or rerouted at numerous points (ibid.: 168-69).

Underlying these decision points, too, are the predilections, biases, and leanings of decision-makers. General supporters will articulate a narrative that allows prisoners "their day in court," whereas those generally antagonistic (whether openly or not) tend to conjure up a narrative based more on constitutional readings that limit discretion. The result is that more petitions by inmates are denied (ibid.: 165-90).

Constitutive penology, then, enables us to see opposition in terms of various narratives in conflict. Which narrative is given priority is not without importance, for prioritizing, it decides on the prisoner's petition. And for the "outside" world, legal viewpoints are seen as what really happened, while other narrative constructions are denied their legitimacy. It is with this in mind that we might appreciate Zwerman's observation of the high-security unit at Lexington. He claims that practices there by prison officials "may be viewed as a first effort to develop a strategy which insures that a critical analysis of political crime will have no place in the formulation of correctional policy and practices with respect to political prisoners" (Zwerman, 1988: 41). Thus, the critical questions become reduced to a battle of discourses over truth claims, with the victor being the one whose discourse explains the "what really happens." As Thomas (1988: 184) has shown, decision-making behind prisoner litigation has more to do with pragmatic, bureaucratic functioning: "such organizational goals as fiscal restraints, control of prisoners, stable prison administration, and face-saving denial of culpability dominate the state's strategy of settling cases." Thus, resolving prisoner litigation has little to do with *bona fide* issues, but much to do with the exigencies of the prison bureaucratic apparatus, with the prevalence of stabilized, readily available accounts, rationalizations, legitimation principles, and explanatory constructs that await appropriation and application. Given an outwardly unexplainable event, readily available, "packaged" explanatory narrative constructs exist. As Thomas poignantly states, the actual work of acting on cases occurs not so much through rule-following as through enacting various contexts of action that justify how a particular group can attain its own ends rather than the ends of "justice." (p. 188)

This process has its parallel at a macro-level in Foucault's (1977) extensive "excavations" of changing and conflictive discourses, which oftentimes are resolved by one gaining ascendancy. Laclau and Mouffe (1985) have also indicated how historical upheavals by themselves remain ripe for articulation; however, otherwise "floating signifiers" must be articulated in a coherent, narrative form (see, also White, 1973). As Laclau and Mouffe (1985: 154) have said, "there is no relation of oppression without the presence of a discursive 'exterior' from which the discourse of subordination can be interrupted." Further,

it is only from the moment when the democratic discourse becomes available to articulate the different forms of resistance to subordination that the conditions will exist to make possible the struggle against different types of inequality. (ibid.)

Moreover, before even this process has taken place, a new notion of formal equality, an imaginary construct, must have been established.[7]

ALTERNATIVE PROGRAMS AND CONSTITUTIVE PENOLOGY

Alternative programs to prison, those that ostensibly list as their manifest goals reintegration or conciliation, also can be conceptualized as arenas where opposing discourses compete for dominance. Reality construction is constituted by everyday discursive practices in which ideologically laden signifiers are given sustenance. Both conventional criminology as well as much of critical/radical criminology has overlooked the effects of the clash of divergent discourses, even as the same agent may use two or more discourses to explain his/her actions, one at the private level, one at the public level. So, for example, even though an interviewed inmate may be asked for his/her personal beliefs, this may operate at a different level than the discourse that lies behind actual behavior itself (Muir, 1977; see also, Gilsinan, 1982; Manning, 1988). Asking guards to explain their actions after the fact may even crystallize a rendition of reality in accord with conventionally understood practices. Prevailing dominant discursive practices may act as explanatory constructs of otherwise perceived disorderly, unexplainable events. Consider, again, Mastrofski and Park's point (1990: 489) that "asking police officers [and guards] to undergo a form of instant replay self-analysis creates a greater tendency to rationalize than they would otherwise have."

Community mediation attempts, as Baskin (1988: 105-10) has pointed out in the tradition of Mills (1959), to neutralize conflict by reducing social problems to a discourse of *individual* problems; interpersonal disputes are reduced to a discourse of hedonistic individualism and the failure in communication, whether the problem is sexism, racism, poverty, etc. Additionally, motivational patterns associated with commodity production and consumption are given articulate and preferential form (idealized expression). But again, we see human agents maneuvering various discourses for ascendancy and dominance. Baskin's insightful article on community mediation can be conceptualized as a statement concerning how a particular discourse, conveying a particular ideology, encroaches on other narrative constructions of social problems. Establishing the "what happened?" is situated in a psychological, mental-health discourse rather than in a political discourse, thereby shifting attention away from critical examination of the social structure. Community-based corrections, and with it their attendant, particular narrative constructions, then, become increasingly pervasive (Baskin, 1988: 106) and permeate every detail of private life.

A constitutive penology focuses on agents embracing particular discourses rather than others in constituting reality, in creating order out of disorder. Agents do not merely participate in nominalistic exercises; rather, attributing structure is a discursive undertaking, the construction of the object itself. Given this, a fundamental instability exists and potential alternative articulations may take place (Zizek, 1989: 89-92). Laclau, for example, has poignantly stated that,

> if the unity of the object is the retroactive effect of naming itself, then naming is not just the pure nominalistic game of attributing an empty name to a preconstituted subject. It is the discursive construction of the object itself...[If] the process of naming of objects amounts to the very act of their constitution, then their descriptive features will be fundamentally unstable and open to all kinds of hegemonic rearticulations. (cited in Zizek, 1989: xiv)

Academic penologists as well as policy-makers often tap into a metatheory, and a divergent one from the actual world experienced by the lawbreaker and law-enforcer. On the other hand, it very well may be that some inmates do in fact internalize a conformal discourse,[8] even to the point that it comes to replace previously internalized linguistic structures. These "rehabilitated" subjects are often paraded as showcases of success. Others may, after experiencing more failures at "rehabilitation" (double failures), or those who may see that the formal court and prison structures are nothing less than the extension of the street scene, may incorporate an alienated discourse replete with fatalistic views of life. Yet others may, under the same conditions, reinforce their preprison instrumental discourse and become more dangerous, yet more elusive criminals. A smaller group, those who espouse an oppositional discourse with elements of a replacement discourse, may develop. Theirs is a contradictory state, both opposing and, even in so doing, reifying structures of domination (Henry and Milovanovic, 1991; Milovanovic and Thomas, 1989; Bannister and Milovanovic, 1990).

In sum, neglected in the penological literature is an analysis of the cognitive structurations that work on the level of discursive practices. Absent this, theorists are left to constitute renditions of "what happened?" whether in prison uprisings, street disturbances, or outright political acts of rebellion that may be only partial accounts of the totality of their experience.

DIAGRAMS OF POWER AND CONSTITUTIVE PENOLOGY

Rothman's (1971) classic investigation of the "discovery of the asylum" indicated that architectural designs are often the reflection of changes in ideological positions that are in turn connected with the industrializing order. But once constructed, the ideology connected with the architectural space becomes the operating background, a linguistic structure within which discussion, resolutions, and policy are formulated. Foucault (1977), too, has indicated that the rise of panopticism is connected with materialistically grounded, changing needs of a political economy. Discourses that are generated from these sources can then appear relatively autonomous, being continuously reaffirmed in their use (see, also, Manning, 1988: 207; Milovanovic, 1988a). These discourses, too, can permeate various domains, otherwise unconnected with the original source. Gary Marx (1988), for example, in studying the new techniques of police surveillance in America, sheds light on how Weber's principle of rationality, and Foucault's panopticon, could extend to all domains of society.

Agents in their everyday activity are located within fluctuating spatiotemporal coordinates and thereby are provided with diverse sensory data and imageries. Imageries and sense data are infinite, whereas their expression is found in a finite discourse. Different finite discourses provide different ways of expression; and in fact, also to substantial degrees, structure expression (Whorf, 1956; Manning, 1988). Architectural designs, unintended living arrangements, technological apparatuses, random change (chaos) on the one hand, and more clearly articulated ideologies on the other, with more intermediary latent forms of expression such as generated by the logic of commodity fetishism, provide primordial sense data that may be categorized, posited, and placed in meaningful arrangements (see, for example, Manning

1988; Thomas, 1988). But, as Deleuze (1988) and Foucault (1977) have indicated, power permeates all relations; power, too can only be defined operationally (Deleuze, 1988: 27). Power finds its expression in particular forms, in "diagrams of power" (Deleuze, 1988: 34-44, 72-3). The diagram "is the map of relations between forces, a map of destiny, or intensity, which proceeds by primary non-localizable relations and at every moment passes through every point..." (ibid.: 36). Diagrams of power are imbedded within discursive practices. Thus various linguistic coordinate systems provide alternative crystallizations of power relations. Agents finding themselves in, or inserting themselves within these power relations reproduce its essential themes. Consider Gilsinan's (1982) point as to the functions of punishment:

> It is an attempt to convince people that the decisions made about others are not only rational, logical, and coherent, but are in fact the only decisions that can be made given the "reality" of the situation....Punishment is the ultimate means of confirming the accounts of particular groups in society. (p. 84)

Penologists, academic theoreticians, policy-makers, as well as operatives (guards, counselors, etc.) on the one hand, and clients (inmates) on the other, in their daily activities, take up residence in various discourses. We are suggesting that a constitutive penology would examine these changing as well as already stabilized/crystallized discursive subject-positions (see also, Smith, 1988; Deleuze, 1988: 55; Pecheux, 1982). Criminologists, policy-makers, and administrators on one level and operatives (guards) on the second, are catalysts in sustaining and stabilizing systems of linguistic relevancies, which in turn become the background linguistic relevancies to which inmates must adjust while invoking both those they have imported and generating others anew. For Gilsinan (1982: 236): "Within the arena [criminal justice], different social worlds struggle for recognition and legitimation, so that the process of justice results in a number of decisions about whose world view will prevail." Thus some prisoners incorporate (conformal discourse), some oppose (oppositional discourse), some become alienated (alienated discourse), and some have been provided reassurance for their preprison, utilitarian and self-justifying frame (instrumental discourse). The latter, ironically, contributes to the "virulent" subject (Athens, 1989: 72-9), one who often has strongly espoused the instrumental rhetoric at a private level, which makes easier future criminal activity by the very rhetoric replete with rationalizations and neutralizations.

CONCLUSION

We are not offering here a form of linguistic determinism. On the contrary, we argue that several discourses are recursively generated, their boundaries often blurred, and that they can be seen as providing alternative signifiers in constructing reality and in making truth claims about reality. Subjects, whether prisoners or "free world," construct mind patterns of their daily lives and develop believable (logical) narrative "accounts." Agents situate themselves within a discursive frame, taking up temporary residence within discursive subject-positions that provide a system of linguistic relevancies for orientation and for narratively constructing projects/goals. Thomas (1988) has shown how different decision-makers within prisoner litigation suits may make use of various narrative constructions justifying their already assumed decisions. Similarly, according to Manning (1988: 204) operatives engage in "cognitive mapping"; according to Gilsinan (1982) they construct believable "accounts"; and, according to Jackson (1988), they develop narratively coherent stories of "what happened?" Of course, the production and rendering dominant of various discourses has not been fully addressed here, but we have hinted that these are connected with such phenomena as capital logic, bureaucratic imperatives, technological advances, architectural design, phallocentricism, and those, with their particular professional interests in mind, who give these often amorphous and oftentimes contradictory forms idealized expression. We posit that once a discourse is "in place," by which we mean it is repetitiously and routinely reproduced, it provides a framework in the production of particular renditions of reality. From these accounts, an object reality is implied and is constituted through the rendition of that discourse. Accounts are only generated within bounded spheres of floating signifiers always already populated with a voice; such is the creative capacity of human agency that the generation of accounts not only remakes that voice but adds to it, extends it, attenuates it. It is this recursive account-making that constitutes prison policy and prison life.

An adequate penological analysis must begin by examining "the how" of that constitutive process rather than becoming just another builder of the prison edifice. As Zizek (1989: 90) has conceptualized it, "descriptivists [read essentialists] emphasize the immanent, internal 'intentional contents' of a word, while anti-descriptivists [read anti-essentialists] regard as decisive the external causal link, the way a word has been transmitted from subject to subject in a chain of tradition." An alternative discourse, a replacement discourse, may only arise as alternative accounts are given hearing at every level of crime-control proceedings (Gilsinan, 1982: 236). Thomas' (1988: 242-43) argument is a case in point: although jailhouse lawyers may demonstrate rudiments of an oppositional (political) discourse, they do not, typically, pursue abstract political agendas (see also Milovanovic and Thomas,

1989), and neither do "free-world" activists help jailhouse lawyers develop their incipient political agenda. This possibly leads to a stable oppositional discourse (with appropriate "*objets petit a*" reflecting the pains of imprisonment) within which rebels take up oppositional stances in producing coherent, persuasive narrative forms.

However, we also recognize that traditionally, alternative programs to corrections, like alternatives in other spheres of social life, often duplicate dominant forms of expression (Henry, 1985, 1989b). A genuinely alternative, replacement discourse would capture "the fluid nature of criminal violations and the legal processing of such infractions" (Gilsinan, 1982: 243). It would envelope, not just the declarations of policy but the ways its practitioners and policymakers distinguish their reality from the totality. At a more macro-sociological level, it would specify the conditions whereby signifiers are anchored to particular signifieds (Zizek, 1989) within particular differentiated and sedimented discursive regions (Milovanovic, 1986) and whereby oppositional movements are articulated, more often in system-preserving forms (Laclau and Mouffe, 1985). It would require a "bringing back in" of the under emphasized, informal, unofficial, marginalized practices (the unspoken) that are part of the totality of the prison business.[9] This notion, in principle,

> (A)...includes almost every conceivable reaction to an event— individual, collective, structural, material, or immaterial. (B) It implies that response is mandatory, without pre-defining the event as a crime, an illness, or anything else. (C) It invites analysis of the event before deciding or choosing a proper response. [And] (D) ... [I]t invokes the consideration of historical and anthropological forms of dispute settlement and conflict resolution for possible cues to rational forms of response (de Haan, 1990: 158).

De Haan's suggestion is worthy of further examination. It speaks for providing various (repressed, marginalized) discursive practices a forum for genuine consideration. Only with such a comprehension of the totality and the contribution of these excluded parts to the reality-making process is it possible to provide an alternative understanding of the phenomena of crime and crime control in our society. Only from such an understanding of the total constitutive process is it possible to generate a replacement discourse that begins the deconstruction of penology, the correction of corrections, and the ultimate penal policy that is its own demise.

NOTES

1. As well as the publicly documented violence, there is the trade in weapons, drugs, alcohol, prostitution, gambling that Kalinich (1986) found pervasive in prison and which requires necessary connections to the "outside."

2. This hyperreality often appears to be relatively autonomous, with a generated sign-system that is self-referential. Signifiers refer to other signifiers in an endless chain of self-reference, much like trying to look up a word in a dictionary, and then having to look up additional words within the meaning given, followed, perpetually, by looking up yet new words, and so forth. In the process of searching we forget that it is we who are doing the "looking up" and we who give energy to the meanings so referred.

3. The particular discourse is a metatheory reflecting patterns of action that are seen as constitutive of a particular ideological orientation. Particular words, signifiers, therefore have denotative as well as connotative value. They do not reside in a neutral state awaiting instrumental use, but their use calls out a particular rendition of "reality." Agents, therefore, locate themselves within certain bounded spheres of discursive practices wherein can be found appropriate terminology, rationalizations, and justifications. Human agents are not passive to this process. They invoke and recreate preexisting discourse and they innovate, inventing new forms and new applications.

4. See also chapters 2, 9, 10, this book.

5. See also chapters 2, 3, this book.

6. On the honoring of accounts, see Scott and Lyman, 1970 and Blumstein et al., 1974.

7. Cases in point are Pashukanis' notion of the "legal form" and the abstract juridic subject created through the process of commodity fetishism, agents created with universal and formally equal rights, and Poulantzas' notion of the citizen, free, and equal, a creation of the metaphysics of the law of equivalence.

8. Wheeler's (1961) classic study indicated that certainly behavioral conformity is structured in relation to the duration of the sentence (irrespective of how long it is) such that the incarcerated are more conforming at the beginning and end of their sentence than during the middle.

9. For a recent elaboration advocating expanding discourse beyond traditionally narratively constituted punishment and crime debates, see de Haan's (1990: 150-68) offering of the concept of "redress."

Topology, Chaos, and Psychoanalytic Semiotics

INTRODUCTION

Postmodern theory has placed much focus on the nature of dominant discourse and its ability in adequately representing narratives of the disenfranchised, oppressed, marginalized, and alienated. Rather than privileging global knowledge, postmodernists attempt to excavate denied voices. In criminology we have been faced with the question of how narratives and stories are constructed: be they by citizens, witnesses, police; or in reports and testimony, trial proceedings, court opinions, newspaper accounts, and scholarly research. A postmodern criminology is interested in explaining the interconnection between subjectivity and discourse. This approach is also interested in explaining the connection between "foreground factors" and "background factors" (intrapsychic as well as macrolevel) in the etiology of crime. Katz's book, *The Seductions of Crime* (1988), is especially useful here for further refinement. A postmodern methodology, then, needs to provide some conceptual tools for viewing the nature of these interconnections.

Jacques Lacan has been the critical scion for the portrayal of the desiring subject's inseparability from discourse (Milovanovic, 1992a, 1993a, 1993b; Arrigo, 1995a, 1995b, 1996). Sense production, therefore, needs to be explored as well as the intersubjective nature of desire and linguistically articulated demand. We therefore, would like to briefly outline two of the key topological constructs used by Lacan (the torus and the Klein bottle) and indicate the relevance for doing postmodern criminology. Elsewhere we have developed the relevance for doing critical criminology in the application of the Mobius band (1995a), cross-cap (1994a), and borromean knots (1993b; 1994b; see also Chapters 2, 3, this book).

We have also been making initial forays in the relevance of integrating a critically informed psychoanalytic semiotics and chaos theory (Milovanovic, 1993c, 1994a, 1995a, 1995b; Henry and Milovanovic, 1996). Although Lacan had said "mathematical formalization is our goal, our ideal" (1974-1975: 118) his many ideas represented in graphs, topological constructions, borromean knots, mathemes, ideographs, neologisms, algorithms, and metaphors indicated his notion of a "math" was underdeveloped. It would seem that chaos theory offers a useful mathematics more expressive of his ideas. Rather than Euclidean geometry, it seems that Lacan's work in many instances could be situated in fractal geometry of chaos theory. Here, rather than just integer dimensions, we have "in-between" dimensions (fractals). Take for example his borromean knots. Marini (1992: 242) has noted that the subject "is mis-situated between two and three dimensions." Lacan has also talked about a "dit-mension," the situatedness between dimension two and three. This is a fractal. Take also Ragland-Sullivan's view (1990a: 58) of Lacan's various topological structures: "structure is both anticipatory and retroactive; static and dynamic; prediscursive and discursive; regulatory and disruptive." In the parlance of chaos theory, this represents a strong affinity with the notion of far-from-equilibrium conditions within which phenomena are in dynamic flux, producing "structures" that are both taking shape and dissipating, hence the notion of "dissipative structures."

Consider, also Lacan's (1977) "graphs of desire" where numerous looping effects are indicated, each having an interactive effect, not necessarily linear, on any manifest or emerging phenomena. The notion of "iteration," or nonlinear feedback, from chaos is contiguous here (see also Henry and Milovanovic, 1996: 164-70).[1] They share the same ecological space. The relationship between demand and desire, we will also show, has affinities with the quasiperiodic torus attractor. And consider, finally, Lacan's endorsement of the use of vector analysis and plate tectonics used to model geological faults (Lee, 1990: 193). Here continuities and discontinuities can exist side by side (Lacan, 1975-1976: 44). We need not, nor do we claim to, develop a full integration here, but merely suggest some further integration of topology and chaos theory in providing phase portraits of the dynamic phenomena explained in Lacan's psychoanalytic semiotics.

TORUS

The topology of the torus, visually appearing as an inflated inner tube (figure 1a and b), represents the idea that subjectivity is inherently intersubjective. For Lacan, demand and desire of the subject are coupled (the interlaced tori of figure 1b). Here desire can be depicted as the central region of the "inner tubes" with demand winding around the outside of this inner tube, always coupled with desire.

Whereas desire answers to the question of the inherent "lack" in being (*manque d'être*), the price paid for the subject entering the Symbolic order and its promise for mastery and control, demand is the linguistic translations, always illusory, of these desires (Lacan, 1977; Lee, 1990: 58-9, 75-6). Since demand is always addressed to the other, and since the subject always, in the Lacanian schema, searches for the recognition of the other—in fact linguistically articulated demand always has a performative dimension, it calls out an effect in the other—, then the search for recognition lies behind all demands. But demand, depicted as circling around the outside of the torus, never articulates desire precisely (chaos theorists refer to this as a quasiperiodic attractor, see figure 1a). The object of desire, the *objet petit a* for Lacan, is always out of reach, but always finds potential vehicles that partly embody desire. If we look at the interlaced nature of the two tori (see Figure 1b), we also note that the demand of one is for the desire of the other, and vice versa (Granon-Lafont, 1985: 55-6; Granon-Lafont, 1990: 161-7 Fink, 1995: 54).

Figure 1. Torus, Desire and Demand

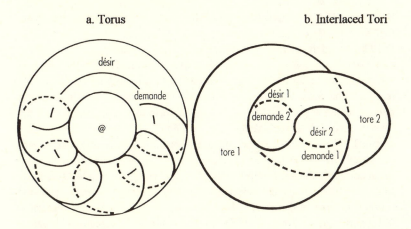

a. Torus   b. Interlaced Tori

(Granon-Lafont, 1990: 164-5)

What this underscores in any attempt in doing criminology, in theorizing within the discipline (i.e., unraveling the determinants of the motivation behind lawbreaking), is that separating the subject, the lawbreaker, somehow from the rest of society and then bringing the "normalizing disciplines" (Foucault, 1977) into play for correction misses the essentially intersubjective quality of subjectivity, and can only be relegated to pure illusory, reifying constructions of the desires and demands of the subjective in a political economy. As we have said elsewhere, our constitutive approach (Henry and Milovanovic, 1996: ix) reflects "our dual concerns of being built while building, of being made while making, of parts making the wholes of which they are constituents." Consider, for example, Matza's juvenile "drifter"

(1964),[2] who seeks to reestablish the "mood of humanism." It is recognition by the other that s/he searches; the recognition that s/he is worthy of not being pushed around. Or consider Salecl's "modes of subjectivization" (1993), where the lawbreaker seeks to be recognized as a subject by the other.

The torus is also the starting point for other topological constructions. Through tracing a figure-eight on the torus, and through cutting and gluing operations, we can construct the Mobius band (Granon-Lafont, 1985: 62-5). The Mobius band can be better viewed as a rectangular strip with a twist, where the two ends are glued together producing a one-sided construction. A soaked-through image would travel around the Mobius band and arrive back in an inverted form. Lacan indicates its relevance: "Human language... constitutes a communication in which the sender receives his own message back from the receiver in an inverted form" (1977: 86; see also chapter 2, this book).

Lacan's late investigative works (post-1974) on the nature of the Borromean knot conceptualized these three interlocking rings (symbolizing the Symbolic, Real, and Imaginary Orders) as tori (Granon-Lafont, 1985: 145-7; 1990: 22). Here we not only conceive of effects produced by the in-between dimensions and spaces, but also, with the tori, we see further holes as constitutive of being itself. Lacan conceded that no one knows what a hole really is. But these tori are interlocked around a center, the hole in being, plugged by *objet petit a* (Lacan's various objects of desire, which offer the illusory potential of overcoming *manque d'être*). Absent the "plug" we are destined to be overwhelmed by the rush of unconscious material that gushes uncontrollably to the surface, to the conscious sphere. Thus it is not just metaphor when alienated subjects talk about an "emptiness inside." Similarly, Matza's (1964) juveniles responded to being pushed around with the consequent onset of the mood of fatalism; with Lyng's (1990) skydivers doing "edgework"; and Katz's (1988) various offenders engaging in moral transcendence—each confronts the divide between order and disorder and takes the leap across "the invitational edge" (Matza, 1969) in hopes of overcoming *manque d'être*.

We could also relate the torus to chaos theory, particularly where "attractors" are concerned. The quasi-periodic torus, for example, as we indicated earlier, provides a phase portrait of two coupled (interacting) phenomena—desire and demand—and how demand always misses its mark, never precisely reflecting desire.

Two connected tori could also be conceived as the "wings" of a particular "strange attractor" called the Lorenz or butterfly attractor (T.R. Young, 1997). Here we could also trace yet another figure-8 analogous to Lacan's notion of *huit interieur*, indicating the orderly disorder in existence: determinacy at the more global (macro) level—a structure does appear taking the form of the butterfly attractor; but, within the "structure" (the microlevel), indeterminacy prevails, for we cannot be precise as to the exact path the traced figure 8 will take. Said differently, the two wings represent outcome basins within which determinacy fails.

Figure 2. Strange Attractor (Butterfly or Lorenz Attractor)

Determinacy and indeterminacy, as chaos theorists tell us, can exist simultaneously, which fundamentally questions many of the suppositions of Enlightenment thought found embedded in modernist theorizing (Milovanovic, 1995a). As T.R. Young tells us (1996), linear dynamics too often assume one outcome basin given some configuration of forces, whereas complexity theory indicates that two or more outcome basins may exist, portrayed by the two tori of a butterfly attractor. With further perturbation these tori can break up, producing further outcome basins. Chaos theory offers the notion of bifurcation diagrams, which explain how 2, 4, 8, 16 and more outcome basins may evolve (for an accessible presentation, see T.R. Young, 1992). Put in a different way, a torus can give way to the strange attractor, which in turn can break up into increasingly complex outcome basins, culminating in total unpredictability. However, with further perturbation, chaos theory notes that self-organization, order out of disorder, can occur within these far-from-equilibrium conditions.

Integrating Lacan's ideas with chaos theory could be illuminating as to how certain crimes can be better explained. Take for example some recent theorizing that is in a more postmodernist tradition (Matza, 1964, 1969; Katz, 1988; Lyng, 1990; Ferrell, 1995a, 1995b; O'Malley and Mugford, 1994; Arrigo, 1996). These explanations focus on the neglected area of "foreground factors" more so than "background factors." Here the focus is on the seductive nature of crime, the sensual, visceral, pleasure, or adrenalin-charged, passion-driven nature of the phenomena and the moral emotions. As Ferrell tells us, "we need a criminology that incorporates understandings of humor and pleasure, excitement and desire, entertainment and emotion, and the entanglement of these human experiences in and around the sensuality of the human body" (1995b: 2). Further, as O'Malley and Mugford tell us (1994: 209), we need a "phenomenology of pleasure" rooted in historical conditions. The phase portrait of these activities could be portrayed by chaos dynamics.

We begin in these various innovative initiatives with preoccupation with "order" (O'Malley and Mugford, 1994; Ferrell, 1995a, 1995b); we find the periodical flaring up of the desire for confronting the invitational edge, the boundary between order and disorder; and here "edgework" is initiated, where the initial bifurcation is experienced. As Ferrell tells it, many crimes (i.e., gangbanging, joyriding, cruising, wilding, as well as what Katz calls "sneaky thrills") "may represent a real, if flawed, escape from and defiance of the powerlessness and subordination which frames their daily lives" (1995b: 4). Excitement and pleasure in these crimes may create "experiential escapes" as well as being alternative modes of meaning and identity construction (Ferrell, 1995b: 4; Lyng, 1990: 869, 871). The initially more stable "point" and "cyclic (limit) attractors" [3] that postmodern society demands — rooted in the demands and effects of clock time, capital logic,[4] and alienation (O'Malley and Mugford, 1994; Ferrell, 1995b; Lyng, 1990), often is the repressive structure that is challenged in "edgework," the process whereby the everyday mundane and rational is confronted. Boundaries are experienced, bifurcations are negotiated, disorder is witnessed.[5] Torus attractors are representative of the dynamics. The development of strange attractors is often the next stage, where greater indeterminacy prevails, and then out of disorder, order will once again prevail as self-organization dynamics run their course (see also T.R. Young, 1992, 1997).

Similarly, in a very different discipline, critical pedagogy, Giroux (1992) has advocated "border crossings" in order to develop a discourse of possibility. This "border pedagogy" is such that crossing boundaries is advocated as a means of understanding otherness and of diversity, of "understanding how fragile identity is as it moves into borderlands crisscrossed within a variety of languages, experiences, and voices" (1992: 34). The borderland is what chaos theories would call the area where far-from-equilibrium conditions prevail, where sensitivity to initial conditions assures even a small change will often produce disproportional or nonlinear consequences, and where not point, nor cyclic attractors prevail; rather, the torus and strange attractor becomes ubiquitous. In short, a critical border pedagogy is advocating "edgework," confronting the "invitational edge," and thereby challenging many of the repressive structures in a political economy and in monolithic discourses (where point and cyclic attractors reflecting order dynamics exist, rather than the variability, flux, change, and dissipative nature of structures found in far-from-equilibrium conditions).

In sum we see two lines of innovative argumentation found in recent literature: those attempts at bringing attention to the importance of explaining the foreground factors in various crimes, and those which indicate and advocate border struggles that promise to provide an avenue to new knowledges, identities, and appreciation for otherness. Each can be significantly understood by the use of topology and chaos theory. The torus is this exemplary topological construction, which provides a valuable tool for investigation and for understanding.

KLEIN BOTTLE

One of the least explored topological constructions employed by Lacan is the Klein bottle (Granon-Lafont, 1985: 93-106; Nasio, 1987). It indicates the relationship between a signifier (S1) and the remainder of a signifying chain (S2) (Nasio, 1987: 157). It is a question of how consistency is maintained in a signifying chain, a strung-together ordered sequence of signifiers. The Klein bottle has no border, and is one-sided; an ant traveling on a "surface" would enter the bottle and reappear in inverted form without crossing any boundaries (see figure 3).

Figure 3. Klein bottle

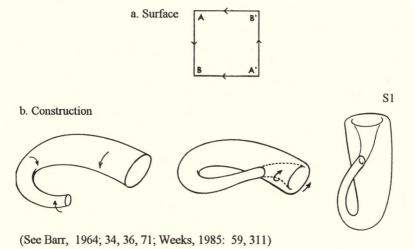

(See Barr, 1964; 34, 36, 71; Weeks, 1985: 59, 311)

The "inside" is directly connected to the "outside"; in fact, they are continuous. The Klein bottle is a useful topological construction for a postmodernist criminology in that it indicates that in narrative/discursive constructions all words produced are infused with some more unconscious ideological material that is embedded within stabilized key signifiers, which provides stability and a sense of permanence to the subject. These can be seen as colored, among other things, by such things as the dominance of the male voice (Φ) in a phallocentric symbolic order, or, for example, the dominance of capital logic in a political economy (Pashukanis, 1980). We can view the "neck" as a conduit for the more unconscious ("inside") infusing the unfolding discourse (the "outside") with desire embodied in unary signifiers that remain always latent.

In figure 3, the line of intersection where the "neck" enters the main bottle appears only in 3D; in 4D, similarly to the cross-cap (Milovanovic, 1994a), there is no line of intersection, and hence "boundaries" are not experienced. In the Mobius band an edge does exist; in the Klein bottle, no edges exist. Cutting a Klein bottle in two produces two Mobius bands (Weeks, 1985: 75; Barr, 1964: 62-77). The Mobius band, cross-cap, and Klein bottle are homeomorphic: the Mobius band, with transformations, can be used to obtain both the Klein bottle as well as the cross-cap (Frechet and Fan, 1967: 44).

The Klein bottle shows the connectedness or the coupling of a pair of signifiers: S1, which Lacan here refers to as the "unary signifier" (the primordial representations of various drives that allow these drives to be represented linguistically), with S2 the "binary signifier." For our example, S2 represents knowledge embedded in a narrative (chain of signifiers). Unary signifiers are necessary for they are the avenue for the expression of demand. The reoccurrence of dreams, symptoms, and slips of the tongue is the play of the signifying pair (S1 and S2). We extrapolate from this to say, so too ideological constructs (the notion of the "reasonable man in law," the juridic subject) that have been internalized (the imposition of "maps" coordinating the flow of desire, see Milovanovic, 1995c) from the political economy and various state ideological apparatuses (consider the discourses of the university and master, Milovanovic, 1993b, 1993c; Arrigo, 1995a, 1995b).

The unary signifier exists outside of discursive chains, but constantly asserts itself. It has some affinities with Derrida's notion of the "trace" (1976; see also Balkin's application to semiotic production in law, 1987). The Klein bottle indicates this "asserting" of the unary signifiers; it is everywhere present. In other words, Lacan's algorithms for metaphor and metonymy (1977), the two coordinating axes of unconscious production of signifiers and signifying chains, the unconscious structured like a language, implicates the assertiveness of the unary signifiers: it remains a "trace" that continuously colors all other signifiers and signifying chains (Nasio, 1987: 37-9, 41, 66-9, 157-8).

In sum, the unary signifier gives consistency to any signifying production; it conveys the unique "truth" of any subject into the discursive chain being produced. S2 (knowledge, the binary signifier) can *be* only if S1 (the unary signifier) exists and persists (i.e., Lacan's notion of the "insistence of the letter") (Nasio, 1987: 39). The Klein bottle represents a "folding back" (the "neck"), which represents the movement of the unary signifier asserting itself in any discursive chain under construction (Nasio, 1987: 158). This is represented as the S1 appearing at the "mouth" of the bottle. The "mouth" is misleading because it really represents the S1 being further folded back, having an effect on all other S2s which, for purposes of illustration, could be visualized as the "outside" surface of the Klein bottle. This folding back can also be envisioned as implicating iterative processes. Iterative loops, in other words, always produce "more than one" (*Un en plus*); what returns is always greater than what started the journey.

Since the Klein bottle is constituted by two Mobius bands attached at their borders, then what is implicated here is Lacan's two algorithms said to coordinate semiotic production within the sphere of the Other: the algorithm for metaphor whereby one signifier is replaced by another (the movement along the Mobius band and the return in inverted form); and also the algorithm for metonymy associated with the displacement of desire along a discursive chain (for Lacan, "desire *is* a metonymy," 1977: 175; see also Nasio, 1987). The lightning-quick movement along the figure-8 of the Mobius band also indicates how consistency is maintained through repetition (Nasio, 1987: 206-8), although any text/narrative is inherently unstable as the effects of metaphor and metonymy will be felt. The return of the previous psychic material now in inverted form can be seen as having undergone iterative transformations: with each journey along the figure-8 the new is always different from the past as myriad interacting effects will be at play. Consider Balkin (1987: 775): "The history of the law is iteration; the development of law is the development of legal materials, which are subjected to new interpretations as we read them over and over again in different factual, historical, and political contexts."

The relevance of the Klein bottle for criminology is again to look at how an utterance is constructed and how in its entirety it remains consistent: it is immersed in ideology and these ideologies have their effects in all discursive productions. But the Klein bottle also indicates that all discourses, whether by a witness to a crime, a police officer making a report, a lawyer constructing a legal case, a judge ruling on a case, a probation officer making a presentence report, a guard writing up a "ticket" on an inmate, a criminologist creating a theory of crime — all will find that their unfolding discursive chain will develop with the appearance and continuous effects of the unary signifier being ubiquitous. In fact, ideology, criminal conceptions, stereotypes, and identities can be seen as being created and re-created continuously because of the influence of the "folding back" character portrayed by the Klein bottle. Consider, for example, Jackson's (1988) "narrative coherence model." Here guilt or innocence determinations are often a function of presenting plausible stories constructed in dominant discourses that jurors can relate to (see also Bennet and Feldman, 1981).

Balkin's (1987) accessible discussion of Derrida's ideas of "differance," the "trace," and iteration as applied to law is useful here. What is pointed out is that ideological constructs continuously reassert themselves in legal narrative constructions. Similarly, Pecheux's (1982) notion of the "intradiscursive," the more covert structure always residing in potentiality that provides supportive statements for a particular discourse in the form of "it is so because...," "in other words...." This provides consistency and a degree of permanence. Said differently, more persuasive statements made in various discourses can always summon up supporting validity claims that more often remain in unverbalized states of potentiality. This is quite apparent in law, because of the assumed linear support found in the principle of *stare decisis*. Presentence investigations (PSIs) done by probation officers would be ripe for investigating how dominant linear conceptions of cause (e.g., onset of crime) make their way into reports that have effects on the "in or out" decisions by judges. Again, we see the effects of the infusion of an unfolding discourse with ideological content embedded within the Other.

DISCUSSION
Integrating critically informed psychoanalytic semiotics, topology and chaos theory offer much potential for developing new insights in doing postmodern criminology. Mainstream criminologies, those perspectives that accept uncritically a modernist framework, are too often preoccupied with "background" factors and not sufficiently with "foreground" factors. Recently, several forays into placing foreground factors center stage are emerging. Works by Katz (1988), Lyng (1990), O'Malley and Mugford (1994), Ferrell (1995a, 1995b) as well as earlier suggestive and anticipatory works by Matza (1964, 1969) provide provocative analyses that center on the visceral, sensual, pleasure, seductive, adrenalin-charged, passion-driven, and emotional aspects. O'Malley and Mugford's (1994) call for a "phenomenology of pleasure" certainly points the direction. Lacan's psychoanalytic semiotics is well situated for explaining many of these complex, dynamic, often contradictory visceral factors at play. Chaos theory offers further conceptual tools: nonlinear developments, feedback mechanisms, disproportional effects, the existence of determinacy and indeterminacy at the same time, and various methods of mapping dynamic phenomena such as phase portraits in doing complexity analysis (see also chapters 10, 11, this book). Topology theory provides a

"rubber math" that suggests ways of modeling complex phenomena. Lacan's use of the torus, Klein bottle, Mobius band, cross-cap and borromean knots is not only for expository purposes, but is suggestive when used as tools for discovery.

What is still needed in criminology is an integration of background and foreground factors. For sure, foreground factors have been neglected and recent studies indicate some crimes can be explained by these factors. However, these must be connected with the play of background factors (see figure 4).

Figure 4. Foreground, Background Factors and Iterative Loops

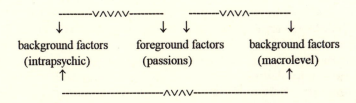

background factors	foreground factors	background factors
(intrapsychic)	(passions)	(macrolevel)

(Where squiggly lines represent "iterative loops," or nonlinear transformations. For a suggestive model, see, Gregersen and Sailer, 1993 where nonlinear polynomials [and as an extension, algorithms] are offered. See Henry and Milovanovic, 1996: 168-70; see also chapter 11, this book).

Background factors have two specificities: macrolevel, and intrapsychic. Macrolevel are structural factors that are conditioned by historicity and political-economic determinants. Intrapsychic factors concern the functioning of the Other, the unconscious structured like a language. Here Lacan's Imaginary, Real and Symbolic Orders are implicated. We hasten to add, consistent with constitutive theorizing, these two "levels" may be presented as dualities for exposition purposes, but are better conceptualized as mutually interpenetrating and constituting; they are coterminous.

The first level of background factors, the intrapsychic level, concerns the Other. The torus is useful in portraying how demand is a linguistic attempt in embodying desire but always missing the mark. From demand particular drives develop; in fact, language, for Lacan has a performative dimension—it is the basis of action-effects. The interlaced tori also indicate how foreground factors for one can be background factors for the other; in fact, this is why subjectivity is inherently intersubjective in orientation. The Klein bottle is useful in depicting how the "inside" has effects on the "outside." The psychic apparatus, as Lacan has well demonstrated in his "graphs of desire" (1977), schema R (1977), and borromean knots (Milovanovic, 1993b), is constituted by Imaginary, Real, and Symbolic order effects. Thus the various forms of deviance that Katz (1988) explains need to be also traced to the more hidden factors residing within the unconscious — the play of metaphor and metonymy; the effects of various imaginary constructions of self and others; the various objects of desire seen as offering the ability of overcoming the lack-in-being; narcissistic strivings; the law-of-the-father; the unary signifier; the nonlinear looping effects indicated in his graphs of desire, etc. Most notably, Lacan's dialectical analysis of aphanisis (1981: 203-29), the appearing and disappearing of the subject (the "fading of the subject"), whereby the subject ($) is replaced by a signifier (S), which now stands for the subject for other signifiers, is relevant. Here the subject has been embodied in an object, has been "objectified," much like the process Katz (1988) as well as Matza (1969) explains as the necessary step in being "pacified," whereby the subject is released from the moral binds of the law. In this state the subject will be what circumstances dictate (determinism).

For Lacan, a signifier represents a subject for another signifier. The subject ($) has disappeared from the scene and its representative, a signifier (S), is now caught in the inherent logic of various discourses. Similarly, Katz's and Matza's pacified subject will now exhibit or give the appearance of determined behavior. Consider for example Katz: "one feature of the typical homicide, then, is its character as a self-righteous act undertaken within the form of defending communal values....[t]hese killers were defending both the morality of the social system and a personal claim of moral worth" (1988: 18-9). Here the subject is inserted in conventional discourse as a signifier that now represents the subject for another signifier.

Reflecting Nietzsche's idea that the subject is better conceptualized in terms of the "deed" rather than the "doer" and that "semiotic fictions" are plentiful for ex-post-facto attributions of agency, Katz has argued that asking many who engage in more passionate forms of crime "why do they do it?" will be responded to by self-justifying rhetoric (1988: 7). For Katz, the task is

> to specify the steps of the dialectic process through which a person empowers the world to seduce him to criminality....For a person to experience being influenced or determined, he must lose a reflective awareness of the abiding, constructive workings of his subjectivity. Thus, part of the challenge is to recognize steps in raising a spirit of determinism that are sufficiently subtle that their contingencies go unnoticed (1988: 7).

Katz is concerned with seductive forms of crimes whereby a person remains in limbo between being in and out of control, subject and object (see also Matza, 1969). Lacan's work, unlike most in criminology, is particularly well situated in explaining how the subject's drift to an object state unleashes the various passions, drives, and desires emanating from the intrapsychic structure. A person is temporarily released from moral constraints, experiencing a "moral transcendence." The Klein bottle as well as several other topological constructions employed by Lacan are useful in indicating the effects of these processes. This topological construction provides a conceptualization of the foreground factors being affected by background factors (i.e., intrapsychic factors, not all of which are accessible to consciousness).

The second level of background factors concern macrolevel determinants. Macrolevel factors shape or frame contexts and within these contexts foreground factors will be played out. Consider, for example, Katz's specification noted above that the killer is often defending both the morality of the social system as well as his personal claims to moral worth. These notions of morality have historical and political-economic determinants. Consider also Katz's (1988) explanation of "righteous slaughter." A key factor in minimizing the development of spiraling linear emotions, which are often punctuated by nonlinear events (i.e., rage and violent attack), is the existence of an "escape" option — a fantasized other place, other times, other people, where this spiraling humiliation being suffered can be overcome, where one is free of humiliation (Katz, 1988: 22). It could be, however, that since life chances are differentially distributed as a function of socioeconomic class, some people will be situated where there is no other place to go: here the escape option is reduced and further escalation is likely. The key point here, again, is that the foreground and background factors are both at play (see figure 4 and the various iterative loops). Nietzsche, contrary to O'Malley and Mugford's (1994: 209) rejection, is certainly a useful figure in this postmodern analysis, but in combination, as they insist, with an understanding of historical conditions. As they point out, the promise of integrating foreground and background factors "can be realized by connecting abstract general arguments to concrete matters of differential access to resources and experiences. As a consequence of the inequality of resources in society, some of the ways of transcending mundane life are more open to some groups of people than to others" (1994: 209). For them, a "historically contextualized phenomenology" would better connect agency with structure. Certainly they are on the right track. Their exclusive reliance on conventional modernist theory, however, can not provide them with a vantage point for doing the complexity analysis that is needed.

Elsewhere (Henry and Milovanovic, 1996: chapters 4, 8, this book), we have offered a direction, constitutive criminology, which explains the parallel and interpenetrating factors at play in much emerging phenomena. Background and foreground factors cannot be easily separated as autonomous spheres. This position builds on many of the insights of psychoanalytic semiotics, chaos theory, topology, gender analysis, and Hunt's idea of "relational sets" (1993: 295). From this we have developed the idea of "constitutive interrelational sets" (COREL sets) whereby foreground and background factors find themselves mutually influencing each other, but in often nonlinear ways (see figure 4 and the iterative loops reflected by the squiggles, Henry and Milovanovic, 1996: 153-80; see also chapter 11, this book). Thus codetermination and interrelationship exist. As we have put it: "crime is the ongoing, recursively produced outcome of numerous different contexts of interrelationship, wherein human subjects progressively lose sight of their productive contribution, and increasingly invest in that which they produce to the point of some becoming excessive investors....[w]e see these relationships not as deterministic but as dialectical...our constitutive dialectics assumes nonlinear developments" (1996: 170-1).

The interrelationship between subjectivity and discourse, as well as between agency and structure generally, particularly when pointing out nonlinear effects, can be specified by our notion of COREL sets. Lacan's various conceptual tools offer ways of conceiving the desiring subject and also provide insights for explaining foreground factors that are at play. Lacan's background factors, such as the Symbolic, Real and Imaginary Orders, certainly must be placed in an historical and political-economic context. In other words, even though he provides a key and convincing explanation of the relationship between subjectivity and discourse, he lacks a sufficiently materialistic analysis. Doing postmodern criminology demands this further integration. This is the challenge of our times.

We need not go further in this direction here. We only stress that in doing critical criminology from a postmodern perspective, foreground and background factors must necessarily be integrated for a bonafide statement in explaining crime. Our presentation of the torus, particularly the intersubjective nature of desire and demand, and our examination of the Klein bottle indicating various looping, or nonlinear feedback effects, indicate some useful conceptual tools worthy for integration toward the end of better explaining phenomena in criminology.

CONCLUSION

Topology, chaos theory, and psychoanalytic semiotics are only beginning to be integrated. Much promise exists for these novel conceptual tools for critical examination in the social sciences. We have offered a modest beginning integration.

NOTES

1. The notion of iteration encompasses the idea of disproportional effects and sensitivity to initial conditions. Even a small input of .0001, when iterated continuously, may produce unpredictable results, fundamentally challenging modernist thought privileging linearity.

2. Matza (1964) explains the onset of delinquency by indicating that juveniles, because of their status, periodically feel that they are pushed by forces beyond their control. This "mood of fatalism" in combination with the company of peers similarly situated and with the exposure to a discourse of neutralization often found in juvenile subcultures, releases the juvenile from the moral binds of the law, and frees him/her to commit delinquent acts. The delinquent act often reestablishes the "mood of humanism," where the juvenile regains his feeling of being in control. Matza says that juveniles intermittently drift between nondelinquency and delinquency and in their late teens often "mature" out of delinquency, which he calls maturational reform.

3. See also chapters 2, 10, 11, this book.

4. Pashukanis (1980), extending on Marx's fetishism of commodities principle, indicated that the legal subject undergoes the same transformations from use-value to exchange-value. One form of capital logic is the "law of equivalence" by which the concrete is replaced by abstract. Capital logic is the primordial principle in competitive capitalist modes of production.

5. See also chapters 10, 11, this book.

PART 3

Emerging Postmodern Methodologies: Integration and Application

Chaos and Criminology
Phase Maps and Bifurcation Diagrams

INTRODUCTION

In this chapter we present alternative, more postmodernist ways of conceptualizing dynamic systems. We want to go beyond the rather simplistic linear "path analysis" models that are offered by the modernist sciences and particularly by empiricist criminologists. These cannot account for chaotic phenomena. Toward this end, the notion of a phase portrait will be presented. This will be followed by a presentation of one form it may take, the bifurcation diagrams. These indicate how complex systems may "fork" into more than one possible outcome basin, even given the same parameter value, which is said to be affecting the system. Finally, we shall apply the bifurcation diagram in doing critical criminology.

The notion of a phase map, or phase portrait, indicates how complex interactions take place over time. Various trajectories, reflecting the interacting variables in effect, can be traced through "phase space." Variables change in complex ways and affect the state of the system at any particular time. Every "point" in phase portraits represents a description of the dynamic system in one of the possible states. To understand the state of the system at any particular time, we need at the minimum two spatial coordinates and two variables reflecting the momentum of the system (e.g., how fast it is going in a particular direction). For the state of the system in three-dimensional space, the traditional x,y,z grid, we need to create a fictitious space that represents it in its various moments. Thus, on the one hand, we have an actual dynamic system changing over time, and, on the other, its representation, the phase portrait.

The phase space is not real, but a construction that helps us to understand changing complex systems over time. Add more variables that are said to affect the system and we have a phase space of greater than three dimensions. Each variable corresponds to a dimension of the phase portrait (map). Riding a bicycle, for example, implicates many dimensions or variables. The interactions among these variables produces certain areas on the phase map toward which the system tends. In other words, complex systems tend to settle down to some region in phase space. These are called the "attractors" of the system (i.e., point, limit/cyclic, torus, strange attractors). Modernist thought has been preoccupied with two of these attractors: the point and limit (or cyclic, or periodic) attractors. Postmodernist thought, on the other hand, indicates that the quasiperiodic torus and strange attractor are often at play in dynamic systems.

A swinging pendulum is illuminating. Below we will develop the phase space of the "simple" swinging pendulum with frictional and nonfrictional forces at play. We will then move on to indicating how one phase map, that of the bifurcation diagram, can be a useful conceptual tool in understanding complex systems, and for doing complexity analysis in criminology.

PHASE MAP (PORTRAIT)

Linear systems, as often portrayed by path analysis, have been dominant in criminological thought. Chaos theory offers nonlinear models and ways of mapping them. Nonlinear systems tend to settle down to some pattern over time. This settling-down phenomenon results in four major patterns that can be located on "phase maps" or, as they are sometimes called, phase portraits. Point attractors are those where phenomena settle down to some region approximating a point. Cyclic attractors (or limit attractors) are those that converge to an oscillating cycle. Torus attractors (looking much like inflated inner tubes) are those where one witnesses quasiperiodicity. Chaotic attractors, the butterfly attractor being the most prominent, are bounded (have global stability), but internally, trajectories are unpredictable (local indeterminacy). Here a very small change in some crucial control parameter, even of the magnitude of a difference of .0001, after a number of iterations, will produce unexpected results. This, of course, is the much-stated notion of "sensitive dependence on initial conditions." The simplest phase map presented in the literature that is instructive is that of the movement of a pendulum (Briggs and Peat, 1989: 34-7).

Consider the complexity involved. We start the swinging pendulum at some region in space (see figure 1). We note that it picks up speed, reaching a maximum at the bottom, after which it slows down, then stops, and returns in the other direction, again picking up speed until stopping once again to return to another cycle. Note also that correlated with the different speeds are different distances covered by the pendulum. We could have, hypothetically, a pendulum with no frictional forces (and a small motor) at play, or with frictional forces at play. Now the task is one of how to accurately map this interaction between momentum and position. First, we create a phase map where the horizontal axis will reflect momentum and the vertical position.

Here we have one degree of freedom: it moves from left to right. Second, we plot the trajectory of the pendulum swinging on the phase map (figure 2). At B the momentum is zero and the displacement is the furthest (F corresponds to this at the other end); at D and G a maximum momentum exists, with zero displacement.

Figure 1. Swinging Pendulum   Figure 2. Phase Map of Swinging Pendulum

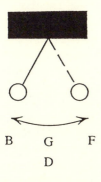
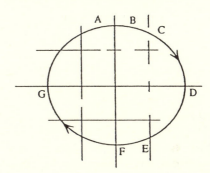

What is traced out is a trajectory in phase space that would be called the cyclic attractor (with no frictional forces and the aid of a small motor) (see also figure 4d). Note that with a greater initial push on the pendulum, a larger circle or amplitude would result. Without the motor and with frictional forces the pendulum will slowly come to a halt and thus be represented by a point attractor (see also figures 4a, b). If we added another dimension, say the pendulum also vibrated while in its swinging motion, and if each of the vibrations were correlated precisely (by a specific ratio) with the left-right movement we could trace out a periodic torus where the two movements are coupled as they move around the outside surface.

If the vibrations were more erratic (nonratio), we would have a quasiperiodic torus attractor (figure 4f; see also our application in chapter 9). Here we have a two-dimensional depiction of a 3-D system. Let us turn to a consideration of one phase map, the bifurcation diagram. (In the following chapters we will consider the Mandelbrot set, catastrophe models, and other meta-models.)

BIFURCATION DIAGRAM AND ATTRACTORS

Nonlinear dynamics make use of nonlinear equations. Results of the computation process are feedback into the equations for recomputation (iteration), the answer to which once again is feedback into the equation, etc.

One classic example (the "logistic map" or the Verhulst formula) is to be found with the growth of gypsy-moth populations from year to year (Briggs and Peat, 1989: 53-65, 66-71; Barton, 1994; Peak and Frame, 1994: 161-86). The formula is given by $x` = x + bx(1-x)$, where $x` = x_{n+1}$ and $n = 0,1,2,3...$ In other words, this represents the steps in an iterative sequence; or rewritten with subscripts to indicate iteration from one time to another, this formula is $x_{n+1}=bx_n(1-x_n)$; or differently, to indicate iteration from one time to another, this formula can be rewritten as $x_{n+1}= (1+b) x_n-bx^2_n$ (where x_n is multiplied by itself and produces feedback or the iterative effect). The left side of the equation represents this year's population, the right side last year's. And where x_1 represents the first value (iterate) to be iterated.

The vertical axis (figure 3) reflects normalization (a simplification device) as ranging from between 0 and 1. It represents the state of the system where 1 represents the largest possible value. B is a constant expressing the rate of birth that potentially would occur if the food supply was continuous (in practice it is really a contingent factor); it will vary from 1 to 4 along the horizontal axis. This factor, therefore, is called a parameter. For some values of "b," the dynamic system will reach equilibrium, a steady state; for higher values we find that the dynamic system may have two possible outcomes (called "outcome basins"); for yet higher values, four outcomes; for even higher, eight outcomes, etc. This sequence, two to four to eight, is called period-doubling. Chaos, defined here traditionally as unpredictability, will occur at the universal value of b=3.57.

These equations show extreme sensitivity to initial conditions, and, because of feedback, nonproportional effects. Without going into the details of the mathematical computations (see Briggs and Peat, 1989: 53-65; see also, Peak and Frame, 1994: 161-86; Peitgen, Jurgens and Saupe, 1992: 195-267), diagraming various iterates as b ranges from one to four, the parameter values, shows that "bifurcations" or splittings occur at several key points (figure 3).

Figure 3. Bifurcation Diagram

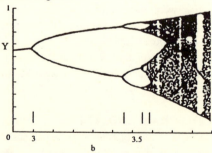

We need first to run a number of iterations to see the pattern that will emerge. At different parameters (b-values) we shall see for even the same value two or more outcome basins may arise at bifurcation points. At values less than b=3 we see traced in figure 3 a horizontal line from the y axis until a forking; here the results of iteration produce a steady state, or a point attractor; said in another way, the population growth of the gypsy moths remains at a constant value. At the value b=3 we note the first bifurcation. This means that two possible outcome states (outcome basins) are now possible, i.e., results of the computation move back and forth between two values (i.e., a normally law-abiding person, may with declining income attempt to supplement it illegally, hence oscillating between two states). We have a cyclic attractor. At the value of approximately b=3.45 we see a second bifurcation and four outcome possibilities (i.e., the person may add child/spousal abuse and excessive drinking as further outcome behaviors and fluctuate among these states). At the next instance a torus attractor develops. At 3.56, eight periods or outcome basins; at 3.59, sixteen, and so forth. A strange attractor begins to emerge as we approach the limit of the bifurcation sequence. A limit is reached at approximately 3.6, where the outcome basins become infinite; no prediction here is possible.

We then note white vertical bands that indicate "intermittancy" or periodicity once again emerging; or order out of disorder (see figures 3 and 4j): said differently, "self-organization" (for example, consider Matza's deviant juvenile who undergoes "maturational reform," 1964; or consider "spontaneous remission"). This pattern is sensitive to initial conditions; thus, if our x value is off by as little as .0001, divergences are expected after several iterations. This bifurcation diagram has appeared again and again in a variety of studies, leading chaologists to conclude that it may also be relevant to the social sciences, and for our purposes, criminology (T.R. Young, 1991a, 1991b, 1992; see also Smith and Comer, 1994). In order to demonstrate the applicability we will provide two examples, one dealing with Matza's theory of delinquency and "drift," the other as to how a cultural revolutionary may be a catalyst in the generation of a new discourse, a replacement discourse that counters hegemonic practices.

In modeling behavior (bifurcation phase portraits), Abraham (1992) has indicated that we need to tease out the relevant variables of some theory. This process is referred to as "dimensional reduction." Although there are some qualifications as to its precision (Mandel, 1995), social scientists progress by operationalizing their terms. (For a useful discussion of collapsing multivariate into univariate indices, see Oliva, Day, and MacMillan, 1988: 375.) We identify the key "control parameter," the dominant factor at play in having an effect on some phenomena under investigation. We then identify the interacting variables at play. In other words, in each frame (state space) we have a phase portrait indicating how the variables interact, given some control parameter, and what results.

In this phase portrait of a complex system changing over time, a series of vectors reflect different effects; these are seen as trajectories (see figure 4, cell "a"). We may have two, three or more dimensions in our phase portrait. We may, for example, review some criminology literature and hypothesize two key dimensions at play. A third interacting variable, the rate of change, indicates that the other influencing factors change at different rates, and hence trajectories may arrive at some region in the respective frames at different rates (note in figure 4, cell "b," that the trajectories are longer). A loss of a parent or a close friend may place the person in a new region in state space and the diagram suggests that there will be a movement (the trajectory) toward the attractor (e.g., the person's more "normal" predispositions and tendencies). In figure 4, cell "c," there is indicated a slower return, portrayed as a centripetal spiraling. Each cell represents a "state space" of a dynamic system over time. Cell "d" indicates that the person cycles through a greater range of moods, but does not return to his previous, somewhat more point-like attractor. This new cyclic attractor can also increase or decrease in amplitude.

Of course, other "intervening" variables and other influencing factors might effect the vectorfield, thus necessitating more dimensions in the basic model here being developed. Each of the factors can be described by a differential equation, with at least one being nonlinear (Abraham, 1992: 45). According to Abraham,

> these trajectories may be considered as the integration of the vectors and the vectors in turn can be considered as the differentiation of the trajectories, and that for trajectories with sufficient order to them and satisfying a few other simple properties, the rules defining the vectors can be given by a set of simultaneous ordinary differential equations. Each variable is coupled to, or influenced by the other. (1992: 27)

Therefore, the rate of change of any particular contributing dimension (variable) may depend, in part, on a number of other intervening variables which might, as Abraham suggests, contribute to the nonlinearity and to the bifurcations in the dynamic system (1992: 45). Thus each state space is a product of a network of interacting relationships. In anticipation of chapter 11, creative and fruitful investigations in a postmodern criminology may integrate the notion of iterative loops into the bifurcation diagram. The notion of COREL sets (Henry and Milovanovic, 1996) could also better conceptualize these networks of interacting relationships. Much integration awaits the interested postmodernist criminologist in this direction.

We should also mention that this is merely a model. One of its limitations is that point-like states (as in the point attractors in figure 4a) are better conceptualized as regions, patches, or moments, consistent with what quantum mechanics tells us about indeterminacy when trying to specify location and momentum at the same time. Coupled with the central idea of chaos concerning "sensitive dependence on initial conditions," we can never, then, precisely predict results.

The bifurcation diagrams have been used by Abraham (1992) to present phase portraits of Carl Jung's dynamics of the psychic apparatus, the relationship of self-image and mood, therapeutic implications in the relationship between self-control and dependency, and cognitive motivational theory. In each case, Abraham has indicated how the various attractors appear as the control parameter varies. Let us now turn to two applications of the bifurcation diagrams to criminology.

MATZA, DELINQUENCY AND DRIFT
Matza's theory of delinquency (1964) indicates that the juvenile normally "drifts" between convention and crime. The juvenile, because of her/his status, finds at times that s/he is "pushed around," which is experienced as a "mood of fatalism." Episodically, within the "situation of company" (peers) and within a context where neutralizations for releasing oneself from the moral binds of the law flourish, s/he is free to commit delinquent acts. These key parameters can be located on our bifurcation diagram in figure 4.

Figure 4. Bifurcation Diagram and Matza's *Delinquency and Drift*
← control parameter: "being pushed around" →

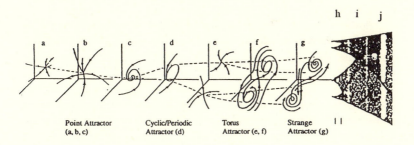

(Adapted from Abraham, 1992)

Our control parameter is "being pushed around." The x-axis represents neutralizations; the y-axis, the situation of company; and the z-axis, the rate of change between the two interacting factors.

We could provide other examples, such as Cressey's embezzler in *Other People's Money*, where the control parameter would be "nonshareable financial problems"; and where x = neutralizations, y = opportunities and skills, and z = rate of change. Hence we could apply this phase portrait to "blue" and "white" collar crime.

In figure 4a, we start with a hypothetical situation in which the juvenile experiences some modicum of being pushed around, indicated by vectors that spiral to a point (region, patch, or moment). This point attractor indicates that the juvenile is in somewhat of a homeostatic balance between the "mood of fatalism" and the "mood of humanism." The effects of exposure to the situation of company and neutralizations, although at times locating the juvenile at a distance from this more likely moment (point attractor), are not so consequential as to produce a delinquent act. The Schwendingers, for example, indicate other offsetting "moral rhetorics" that may be at play (1985: 141).

In 4b we note the trajectories, or vectors, are longer, indicating that the control parameter, "being pushed around," is increasing in intensity resulting with the juvenile beginning at a further distance from her/his more normal or bounded state (region). In 4c we note that "being pushed around" has increased further in intensity and now the juvenile takes longer (the spiraling toward the point, or better, region) to return to her/his more normal disposition. The juvenile is coming into an increasing influence of "the situation of company" where lawbreaking is encouraged, and of available neutralizations that release the juvenile from the moral binds of the law. At this moment, the juvenile maintains predominantly law-abiding behavior. Figures 4a, b, and c represent "point attractors."

However, we note that in 4c the first bifurcation has begun to develop (the diverging dotted horizontal lines). Two outcome basins result; meaning, the juvenile, given the prevalent neutralizations and being in the situation of company, is now free to entertain law-abiding *as well as* law-breaking behavior. In 4d we note a greater amplitude (variability) in behavior, and the juvenile does not return to a point (or region) any longer; s/he exists within a greater range of possible activities; this is the "cyclic" or "limit attractor." In 4e, because of even more increased intensity of "being pushed around," the juvenile fluctuates between two states (two point attractors); in one, experiencing the freedom to commit "infraction," in the other, to maintain law-abiding behavior.

With yet even a greater feeling of being pushed around, a new bifurcation develops in 4e and the juvenile's behavior now fluctuates in a yet more unpredictable manner between two states, expressed by the "torus attractor" (4f), and then, with even more of an increase in being pushed around, the chaotic attractor of figure 4g appears. As Matza tells us, "The delinquent *transiently* exists in a limbo between convention and crime, responding in turn to the demands of each, flirting now with one, now the other, but postponing commitment, evading decision...he drifts between criminal and conventional action" (1964: 28). It would be difficult to predict within which state the juvenile is found at any particular moment. But this does not end the story. One of Matza's important contributions is to show that most juveniles do not go on to becoming committed to their delinquent acts; they grow out of it, they undergo "maturational reform" (1964: 25). In our diagram, we note that in region 4j there is a vertical white band that indicates, for chaologists, "intermittency" or "order out of disorder." Spontaneously arising is a maturing out of the delinquent enterprise.

In this bifurcation sequence, 4a through 4e would be well within the modernist paradigm and explained accordingly (much prediction exists). In 4f through 4j we enter far-from-equilibrium conditions (Prigogine and Stenger, 1984), and the postmodernist framework better explains what will take place. Here, things are uncertain, not totally predictable, and in a state of flux (the area where we find the torus and strange attractor). Indeed, as labeling theorists have indicated, attempts at arresting the process inadvertently may focus exclusively on one wing of the butterfly attractor (law breaking) and hence produce the forces for the occurrence of the secondary deviant (the "committed" delinquent in Matza's view) and deviance amplification. This model is also suggestive of policy implications as to intervention strategies, i.e., social policies of empowering youth, such as summer programs and creative strategies in offsetting neutralizing discourses.

REPLACEMENT DISCOURSES

Let us provide a second example, one that professes to account for the development of new master signifiers and the emergence of a replacement discourse. Much literature in postmodernist analysis has indicated that the desiring subject is trapped in alien, repressive discourses within which narrative constructions disallow full embodiment of desire, or more concretely, disallow constructions of local knowledge. For example, critical-race theorists note victims of hate speech often do not have a discourse to represent their injury (Matsuda et al., 1993; for feminist prison literature, see Howe, 1994; Carlen, 1990; for jailhouse lawyers, see Milovanovic and Thomas, 1989). In the use of the dominant discourse, what often results is the reconstituting of dominant global forms. Narrative constructions by disenfranchised place them at risk to negative interventions by social-control operatives and mechanisms (see, for example, in police literature, Gilsinan, 1982; Manning, 1988; in law, Yngvessen, 1993; Bennet and Feldman, 1981; Arrigo, 1993a, 1993c, 1994, 1995a, 1996). Bail decisions as well as presentence reports would also place some more at risk due to the form of narrative constructions in use. Absent, too, a more local (indigenous) discourse that better reflects nuanced, contextual factors, adequate understanding of various forms of crime development and possible social-change strategies are minimized.

The challenge for postmodernists has been to develop an alternative replacement discourse. "Standpoint epistemology," without more, will not do, for it still asks repressed subjects to construct narratives out of the dominant discourse, hence reconstituting the form and embedded ideology. We shall draw from Lacan's influential work on the four discourses (1991a; Bracher, 1988, 1993; Fink, 1995; Milovanovic, 1993a; Arrigo, 1995a) in combination with Freire's work (1985) on a dialogical pedagogy in indicating the wherewithal for the beginnings of replacement discourses, those constructed by indigenous populations with the cultural revolutionary (Unger, 1987) playing the part of a coproducer and catalyst. Lacan's four main structured discourses are offered to indicate the nature of domination, education, rejection, and revolt embedded in discursive structures. We shall use the example of some colonizing power that is inflicting its master signifiers (and global knowledge) on some indigenous population. This is suggestive for creating strategies for empowering disenfranchised defendants before the court. We have identified as our control parameter the effects of the postmodern society specified by O'Malley and Mugford (1994) in terms of three factors: alienation and "hyperreality," clock time, and commodification. We shall collapse these into one composite dimension.

Lacan has lectured that the desiring subject has various commitments to the dominant discourse within which s/he must insert her/himself in constructing reality and embodying desire. Consider, for example, how victims, offenders, police, lawyers, judges, probation officers, guards, journalists and criminologists often find themselves operating within a particular paradigm. The dominant discourse, in Lacan's view, embeds dominant knowledge indicated by his notation, S2. Dominant premises, concepts, truth claims, logics, etc., are embedded in master signifiers, those which have a more permanent hold on the unconscious, and indicated in Lacan's notation as S1. These S1s begin to take on a more amorphous form prior to the entrance of the subject into the Symbolic Order (language), and are subsequently molded by a political economy. Only in the most formal sense can they be regarded as words. They are "identity-bearing words" (Bracher, 1993: 23). There are various degrees of commitment or bonding to these master signifiers.

Accordingly, in our bifurcation phase portrait, our x-axis will be identified as "identification/disidentification" (that is, degrees of connectedness of the subject with her/his master signifiers, S1); the y-axis, expression of desire in master signifiers; and the z-axis, rate of change. Desire can be more embodied in master signifiers of "abstract language" — the various discourses available (elsewhere we have referred to these as linguistic coordinate systems, Milovanovic, 1994c, i.e., legal, scientific, street, religious, clinico-legal, etc.); or relegated to the "material language" of the body, a more unstructured and amorphous discourse, what Lecercle identified as "délire" (1985). He has shown how délire is often expressible by poets, novelists, linguists and mental patients (see also Kristeva's notion of the "semiotic," the preverbal organization of instinctual energies, 1980).

Lacan's four structured discourses include four positions and four terms. We have elsewhere provided more detail as to the four respective discourses' construction, so we shall proceed by providing only more summary statements (Milovanovic, 1993a, 1994c; other applications have been to pornography, antiabortionist debates, political campaign rhetoric, see Bracher, 1993; and to rape and the disordered criminal defendant, see Arrigo, 1993a, 1994, 1996).

Let us begin with a hypothetical example of a colonizing power that has claimed a particular territory as its own (Australia's experience and the U.S.'s experience with the indigenous populations) and has imposed its culture, language, and symbols on the aboriginal peoples. In figure 4a above, we would expect that through the impositions of the ideological state apparatus (Althusser, 1971) the subjects will remain relatively committed to the dominant master signifiers (S1), with an occasional disidentification (the trajectories, or vectors). Here, too, we might expect some continuous maintenance of or yearnings for their indigenous voices in a "material language." The discourses of the university and master would assure that master signifiers are given greater credence in narrative constructions. The *discourse of the university*, represented as

$$\frac{S2}{S1} \rightarrow \frac{a}{\$}$$

is such that the sender of the message (the left side of each of these structured discourses) offers S2, a body of knowledge (here the colonizer's) to the other (the right side represents the receiver and enactor of some message received), who is relegated to constructing narratives, within which her/his local knowledge and desire are excluded. Consider, for example, various operatives of the criminal justice system offering clients a bureaucratic explanation (narrative) of their despair (Manning, 1988; Arrigo, 1994; Yngvessen, 1993). The subject, $\$$, remains in an alienated state. The "a" represents the *pas-toute*, the not-all, the left out; it is translated as the "more than enjoyment" by Lacan; it is the excluded voice. The indigent enactor, by accepting the imposed clinical, legal, therapeutic, or other bureaucratic knowledge, thus recreates and legitimizes (be it inadvertently) dominant, or global knowledge.

With an increased hegemonic imposition of global knowledge, even as the effects of the emerging postmodernist society make themselves felt (alienation, commodification, clock time, hyperreality), the desiring subject will at times resist, but is quickly put in her/his place by the *master discourse*, represented as:

$$\frac{S1}{\$} \rightarrow \frac{S2}{a}$$

Here master signifiers are offered to the other, the indigenous population, from which a body of knowledge (S2), the colonizer's, is created, i.e., hegemony; it is also the basis of interpellation. This leaves something left out, the *pas-toute*, the "a," which nevertheless supports the key premises or truth claims of the colonizers, S1. With continued domination, we have perhaps "c" in figure 4, meaning that the aboriginal subject begins to increasingly alienate and disidentify her/himself from the colonizer's master signifiers, but yet returns at some point, for how else to communicate? In *his* courts? In *his* school system? In *his* media? In *his* criminal justice system? In *his* various bureaucratic apparatuses?

We note, however, that a bifurcation has begun to develop in figure 4c which can be interpreted as the beginnings of the *discourse of the hysteric*, represented by Lacan as:

$$\frac{\$}{a} \rightarrow \frac{S1}{S2}$$

Here the "hysteric," which we expand with Bracher (1988, 1993) to mean the questioning, despairing, challenging, protesting, complaining, and alienated subject ($), has further disidentified her/himself from the colonizer's master signifiers and begins to delve more often in the material language of the body, a situation ripe for the colonizers to offer psychiatric, social work, and religious services on the one hand, or outright imprisonment on the other. The despairing subject (the left side) is offered only master signifiers (S1) from which to construct a body of knowledge (S2) (i.e., clinical categories, stereotypes, various classification mechanisms offered by different components of the criminal justice system and other bureaucracies, and other dominant conceptions; see for example Yngvesson's study of the poor and working-class subjects before the court, 1993). This contribution of a body of knowledge answers the call for a degree of security and stability and a sense of a "stable, meaningful, and respectable identity" (Bracher, 1993: 67).

The dominant discourse and body of knowledge continues to be reconstituted, even inadvertently, by those most repressed (for an example with jailhouse lawyers, see chapters 5 and 6; for activists before the court see chapter 7). Moreover, the "blaming the victim" ideology (S2) is continuously reconstituted by this discourse. In affirmative-action law, for example, we have seen since *Brown v. Board of Education* that first an interest by the higher courts in "conditions" that lead to inequities and biases was dominant, but later, especially beginning with about 1970, a reformulated framework has become dominant. The courts have moved away from articulating conditions, to a framework in which specific offenders ("bad apples") are now the focus of attention.

With increased imposition of hegemonic knowledge, we may enter figure 4e and 4f where the indigenous subject lives a schizophrenic existence, at times speaking the dominant discourse, constructing narrative as they should be, even evading the controlling influences of a repressive state apparatus; at other times, at private moments, the délire, the material language of the body yearns for expression and asserts itself. But expressed in an unrecognized form (by the standards, criteria, and rationality of the colonizer), the subject is at risk for her/his "irrational" behavior, and what awaits is an army of correctors, the disciplining machine (Foucault, 1977; for a feminist form of disciplining, see Howe, 1994).

What is to be done? How does one develop a more responsive discourse? More responsive master signifiers? Without at the same time developing new static forms of expression? In prison literature, how to respond to Spivak's assertion (1988: 307) that there exists "no space from which the sexed subaltern [prisoner] can speak"?

The answer begins with Lacan's fourth discourse, the *discourse of the analyst* (at 4g),

$$\underline{a} \rightarrow \underline{\$}$$
$$S2 \quad S1,$$

but not by itself. At this point we need further integration. We draw from Paulo Freire's work (1972, 1985) on dialogical pedagogy, which recognizes the dialogical quality in the production of new signifiers and knowledge. We also draw from a combined discourse of the analyst and hysteric to indicate that the cultural revolutionary should remain transparent to the subject s/he works with; teacher becomes student; student becomes teacher (see particularly the recent "narrative therapy" movement, White and Epston, 1990; see also Arrigo's application for "deconstructing classroom instruction," 1995b).

Lacan's initial idea was that the analyst, the left side of the formulation, would offer the "a," the left out, to the other, the hysteric ($), who then would see the uselessness of her/his previous master signifiers that keep up the despairing condition. The "hysteric" begins to more actively disidentify her/himself from these master signifiers in slowly creating new ones. In Figure 4e-g, we see these phase spaces indicating the subject as being high on the x-axis and y-axis, with an increasing rate of change on the z-axis. The literacy-campaign worker (Freire, 1972), cultural worker (Giroux, 1992), analyst (Lacan, 1991a), or cultural revolutionary (Unger, 1987) acts as the catalyst in increasing the rate of change and encourages "border crossings" (Giroux, 1992) and the development of new master signifiers.

The sensitive analyst (or cultural revolutionary or literacy campaign worker), in turn, would recognize again what is still left out, accumulated as the S2, and offer it to the "hysteric," who in turn would continue the process of alienation, disidentification, and actively reconstituting new master signifiers. This could be expressed in Figures 4e through 4g in our diagram above. In other words, the subject would find her/himself at times in two states, one in which previous master signifiers are used in constructing various narratives, the other where new master signifiers are in the process of creation. This fluctuating state (border crossings) is unstable. The subject floats or drifts between the two, as in the chaotic attractor.

Freire's work supplements Lacan's. It roots Lacan in material conditions of continuous struggle. The sign becomes "decidable" in real struggles in a political economy (McLaren, 1994a; Ebert, 1991a, 1991b; Zavarzadeh and Morton, 1990; Volosinov, 1986; Giroux, 1992). For Freire, speaking "true words" can only take place when action and reflection are combined (1972: 57-67). In engaging in the production of "true words," subjects change the world; they become active subjects in becoming.

Freire develops his strategy on how to approach illiterate populations, and how to raise their level of literacy without imposing the master discourse. In his dialogical pedagogy, the cultural revolutionary, working with the indigenous population, produces a "conscientization" (for an application to an alternative instructional paradigm for criminal justice and legal studies education, see Arrigo, 1995b). In this process, cultural revolutionaries working collaboratively with the indigenous together decodify key master signifiers, in indicating how they are often connected with hegemonic rule, and recodify through "an authentic process of abstraction." What begins to emerge is a body of alternative master signifiers, a replacement discourse, a "language of possibility" (Giroux, 1992). For Giroux, revolutionaries should be active "border crossers." Here, "as part of a radical pedagogical practice, border pedagogy points to the need for conditions that allow students to write, speak, and listen in a language in which meaning becomes multiaccentual and dispersed and resists permanent closure" (1992: 29). Our position, which integrates the cultural/symbolic with concrete historical conditions of oppression, meets the challenge of postmodern critics such as Held (1995), who sees postmodernist analysis advocating the "death of the subject."

These replacement discourses are "new languages capable of acknowledging the multiple, contradictory, and complex subject positions people occupy within different social, cultural, and economic relations" (Giroux, 1992: 21). In other words, there is no "death of the subject" as in the skeptical forms of postmodernism. The subject is constituted in multiple sites of struggle. The new master signifiers are not static, but rather "less absolute, exclusive, and rigid in...their establishment of the subject's identity, and more open, fluid, and processual: constituted in a word, by relativity and textuality" (Bracher, 1993: 73).

This emerging replacement discourse is opposed to all calls for the master: it is "a continuous flight from meaning and closure, in a displacement that never ceases" (Bracher, 1993: 73). Within this discourse subjects can establish "contingent universalities" (Butler, 1992), which can then become the grounds for social movements (Mouffe, 1992; JanMohammed, 1993; Henry and Milovanovic, 1996: chapters 8, 9). It is the beginning of a "border pedagogy" and a "language of possibility" (Giroux, 1992). And it answers Butler's call "to locate strategies of subversive repetition" (1990: 147).

CONCLUSION

Complexity analysis necessitates the development of better conceptual tools than are currently being offered by the modernist sciences. A postmodern perspective finds itself with the task of discovering, refining, and applying these tools. Doing postmodern criminology will certainly benefit from such conceptualizations as phase portraits and bifurcation diagrams. Previous criminological theory can be portrayed and new insights can be developed. Those doing more empirical forms of research will find useful forms of portraying the complex movement of interacting variables. And those pushing ahead on the theoretical front will be armed with more powerful tools of critical inquiry.

Chaos, Meta-Modeling, and Criminology
Iterative Loops, COREL and Mandelbrot Sets

INTRODUCTION

Those interested in modeling complex, dynamic, and especially nonlinear systems over time find a need to visually present their findings. The bifurcation diagram (see chapter 10) is one visual aid, and its mappings are suggestive for further hypothesis building and testing. In this chapter we want to show how criminological phenomena can be modeled and portrayed by the Mandelbrot Set. This is a suggestive exercise. Postmodern methodologies are only in their infancy of development, and, accordingly, new methodologies will certainly take time to build. We draw much inspiration from Gregersen and Sailer's recent article (1993), which shows how chaos theory can be applied to the social sciences, how to develop metal-models, and how the Mandelbrot Set is illuminating for understanding chaotic phenomena (see also Pickover, 1988; Sinanoglu, 1981). We also draw, for an example, from our *Constitutive Criminology: Beyond Postmodernism* (1996), where the notion of COREL sets was developed in mapping parallel and interlocking dissipative structures and their effects.

META-MODELING

In mapping phenomena, Gregersen and Sailer (1993) have developed a useful modeling technique whereby complex, dynamic phenomena in movement can be visually presented, particularly those exhibiting nonlinear dynamics. They suggest we start with a very simple iterative loop (see figure 1). Note the "squiggle" which represents some nonlinear transformational law at work. An iterative loop portrays how nonlinearity proceeds by way of iteration.

Consider, for example, how words are continuously iterated in new contexts producing ever new nuanced meaning, or think in terms of self-reflection, witnesses' recollections, or the mythical notion in law of some Founding Father's "original intent," or, generally, how texts are continuously reinterpreted (see also Derrida, 1976; Balkin, 1987).

Figure 1. Simple Iterative Loop

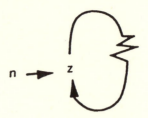

What this means is that starting with some state vector, z, at time t, we then allow iteration to proceed (the computation of the transformational law said to be at work), which produces a new state, z_{t+1}. With an additional iteration, a new state results, etc. It is a continuous method of taking the results of a computation and again recomputing it. Capturing the movement of the phenomena at any of its states, is to do cross-sectional analysis — that is freezing dynamic systems — but at a cost of losing an understanding of the overall dynamic movement over time. This iterative loop can be expanded to include other influences (see figure 2).

Figure 2. Modeling Chaos, the Mandelbrot Set, and Crime

Phenomena   Meta-Model   Mandelbrot Set (2-D)   Mandelbrot Set (3-D)

(Adapted from Gregersen and Sailer, 1993; Pickover, 1988)

We could also identify another state vector, the environment within which the first is embedded, as u_t. Thus the system's state at a particular time $(t+1)$ is reflective of the environment state, u, at time, t, plus the system state, z_t (Gregersen and Sailer, 1993: 780). To indicate how two iterative loops interpenetrate each other, the structural coupling property, observe what appears under the heading, "meta-model" in figure 2.

Take a modernist theory: Cressey's explanation of the embezzler in *Other People's Money*. Cressey's examination indicated that embezzlement takes place if three factors are found: a nonshareable financial problem, neutralizations present in the work environment that rationalize theft, and opportunities and skills. We could see x representing a nonshareable financial problem (an attitudinal variable); y, the immediate work environment (opportunities to embezzle, prevalence of rationalizations). Perhaps u_x and u_y represent some external environment conditions, say economic conditions and unemployment rates. Thus our meta-model suggests that to understand the occurrence of embezzlement, we look at the interactions between x and y (and keep in mind the squiggles between these two factors), and the effects of the external environment.

This meta-model could be represented in a dynamic way by the Mandelbrot Set, which is based on a polynomial that is repeatedly iterated. We will have more to say about transformational polynomials that indicate the various states in our hypothetical example of embezzlement below, but we must first briefly describe the Mandelbrot Set and its relevance.

MANDELBROT SET

Benoit Mandelbrot, inspired by some mathematical puzzles on nonlinear dynamics posed by the great mathematician Poincare, was to stumble across a huge discovery in the early 1980s. By iterating simple algebraic expressions, he was to go on to do further investigations with complex numbers and complex planes, in the end discovering what mathematicians have called one of the most complex objects in mathematics, now called the Mandelbrot Set. This portrait is created by a rather simple looking expression: $Z_{n+1} = z_n^2 + C$, where n+1 represents the new; z_n^2, the old; and C, a fixed complex number. This is mapped on a two-dimensional complex plane, similar to a Euclidean plane but with complex numbers added. By repeated iterations and mapping in phase space a truly remarkable phase portrait appears, the Mandelbrot Set (see figure 2).

The Mandelbrot Set takes form by way of continuous iterations and plotting of the rather simple formula given above. Start with some initial value, plug it into the algorithm, take the results, map them on the complex plane, replug the results into the algorithm, iterate, map, replug, iterate, map, etc. What unfolds is that some results, when mapped appearing in a spiraling orbit, remain within a bounded region (and are often given a black coloration by a computer); some results, after a number of iterations zoom off to infinity (and are given a white coloration). The former have been referred to as "prisoner sets," the latter, the "escape sets." Now take a higher initial value, iterate, map, replug the results, iterate, map, etc. Continue with increasing initial values and repeat the process. Map each orbit to see if it remains within a confined region or not. The totality of the prisoner sets provides the image of the Mandelbrot Set. We could now iterate various test points to see if their initial values upon further iterations would remain as prisoner or escape sets.

What is also unique is the fuzzy boundaries. The "antennas" that emanate from the Mandelbrot Set, when inspected closely, will indicate infinite complexity, and rather remarkably, the whole structure of the Mandelbrot Set is found again and again with increased maginifications. With 300,000,000 magnifications it still appears.

Okay, so far so good. But what relevance does this have for postmodern criminology? Consider for a moment doing traditional modernist forms of analysis. More specifically, think in terms of regression and path analysis. We take some data and attempt to find the "best-fitting line" and express it in terms of some formula with results that range from -1 to 0 to +1 (Pearson's R, or Pearson's Correlation Coefficient). The best-fitting line is making a prediction. The empiricist would then create path analysis models (see figure 3) and indicate that given some starting value, an expected result would occur with a degree of probability. Although these correlations may be small, they nevertheless are said to be suggestive as to the "independent variables" that have the most "significance" in the onset of some dependent variable. In more complex path analysis what is provided is a series of "partial" correlations that are said to result after holding constant certain effects. In figure 3, for example, note that "stressful family event" correlates with "serious violent offending" by a +0.07, whereas the "partial," "attitudes towards deviance," contributes a +0.31 to "serious violent offending." This linear model implies a "path" of influencing factors from the independent variable through the intervening variables, cumulating in the dependent variable.

Chaos theorists would challenge this linear science. First, consider trying to find the best-fitting line at the boundaries of the Mandelbrot Set. Here, infinite complexity prevails. No best-fitting line exists. Prediction makes no sense. This is not to say that no "order" exists, for we do in fact see the shape of the Mandelbrot Set indicating some patterned "disorder."

Second, two close starting values plugged into the algorithm for the Mandelbrot Set could hypothetically have results, which after say 100 iterations, remain within the prisoner set, but a starting value in between these two could produce an escape set. Two juveniles, for example, being exposed hypothetically to similar environmental conditions, say E1 and E2, could become delinquents, but another juvenile who finds her/himself in environmental conditions that fall in between E1 and E2 does *not* become a delinquent. Consider, for example, the heavy usage by modernists of Sutherland's "differential association theory," that delinquency is predicted when there exists in an environment, E, an "excess of definitions favorable to violation of law over definitions unfavorable to violation of law." Implicit in this is that if the balance of definitions is favorable to violation of law in E1 and the balance is even greater in E2 then delinquency would occur and what falls in between these two, say E1.5, should also produce delinquency. But clearly the literature shows that this does not always happen. Modernist linear analysis would find this hard to explain.

Third, in regression-analysis, often a few independent variables would be judged to explain most of the variance ("variance explained"), and other factors would be discarded for their minuscule contribution. Chaos theory would argue that these "insignificant" factors could have disproportional result when undergoing continuous iterations. A racial slur may be psychologically iterated by the recipient over time to produce long-lasting injury (see Matsuda et al., 1993); one person's "small" contribution to politics may have disproportional effects (i.e., the "butterfly effect"). Discontinuities, for linear science, are difficult to account for. Chaos theory, on the other hand, explains that determinacy and indeterminacy can live side by side.

We want to now turn to some insights generated by Gregersen and Sailer (1993) on transformational polynomials and suggest the relevance for a postmodern criminology.

TRANSFORMATIONAL POLYNOMIALS

Gregersen and Sailer's suggestive study also indicates that we should consider the "law(s)" (or principles, formulations, algorithms, etc.) established for understanding the phenomena under study. In other words, the transformations from one state to the next. The bifurcation diagram (see chapter 11), for example, is based on an iterated polynomial. In their study, they would like to suggest an isomorphism between chaos found in deterministic equations with their nondetermined results, with social-science phenomena undergoing iterations. They provide an example of polynomials that could hypothetically summarize the interrelationships. This is their "fanciful part" — merely suggestive. Much good intellectual debate assuredly awaits about the efficacy of this suggestion, and should produce important contributions to the literature. For now, we want to trace out the suggestions by Gregersen and Sailer for a postmodern criminology.

In their example, they would like to model the relationship between a worker's behavioral commitment (x_t), attitudinal commitment (y_t) and the work environmental supports, where u_x = co-worker relationships, and u_y =

formal reward system. In their "fanciful part," they make use of a polynomial in noncomplex math: they offer: $x_{t+1} = x_t^2 - y_t^2 - u_x$ and $y_{t+1} = 2x_t y_t - u_y$, where $t = 0,1,2,3,...$ and where the environmental state vectors, for simplification purposes, are held constant, $u_t = u$. Again, these would represent the transformational law said to account for the movement from one state to the next.

We could now use the logic developed previously concerning the prisoner and escape sets and indicate the importance of the Mandelbrot Set for postmodern criminology. If we start at some set of coordinates representing the state vector at time t, then proceed to iterate and observe the results, we can plot the outcome on a phase map and end with a Mandelbrot Set in two-dimensions (2-D). We could also portray it in 3-D, where the vertical axis would represent iterations (figure 2). In other words, by iteration we will find some results that converge after a set number of iterations to the black region (the Mandelbrot Set); other starting points, however, after the same number of iterations, diverge to the white region. Again, the iterative polynomial is deterministic, but the results are not always so.

Gregersen and Sailer suggest that although on first view iterative polynomials might seem only relevant to the natural sciences such as population growth models, they can also be used to approximate functions in the social sciences that appear chaotic (1993: 779). In the natural sciences, the manifestation of chaos is now well established. The social sciences are beginning to identify more and more chaotic systems. Gregersen and Sailer suggest that two indicators for the existence of a chaotic system are: (1) "highly iterative, recursive, or dynamic structures that change over time," and (2) "highly discontinuous behavior in the system" (1993: 779).

Let's develop an example of the usefulness of the iterative polynomial to criminology. In our example of the embezzler, we could label the three factors identified by Cressey as x, y (x representing nonshareable financial problems; with y being a collapsed variable standing for the work environment offering two factors, opportunities to embezzle, and neutralizations/rationalizations), and environmental factors u_x, u_y. (Perhaps the former could represent the national employment picture, the latter the firm's competitive standing.)

We then apply the logic of an iterative polynomial (the "fanciful part") and compute the results with various starting values. Recall, the iterative polynomial in this example represents the development of embezzlement. Again, this is the "fanciful" part of our application. We note here that Lacan has often made use of mathemes and algorithms that are presented not for strict mathematical adherence, but more as suggestive. Cressey had indicated that where there exists a "nonshareable problem," "opportunities" to embezzle, and "neutralizations" found in the vocabulary (discourse) of the work environment, there would also be embezzlement. We will also add that each of these three variables could range along some dimension. In iterating the polynomial, the points that constitute the Mandelbrot Set (the black region) are the results of the iterated polynomial (representing the laws of transformation) and indicate those occurrences where in fact embezzlement does occur. The "escape sets," or the divergent set, are those white areas surrounding the Mandelbrot Set, and in our example represent behaviors that are not embezzlement. These could include law-abiding behavior, as well as other forms of social harm (i.e., child, spouse abuse, etc.) or self-harm (i.e., suicide).

What chaos theory suggests is that we can start with two state vectors found in similar environments and both might end, after iteration, as prisoner sets (i.e., embezzlement), while a third state vector found *in between* these two might, after iteration, have results quite different than what would be expected. In other words, we would have expected that the in-between starting values should have resulted in the convergent (prisoner) set also. However, deterministic equations are producing unpredictable results, i.e., the first two being in the convergent set, the third in the divergent set. These discontinuities cannot be adequately addressed by modernist thought.

Even in increasing the sample size, as Gregersen and Sailer suggest, there will still exist "a very large number of cases where arbitrarily similar actors can display radically different behaviors" (1993: 783). Thus, rather than a preoccupation with "prediction" in systems exhibiting chaos, chaologists suggest that better "understanding" can take place and the discontinuities can be modeled by meta-models and such exotic-appearing portraits as the Mandelbrot Set.

FRACTAL BOUNDARIES

What is also most interesting about the Mandelbrot Set is its boundaries. Note how jagged they are. They are *fractals*: they represent fractions of a dimension. Normally, in Euclidean geometry we have a point representing zero dimension; a line, one dimension; a plane, two; and a sphere, three; in fractal geometry we can have "in-between" dimensions, literally opening up an infinite space. Continuous zooms (magnifications) on the borders, up to 300,000,000, will show that these boundaries are infinitely varied (see Peitgen, Jurgens, and Saupe, 1992: 453) and no "best-fitting line" as in regression analysis can possibly accurately capture the phenomena. No prediction is possible at the boundary; at best the social scientist can have *explanation* as her/his goal (Gregersen and Sailer, 1993). This is not necessarily to discount the usefulness of quantitative methodology, for, as T.R.Young (1991a) and Gregersen and Sailer (1993) have indicated, critical is the decision of what region of phase space one samples. Near the boundaries, understanding, not prediction, is the goal, a case for ethnographic research.

The significance of the jagged boundaries can be related to approaches that have affinities with a postmodernist analysis. Consider: Matza's "drift" theory and the "invitational edge" (1964, 1969); Lyng's "edgework" (1990); O'Malley and Mugford's "phenomenology of pleasure" (1994); Ferrell's political economy of criminal pleasure (1995b); Giroux's "borderland" (1992); Peirce's "pure play" (1965); Irigaray's call for a "mimesis" (1985); or Cornell's call for alternative "myth making" (1991). The boundary region, the borderland, is the area of indeterminacy where subjects may, with but little perturbation, find themselves in one basin of outcome rather than another. Here the much celebrated regression analysis fails us. It is the region of imaginary play, pleasure, excitement, and alternative embodiments of desire.

TROUSER DIAGRAMS AND COREL SETS

Trouser diagrams, Figure 3, have been developed by cosmologists to better explain "particle" interactions (see Peat, 1988; Bohm, 1980).

Figure 3. Trouser Diagrams

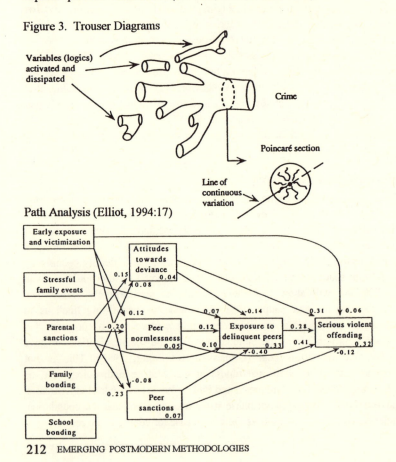

Path Analysis (Elliot, 1994:17)

The better conceptualization is what Deleuze and Guattari (1987) have offered in terms of a "rhizome," a "continuous line of variation"; meaning that along some "line" we have a perpendicular range of variation of some phenomena, which, at any moment in time, cannot be given precise location. Consider here the torus attractor as a representation of global stability but local indeterminacy. We have, in other words, both order and disorder. Compare, in figure 3, the modernist's preoccupation with linear path analysis with the implications of more nonlinear trouser diagrams. Our notion of the COREL set, below, can be modeled by these diagrams.

COREL sets stand for "constitutive interrelational sets" (Henry and Milovanovic, 1996). We could model these by a number of iterative loops that run parallel and are intersecting (for the effects of the intersections of gender, race, and class in criminology, see Schwartz and Milovanovic, 1996; Henry and Milovanovic, 1996: 164-70; Matsuda et al., 1993). A minimum of a 3-D phase space would be needed here. Think in terms of the two-dimensional iterative loops represented under "meta-model" of figure 2, but an additional dimension that runs perpendicular to the two-dimensional plane with various coupled iterative loops that run parallel. Each iterative loop, too, is composed of constituting others, which in turn are connected with a variety of others. There can be no mistake.

Constitutive interrelational sets interpenetrate at different levels with effects, and no particular iterative loop is without many others within it that are constitutive of it. Accordingly, in figure 2, the meta-model would include many iterative loops that intersect, loop, feedback, etc., with each having squiggles indicating nonlinear transformations.

A good example could be drawn from critical race theory (see Matsuda et al., 1993). Crenshaw, for example, in examining various forms of prejudice, notes the intersecting quality that has often been overlooked in the literature. Women of color, for example, are in "double jeopardy." Crenshaw's "intersectional framework" is suggested as a "necessary prerequisite to exploring how this double vulnerability influences the way that violence against women of color is experienced and best addressed" (1993: 112). She suggests that the concept of "intersectionality" "links contemporary politics with postmodern theory" (1993: 114). In critically examining the subordination of women of color, she presents three foci: structural intersectionality, political intersectionality, and representational intersectionality. "These intersectionalities," she continues, "serve as metaphors for different ways in which women of color are situated between categories of race and gender when the two are regarded as mutually exclusive" (1993: 114). We appropriate this under the rubric of "constitutive interrelational sets" (COREL sets), which suggest that a complex, three-dimensional portrait may illuminate the intersecting quality of various influences in the continued subordination of women of color. In other words, we have a dynamic system best understood by complexity theory. Since various interpenetrating iterative loops are active, often the occurrence of a *particular* instance of violence toward women of color could not be predicted as the various iterations work themselves out. In other words, many times violence is not a continuous phenomena. Crenshaw's position would indicate a new form of investigating violence toward women of color. Our meta-modeling could illuminate the various vulnerabilities found in social space.

What best reflects these complex interconnections is the hologram. Bohm has argued how it can uncover the undivided wholeness of phenomena in 3-D, even if a laser light is directed only to a part of a photographic plate (1980: 145-7). As we shall see is also the case with Lacan's topologies, Bohm indicates the importance of the 4-D space dimension. He tells us "the implicate order has to be considered as a process of enfoldment and unfoldment in a higher-dimensional space. Only under certain conditions can this be simplified as a process of enfoldment and unfoldment in three dimensions" (1980: 189).

CHAOS, PSYCHOANALYTIC SEMIOTICS, AND CRIMINOLOGY

Iteration and meta-modeling can also be useful in understanding many of the insights generated from Lacanian psychoanalytic semiotics that sees an inescapable connection between discourse and subjectivity. Although there is no evidence that Lacan drew from chaos theory, especially in light of the fact that most of contemporary theorizing in chaos theory has developed after Lacan's death in 1981, there can be useful reconceptualizing of many of his ideas in light of chaos. This reconceptualization could then supply high-powered analytic tools in doing postmodern criminology.

Let's consider Lacan's notion of the signifier (S) as that which represents the subject ($) for another signifier (S) (see chapters 2 and 9; Lacan, 1977: 316). The use of an algorithm for metaphor and of a topological construction, the Mobius band, are indicative of iteration at work. Lacan's algorithm for metaphor (Lacan, 1977), an iterative polynomial that is more in the form of a matheme rather than strict mathematical form, one of the two operative mechanisms at work in structuring the unconscious like a language, is formulated as:

$$f(S`/S)S \approx S(+)s, \text{ or: } S/S` \cdot S`/x \rightarrow S(1/s)$$

What this represents is how signifiers attain new meaning. S`/S represents how it is that a new signifier, S`, comes to replace and stand for an old signifier, S. Thus, f(S`/S)S represents this movement creating meaning.

The "crossing of the bar," the movement from the top position to the position below the bar, or S(+)s, represents the "poetic spark" that creates meaning according to Lacan. The right-hand side formulation is rewritten to indicate this process. In topological terms, the Mobius band (see chapter 2) represents the same movement:

Lacan tells us that the movement along the Mobius band is such that the signifier returns in inverted form as a "more than one." In other words, this is similar to the notion of an iteration. The signifier, the word, always takes on new meaning in new contexts; it undergoes semiotic iteration (for an application to law, see also Balkin, 1987; Derrida, 1976). Balkin has applied this to show how legal terms undergo continuous change; the call by some legal practitioners for a return to "original intent" of the "Founding Fathers" in defining key clauses within the Constitution, therefore, is illusory.

Since the signifier represents the subject, in Lacan's formulation, then the subject too undergoes this process, always returning in inverted form as a "more than one." What gives stability to the signifier and to the subject is "repetition." This has been previously shown by the use of the Mobius band and the cross-cap with Schema R (see chapter 2).

The signifier, as well as the subject, then, can be more usefully conceptualized as following chaos principles for their very stability: both order and disorder prevail. The subject and the signifier return in inverted form as something new, but yet the old is still maintained as an attractor. This is quite apparent in the continuous effects of symptoms, or even in Lacan's discussion of the borromean knots and *le sinthome* (see chapter 3). Nonlinearity, iteration, indeterminacy, and attractors are implicated in this line of investigation.

This has ramifications in doing criminology. Various stories, or narrative constructions, from witness recollections, police reports, jury decision-making, judicial appeals, etc., are implicated in iterative reconstructions. The initial "what happened" can never be congruently reconstructed in the Symbolic Order; it always returns as a "more than one."

We can see this also in Lacan's complex constructions of the Graphs of Desire (Lacan, 1977; Milovanovic, 1992a). These graphs indicate how the subject is constituted by imaginary, symbolic, and real effects. (A reconceptualization of this is to be found in the borromean knots.) The graphs show how various feedback loops effect other feedback loops, all at once, in producing the decentered subject. Our meta-modeling, constituted by various iterative loops that are intersecting, could represent these complex interlocking structures and effects. The subject is therefore spread out along these complex networks. Attractors are implicated in so much as overall stability ("consistency") does exist; however, indeterminacy prevails at any instance as the intersecting iterative loops produce effects. As Lacan tells us "what the graph [of desire] now offers us is situated at the point at which every signifying chain prides itself on looping its signification" (1977: 316).

Even more suggestive of a chaos integration is Lacan's use of the imaginary number, the square root of -1, to represent "lack." All signifiers are inherently lacking in Lacan's formulation; they are inherently "empty." They "fill up" only in their enunciation. This is particularly so with personal pronouns, which assume the function of "shifters": they gain meaning only in use by a speaking subject. Accordingly, S, the signifier = -1, and the signified, s, = square root of -1, or the imaginary number, i (Lacan, 1977: 316-21). As he tells it, the square root of -1 symbolizes a "signifier of the lack" and, as symbol i in complex number theory, "is obviously justified only because it makes no claim to any automatism in the later use" (1977: 318-9). It represents the "place of jouissance" (1977: 320). In a phallocentric Symbolic Order, the unifying principle, the law-of-the-father, is the phallus representing not the biological organ, but power, potency, the signifier of ecstasy. All signifying production includes as terms, i, and the force of the law-of-the-father. It is what makes the Symbolic Order phallocentric. As Clement points out,

> since it is the signifier of a lack, the phallus is analogous in form to the square root of -1, the primordial imaginary number and generator of the whole field of complex numbers....[it] is literally indescribable...without this generic signifier of negativity, however, no other signifier would exist. It is from this that the phallus derives its generative power (1983: 180).

Lacan is indicating that the imaginary number, i , is not expressible, "but its operation is not inexpressible" (1977: 316). It is what undergoes continuous semiotic iteration in discursive production with effects. Take, for example, Rapaport's analysis of Theodor Fontaine's *Effi Briest* applying the borromean knots and the notion of lack being iterated: "for Lacan the phantasm is always constituted as repetition, and comes into appearance not simply because the Lacanian object (a) is lacking, but because that lack is iterated with special effects in each of the Lacanian topological orders" (1990: 243). Thus for Rapaport, this "dis-appearance is repeated throughout the psychological topology of the Borromean knot in ways that, to some extent conserve what it is that vanishes" (1990: 243).

We can never say what we want and always want to say what we can not. What we say is always more that what we mean. The *i* is ubiquitous in discursive production and in *being* itself. It is for this reason that Lacan also refers to the subject as a fading subject, represented by a capital S with a slash running through it.

This, however, also provides the very opportunity for change, as Drucilla Cornell has argued in her feminist analysis of law (1991). It is because "slippage of meaning" and a "disruptive excess" exist in discourse that we are able to escape from the imprisonment of discourse itself and imagine the possible and to turn a subordination into an affirmation (1991: 147-8, 169, 171, 178).

Finally, Lacan has indicated his very notion of "structure" is not one of equilibrium or homeostasis, but more in accord with far-from-equilibrium conditions (Ragland, 1995: 158, 169; Ragland-Sullivan, 1990b: 58). According to Ragland-Sullivan, his notion of structure is at the same time "static and dynamic," "regulatory and disruptive," "anticipatory and retroactive" (1990b: 58), indicating the very dynamics chaos theory suggests. Just as Carl Jung had suggested the efficacious primordial symbol, the Mandala, in the deeper recesses of the unconscious, functioning much like a master attractor, perhaps, with Butz (1992a, 1992b), we can suggest that the primordial symbol is the Mandelbrot Set.

DISCUSSION

Postmodern criminology has many conceptual tools at its disposal to more sensitively investigate many of the kinds of crimes described as revolving around the visceral, sensual, excitement, emotion, pleasure, and adrenalin rush. Merely using some form of cost-benefit and other forms of "rationality" analysis, as in modernist thought, does a disservice in understanding these forms of deviance. Exciting times await those who take up the challenge of doing postmodern criminology. Several lines of critical inquiry have been suggested that fundamentally challenge the modernist paradigm.

First, the notion of cause has become problematic. The modernist framework is heavily rooted in linear dynamics. Postmodern theory suggests that the cosmos is more chaotic and that nonlinearity is the more dominant force. Our futile search for the "causes" of crime in modernist thought is so because of the underlying truth claim that can not further an understanding of the nature of crime. Discontinuities arise, we have shown, which raise fundamental questions about the findings and conclusions in empirical investigations. A nonlinear assumption may lead researchers to develop models of causation that allow for the discontinuous, the random, the spontaneous, ironies, contradictions, and chance events that have no other explanation. Nietzsche, and Foucault after him, have already suggested this in their historical genealogical form of analysis. The notion of iterative loops and COREL sets suggest novel ways of integrating nonlinear assumptions and overdetermining effects. Critical race theorists' focus on the question of the intersectionality of prejudice, domination, and violence certainly are in this direction.

Second, the notion of the subject in criminology must be reconsidered. The notion of the centered subject, the individual, cannot be supported. It's abstract formulations in such notions as the legal subject (juridic subject), or the empirical, rational, positivistic, or "oversocialized" form must wither away. These conceptualizations have political, economic and historical determinants and implicate point and limit attractors in equilibrium (homeostatic) conditions. These impositions have overlooked the abundance of quasiperiodic tori, strange attractors and importance of far-from-equilibrium conditions. The notion of the decentered subject does not relegate one's existence to passivity, fatalism, and despair; rather, as Nietzsche has offered us, and as many contemporary affirmative postmodernist theorists have argued, the question of decidability of the sign, of contingent universalities, and of alternative replacement discourses are there in potentiality and demand a transpraxis to develop to fruition (see also Henry and Milovanovic, 1996).

Third, narrative constructions in law and at all levels of criminal justice processing (e.g., victim and witness recollections; police, probation, guard reports; story-telling in the courtroom; higher judicial opinion-making) implicate semiotic iterative practices, militating against any objective notion of Truth, Objectivity or the possibility of accurately reconstructing events as they had once occurred. Lacan's "graphs of desire," "cross-cap," and use of the Mobius band indicate the many intersecting contributing factors in various fantasies that we create. These, too, because of "repetition," do repeat themselves — this is what gives stability or constancy to the psychic apparatus; but the journey along the Mobius band always returns in inverted form as a "more than one." Semiotic iterations produce new nuanced meanings and constructions. The past is the past; never to be constructed accurately again. The search for the "objective truth" is illusory. We must recognize the fuzziness, the fractal forms of truths that exist (T.R.Young, 1991a, 1991b). Criminal justice policy would indeed look very much different if this were so.

Fourth, the Mandelbrot Set offers us a novel way to make sense of dynamic phenomena. Recent work in criminology that borders on the postmodernist can be usefully integrated with the dynamics of the Mandelbrot Set. In particular the theoretical investigations that focus on excitement, the visceral, sensual, and adrenalin rush are certainly in this direction. Whether we speak of the "invitational edge" (Matza, 1969), "edgework" (Lyng, 1990), "sneaky thrills" (Katz, 1988), or pleasure (Ferrell, 1995a, 1995b; O'Malley and Mugford, 1994), we note the fuzziness of boundaries that are negotiated; in fact, they have an intrinsic appeal. The boundaries of the Mandelbrot Set indicate the infinite variability that may exist; perhaps, as Ferrell, Lyng, Katz, O'Malley and Mugford have suggested, we need to develop a macrolevel analysis of the political economy of pleasure. We would hasten to add that we need to integrate: (1) this macrolevel analysis, (2) a microlevel analysis whereby subjects confront structured opportunities, and (3) the connectedness between the first two in explaining these various forms of activities and crimes.

CONCLUSION

In this chapter we have been further concerned with postmodern methodologies. We have suggested some directions for further inquiry. Most importantly, for affirmative postmodernists, is their desire for the development of a more humanistic world, one in which diverse desires may have room for embodiment in recognized discourses. Affirmative postmodern methodologies advocate an expansion in presenting "ways of describing possibilities." But this cannot take place by theorizing alone. Active struggle is what creates the "decidability" of the sign. And changes must take place in the Symbolic, the Imaginary and the Real Orders.

Catastrophe Theory, Crime, and Peacemaking

INTRODUCTION

Discontinuities experienced in rather orderly systems are puzzling in criminology. Much of these occur in interpersonal conflicts that undergo escalating dynamics until an abrupt, nonlinear change is experienced (Katz, 1988). Accordingly, along with the importance of chaos theory, and discourse (psychoanalytic semiotics), the third area we would like to offer, as promising to the development of postmodern methodologies, has been linked by Lyotard (1984) to catastrophe theory as developed by Rene Thom (1975; see also Zeeman, 1976; Oliva, Day, and MacMillan, 1988; Oliva, Michael, and Murphy, 1981; Baack and Cullen, 1994; Casti, 1994).

Catastrophe theory has been applied to beams buckling, ships capsizing, prison riots, the fall of communism in Eastern Europe, the collapse of civilizations, stock-market crashes, market competition, bargaining behavior, centralization or decentralization in organizational decision-making, treatment for anorexia, and morphogenesis, to name a few (see generally, Casti, 1994; Baack and Cullen, 1994; Zeeman, 1977; Oliva, Day and MacMillan, 1988).

We would like first, to explain the construction of the "cusp catastrophe generic model" along with some possible applications in doing postmodern criminology. And, second, we will turn to the "butterfly catastrophe" in indicating its importance for conflict regulation, harm reduction, and peacemaking.

CUSP CATASTROPHE GENERIC MODEL

Thom developed a mathematics (topology) that expressed the discontinuities that may arise in deterministic systems. Thom (1975) and Zeeman (1976) have identified seven forms of catastrophes that extend to 6-D space (depending on how many variables are needed); however, with even more variables, higher-dimensional space is required. The mathematics for the catastrophes have been worked out by Thom (1975). These are stated as the "classification theorem." Given, for example, two input variables and a single behavioral variable, then a geometry can be developed relating them to each other in typical fashion represented by a topological structure. If the actual description varies somewhat from this model, it will be unstable and a small perturbation will return it to the more stable form (Casti, 1994: 60; see also Zeeman, 1976: 79-80; 1977: 331-4). Higher-dimensional models can not be visualized easily; nevertheless, the geometry and topology define the movement of the dynamic system and the researcher must study it analytically and perhaps intuitively. Certain devices, such as taking slices or sections, can reduce a higher-dimensional model by one, and thereby allow a better visualization of what is taking place.

A three-dimensional model (figure 1a, b) begins with two independent variables, or "control parameters." One is referred to as the "normal" control variable. The second variable is called the "splitting factor." This factor can be seen as a "moderator" "that specifies the conditions under which the normal factor affects the dependent variable continuously or discontinuously" (Baack and Cullen, 1994: 214). Or, rather than a "normal" and "splitting factor" we could have two "normal factors" that are conflictual influences on our behavioral parameter (Zeeman, 1977: 332-3). An example would be Konrad Lorenz's study of rage and fear as conflicting factors influencing aggression. Together, the control parameters make up the "control space," or C. And then we have some dependent variable, the behavioral parameter, X, under investigation. This is the "cusp catastrophe model."

There are five identified features that indicate the existence of the dynamics of a cusp catastrophe (Thom, 1975; Zeeman, 1976, and lucidly presented by Oliva, Day, and MacMillan, 1988). They are: (1) bimodality (two outcome basins appear), (2) abrupt transitions (sudden movement from one outcome basin to another), (3) hysteresis (sudden changes in one direction are not symmetrical in the other direction), (4) inaccessibility (in the cusp region, two outcome basins appear with an additional middle one being a highly unlikely occurrence), and (5) divergence (initial changes, or perturbations in initial conditions may result in disproportional effects) (Zeeman, 1976: 76; see also Oliva, Day and MacMillan, 1988: 377-8; Baack and Cullen, 1994: 215-6). As Zeeman instructs us, "If any one of them is apparent in a process, the other four should be looked for, and if more than one is found, then the process should be considered a candidate for description as a cusp catastrophe" (1976: 76).

Let's provide an example already in the literature. And then we would like to draw attention to a recent synthesis work by O'Malley and Mugford (1994), which can be modeled.

Lyotard (1984) and Zeeman (1976) give us an example of aggressiveness of a dog (this is the state variable). It is said to be directly proportional to the dog's anger, which is defined as a control ("independent") variable or parameter. When a certain level of anger is reached, it is predicted that an attack will follow. The second possible control variable is fear. But here, when reaching a certain level, flight will occur, the reverse of the first response. We begin at a hypothetical point of stability. Anger and fear are at a minimum. As the two control variables (anger and fear) increase, the two threshold levels (for attack and flight) will be approached at the same time. So far, linearity, a deterministic equation can indicate this. But at the threshold, the dog will switch from attack to flight (i.e., two-periods, or attractor basins, or bimodality). Here we have a bifurcation with two possible outcomes. The dog's behavior is unpredictable; the system is unstable. This instability exists even though the control variables (anger and fear) are continuous. The state variables are discontinuous.

Figure 1. The Cusp Catastrophe Portrait and Postmodern Crime
a. 3-D Portrait

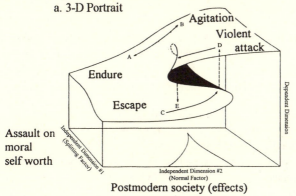

b. 1-D Portrait

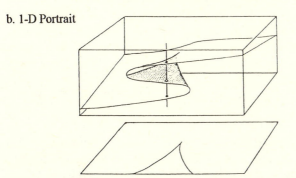

(Adapted from Zeeman, 1976; Abraham, 1992; Casti, 1994)

In the cusp catastrophe model (see figures 1a and b), the state space, or the dependent variable, is the vertical axis and the wavy (upper) plane with a smooth double-fold that is generated. This is the behavioral space. The horizontal 2-D plane represents the control plane (x, y coordinates), reflecting two independent variables. Where the two independent variables intersect we may trace a perpendicular line that extends upward toward the smooth double-folded plane, which represents behavior (the dependent variable). Note the "cusp" region (the folded plane) in the center and its projection (the "bifurcation set") on the bottom surface. This region will be significant in the production of nonlinear effects. The middle pleat represents highly improbable behavior, e.g., neutrality; that is, fear and anger do not cancel each other out. Said differently, this is the region of inaccessibility.

"Folds" are involved where we have one control and one response parameter and hence appear in 2-D. Briggs and Peat (1989) provide the example of blowing up a balloon; at a certain point it bursts; in other words, a catastrophe has emerged. "Cusps," on the other hand, have two control and one response parameter and can be modeled in 3-D. Folds and cusps indicate where outcome values "jump" from one value to another in a nonlinear manner. In other words, at the edge of the fold the outcome will jump to the higher or lower plane; this reflects discontinuous (nonlinear) change (up to that point we had continuous change). This is represented in figure 1a and b as a jump from one plane to another, as in D to C and D to E. This jump can also be conceptualized as a bifurcation. We have two outcome basins (bimodal).

In the figure 1b we see that the vertical line identifies two distinct point attractors. (Bimodality can be traced to the work of conflicting factors or to the splitting factor.) This one-dimensional line represents a portrait, or state space in this 3-D response diagram. Outside of the cusp region there is only one attractor, or outcome basin (see chapter 11), a point attractor (Abraham, 1992; Zeeman, 1976). A catastrophe is defined as "a bifurcation where an attractor appears or disappears" (Abraham, 1992: 11-49; McRobie and Thompson, 1994: 155). McRobie and Thompson have well stated that: "With gradual changes in [a] parameter, attractors generally evolve smoothly, but at certain critical points, called bifurcations, the attractor may split into different attractors or may simply disappear" (1994: 155). The strengths of the generic cusp catastrophe model also pose some weaknesses that we shall discuss below.

CUSP CATASTROPHE MODEL AND CRIMINOLOGY

Let's provide an example, an intriguing synthesis by O'Malley and Mugford (1994) that builds on the work of Katz (1988) and Lyng's analysis of "edgework" (1990). O'Malley and Mugford suggest that both Katz and Lyng are providing answers to "explaining the dilemma of the modern self" (1994: 200), and the effects of the coming of [post]modern society where alienation and the hyperreal (Baudrillard), clock time, and commodification (the law of equivalence, see for example, chapter 7) are being responded to by a search for experiences that arouse visceral, sensual, and emotional states (the "foreground factors"). Thus a more Nietzschian vision rather than just a materialistic explanation of the onset of extreme forms of behavior is offered.

The difference between Katz's approach and Lyng's is that for Katz, the person welcomes the loss of control ("righteous slaughter"), but for Lyng, the person attempts to maintain control under extreme conditions (skydiving). But in both cases the person is subjecting her/himself to extreme experiences in order to develop "mood changes as a form of resistance or escape from the mundane" (1994: 193-4; see also Ferrell, 1995a, 1995b). Perhaps what could be developed here is a triangle of crime: the offender/tester of boundaries or the "invitational edge" (Katz, 1988; Lyng, 1990; but also see Halleck, 1967; Matza, 1964, 1969; Salecl, 1993; Ferrell, 1995b); the corrector (agents of social control, or generally, agents of the disciplining mechanisms spelled out by Foucault); and the reporter (the journalist, cinema producer, criminologist) — the three complete the cycle in these forms of arousals of the sensual. The onset of crime is codeterminous, as we have spelled out in our constitutive theory (see also chapters 4, 8; Henry and Milovanovic, 1996).

In our example, drawing from Katz's (1988) study of "righteous slaughter" and from O'Malley and Mugford's integration (1994), we first identify the dependent variable, located on the behavioral space, as behavior that might result from the interacting effects of the two independent variables (or control parameters) pictured on the control space (here a 2-D plane). The behavioral space may include the states: endure, escape, agitation, and violent attack (see figure 1a). The "normal factor" (control parameter, variable, or "independent dimension") is the emergence of postmodern society and some of its effects: here we collapse O'Malley and Mugford's (1994) three suggestive factors — increasing alienation and hyperreal, clock time, and commodification — into a single variable.

Of course "collapsing" often entails the danger that variables are not necessarily correlated or covarying, an assumption that does not bide well with our notion spelled out elsewhere of constitutive interrelational sets (see chapter 11; Henry and Milovanovic, 1996). But for this example we follow the author's suggestions that they indeed are covarying. Future investigation could attempt to modify the generic model to encompass the various possible integrations and respond to some limitations. We shall return to this in our discussion section.

The second independent variable, the "splitting factor," would be a perceived assault on moral self-worth (Katz, 1988). Thus the increasing effects of postmodern society in interaction with increasing perceptions of assaults on moral self worth could produce an increasing intensity in the emotional state, "humiliation." For Katz, it means "the person is overcome with an intolerable discomfort....[it] takes over the soul by invading the whole body" (1988: 25). In a mild form this would manifest itself by the subject enduring these defilements of self; in greater intensities it may translate into aggressive display, posturing, etc.; and in its most intense forms, humiliation may manifest in rage and violent attack.

In figure 1a, we note that as the normal factor (the effects of postmodern society) increases from left to right, various subjective states will also vary in a linear way (A to B). For example, behaviors that indicate that the subject is enduring the interacting effects of postmodern society and attacks on moral self-worth (upper left quadrant) could move in a linear way towards agitation (upper right quadrant), whereby manifest are lesser harms in installments as well as aggressive display, posturing, verbal "dozens," etc. Here we have continuities.

The splitting factor, assault on moral self-worth, may be a factor for the production of this continuity, or for its discontinuity. The lines CD and DE indicate discontinuous change (i.e., the jumps noted from one plane to another along an S-looking fold). Small differences in the initial conditions, i.e., the initial values, of the normal and the splitting variables may produce divergences. The acceptance of increasing humiliation and the escape option (following Katz, the subject may take comfort in feeling that there will be other times and places where s/he will be free from humiliation) may follow in a linear path but at the double-fold an unexpected radical change will occur. In other words, the acceptance of humiliation and the escape option might be maintained until one reaches the area of the double fold; here humiliation would be transformed into rage and violent attack (Katz, 1988). In figure 1a we see this as the movement from C to D; note the "jump." Of course it could also work the other way: the line D to E indicates a situation where violent attack is imminent but abruptly changes to escape. Thus, we have either an "escape" (D to E) or "violent attack" (C to D) catastrophe (e.g., bimodal behavior).

This model is useful in our understanding of escalating hostilities and violence in various interpersonal situations. Arguments or differences (which often have anger and fear as latent constitutive elements) could initially take on more sober, rational tones, but with an increase in reciprocating incremental assaults on self, may culminate in the cusp region, where an additional small increase of either control parameter may produce an unexpected violent attack. In an increasingly diverse society it would seem that societal-wide strategies need to be devised wherein disputants can safely "walk away" or deescalate from spiraling emotional states (as presented in a currently running public-service announcement, discussed below), allowing cooler discussions of differences to prevail at a later date. We shall develop this in the next section. However, two limitations exist: the entrenched "frontier" ideology of holding one's ground; and unevenly distributed, politically and economically determined "life chances," removing the option of "escape" for many disenfranchised (whereby one can fantasize another time and place where one will not be subjected to the defiles of self). In both situations the spiral may continue. Where hope, possibilities, and life chances in a political economy are vastly restricted, so too the possibilities of defusing escalating hostilities.

Our more postmodern-oriented model, building on O'Malley and Mugford's recent integration, suggests the occurrence of certain kinds of crimes (and edgework) that do not follow linear logic. Rather, discontinuities would likely occur without an external observer being able to predict that from a small increase in the control parameters, crimes, such as those explained by Katz entailing "moral transcendence" would happen. These would be hard to explain. As O'Malley and Mugford tell it, "transcendence appears to involve crossing (or at the very least 'playing with') a threshold or limit between being in and out of rational control in order to experience the self in the grip of emotional or moral forces" (1994: 191). We see much affinity between the previous analysis and Matza's early work (1969) on the "invitational edge" and the necessity of a "leap" into deviance, or in the reestablishment of the "mood of humanism" (1964; see also Salecl's "mode of subjectivization," 1993).

BUTTERFLY CATASTROPHE, LINGUISTIC COORDINATE SYSTEMS, AND CONFLICT REGULATION: PEACEMAKING

In the previous section we applied the cusp catastrophe model in explaining how nonlinear dynamics may lie behind various forms of crime. In this section we want to show how the "butterfly catastrophe" could be used to explain how, out of seemingly polarized positions, a "third way" could arise in various conflict situations. This would be an important addition to those who have focused on conflict regulation, mediation, and resolution. Black (1976), in *The Behavior of Law*, for example, has advocated a "conciliatory style of social control," and more recently a "peacemaking perspective" has been developed within radical criminology (Pepinsky and Quinney, 1991). Neither position, however, has made convincing forays into how "third positions" could develop and how, perhaps, they may attain efficacious institutional status, a degree of stability, in a social formation. Although, ultimately, the particular repressive mode of production must change before real mediation and social justice can take place, we need not wait for the "revolution" while persons are harmfully affected in various interpersonal situations.

We have chosen the butterfly catastrophe because it has clear implications for explaining how "third positions" may theoretically develop. This model has been applied to explaining therapy for anorexia (Zeeman, 1976), to how a "chiefdom" could develop as a society moves otherwise from a centered to a noncentered type of society (Casti, 1994: 76-7), to the emergence of a compromise opinion in the development of war policy as hawks and doves seek to effectuate their respective policies (Zeeman, 1976, 1977), and to the development of an alternative in the debates between those who advocate censorship versus those who advocate "uncensorship" (Zeeman, 1977: 349-56).

CONSTRUCTION

The construction of the butterfly catastrophe can be briefly described. Previously, in the cusp catastrophe model, we had two control parameters producing a 2-D control space, and one behavioral surface reflecting the behavioral states. We thus had a 3-D catastrophe model with a 2-D bifurcation set projected on the control space. We also had bimodal behavior in the cusp region. With the butterfly catastrophe we increase the control parameters by up to four and maintain one behavioral surface, but now with trimodal behavior within a "pocket" region. The intersection and interpenetration of several surfaces produces a "pocket" that suggests a butterfly, hence the name for this generic catastrophe. Here we have a 5-D model, with a 4-D projection of the bifurcation set. Or put in another way, we have a 4-D control space and an additional dimension for the behavioral surface giving us 5-D.

This catastrophe cannot be drawn, but we can do two things to simplify. First, we can take slices, subsets, or sections of the bifurcation set, reducing it first to 3-D and then, with another slice, to 2-D. Second, two of the control parameters, for the sake of illustration, could be suppressed.

The butterfly catastrophe has four control parameters: a, the normal factor; b, the splitting factor; c, the "bias" factor; and d, the butterfly factor. The bias factor alters the shape and position of the cusp. It moves the cusp to the left or to the right, with the vertex pointing the opposite way in each instance. The bias factor also effects the behavior surface in an upward or downward direction The butterfly factor is what is responsible for the third stable form of behavior; it is what makes the outcome trimodal. As the value for the butterfly factor increases, the cusp located on the control surface develops into three cusplike structures, which together form a triangular structure, looking very much like a pocket. By varying "c" and "d," this pocket can be enlarged, narrowed, or deleted. Between the top and bottom sheets of the behavioral surface of figure 1 we would see this additional triangular surface (see figure 3) (Zeeman, 1976: 80; 1977: 336-9; Casti, 1994: 63-9). Keep in mind that figure 3 represents a projection of the bifurcation set onto the parameter plane being affected by "c" and "d."

To actually see this 5-D structure we can draw various 2-D slices of the control space (see figure 2).

Figure 2. 2-D Sections (Slices) of the Butterfly Catastrophe Bifurcation Set

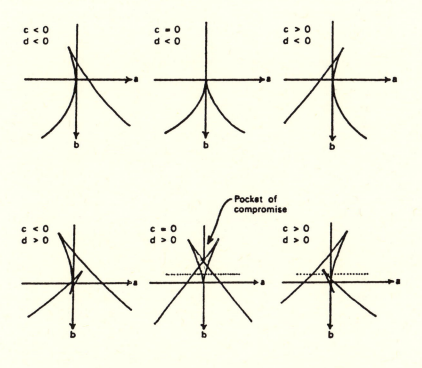

(Adopted from Zeeman, 1977: 337)

"Each section," Zeeman tells us, "is an (a,b) — plane drawn for (c,d) = constant..." (1977: 338). This would indicate what the bifurcation set would look like. In figure 2 note what happens when "c," the bias factor, is less than 0, when it is equal to 0, and when it is greater than 0, while "d," the butterfly factor, is less than 0 (see the top row of figure 2). The cusp swings to the left or to the right. Now consider when we vary "d," particularly when we make it greater than 0. A "pocket of compromise" emerges. Actually, the effect is to produce three cusps (the bottom row of figure 2). The center frame of figure 2, bottom row, shows a V-looking structure indicating three cusps forming a triangular pocket. Again, this is the pocket of compromise.

Zeeman also notes that "the bias factor...tends to destroy a compromise" (1976: 80). Note for example, that the "pocket" is largest when c = 0. When the values of "d," the butterfly factor, are positive, then the pocket emerges and we have trimodal behavior. With "d" being positive, positive or negative values of "c" will move the pocket to the left or right on the behavioral surface and indicate which "wing" of the butterfly is dominant (Casti, 1994: 76).

Figure 3. A Partial Picture of the Butterfly Catastrophe

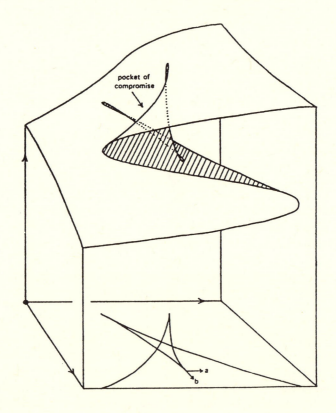

(Adopted from Zeeman, 1977: 338)

The illustrative picture is represented in figure 3. Again, for demonstration purposes, factors "c" and "d" have been suppressed with their effects nevertheless being indicated. Comparing this to figure 1 we see how a new "sheet" has surfaced between the top behavioral surface and the bottom one. Note that as the butterfly factor increases above the value of 0, the "pocket" emerges and grows. The bias factor swings it to the left or right (Zeeman, 1977: 338-9).

APPLICATION TO CRIMINOLOGY

We are now ready to apply the butterfly catastrophe model to doing postmodern criminology. Our goal is to provide some suggestions for how a "peace rhetoric" could act as the "butterfly factor" in deescalating spiraling conflicts in various interpersonal situations and produce a "third way or option," namely, nonviolence. We are only too aware of the escalating nature in the development of violence in "domestic situations," in street-corner encounters, in police interactions with citizens, in guards dealing with prisoners, and generally during various interactions citizens have with the criminal justice system and its operatives. We offer a direction to give further momentum to the development of the conciliatory style of social control, peacemaking, and social justice.

We need first to define our four control parameters. From our previous example, we shall define the normal factor, "a," as the effects of postmodern society, defined in terms of alienation and the hyperreal, clocktime, and commodification or capital logic and the law of equivalence. The splitting factor "b," will be defined as assault on moral self-worth. The bias factor, "c," we will identify as "life chances." Numerous well-established sociological research indicates that life chances are differentially distributed, correlated quite well with structural location in a social formation in terms of socioeconomic indices. The butterfly factor, "d," will be identified as discourse or linguistic coordinate systems (see chapters 2, 3).

The bias factor, life chances, given the effects of postmodern society and assaults on moral self, may contribute to the "escape" or the "attack" option on the behavioral plane in figure 1 (respectively, the lower left and right quadrants). Recall, that if we follow Katz (1988: 22), "when tensions arise on the job, one may feel severe humiliation but there are possible escapes: other people, other times, other social places in which one can expect to be free of humiliation," then the key is an escape option. Two points here are important. First, those subjects who are the brunt of alienation, clock time, and commodification may find their "escape" option greatly limited. And second, as Katz tells it, there are "places of last resort" such as "casual life, affectionate relationships, the weekend and Saturday night, or drinking and cruising Main Street...for the pursuit of relaxed fun" (1988: 22). Here, if one cannot make use of the escape option, there may be perceived nowhere else to go. The attack option may become an alternative consideration. Katz, for example, has shown how spiraling emotions may lead to humiliation, rage, and violent attack. As he tells us, "in some cases...the assailant's rage emerges so suddenly and silently that only when it appears does a preceding experience of humiliation become visible" (1988: 22). This suggests a discontinuity, and hence a catastrophe.

The butterfly factor is identified as discourse or linguistic coordinate systems. In chapter 3, the "elementary cell of speech production" indicated how the subject is intimately connected with discourse. In chapter 2, we indicated this further by explaining the nature of the decentered subject in discourse. Lacan has also provided the four discourses. Following Lacan, a signifier represents the subject for another signifier. The subject, the *parletre* or the *l'être parlant* (the speaking, or speaking being) is intimately connected with the discourse within which it inserts itself to create various narratives. Discourse, in this view, is performative: it produces effects in behavior (see also chapter 2).

Consider, Julia and Herman Schwendingers' (1985) discussion of the different and shifting "moral rhetorics" that are associated with juvenile life. The "instrumental rhetoric" "disregards egoistic standards of fairness" and "assumes people to be engaged in a vast power struggle, with the weak and the powerless as legitimate victims" (1985: 136-7). As the Schwendingers inform us: "...rhetorical devices—words like Punk, Chump, Mark, and Mother fucker—incorporate sufficient meaning to justify illegal acts, especially personal victimization, all by themselves" (1985: 141). The juvenile, therefore, acquires words (signifiers), some of which justify victimization. Consider again the Schwendingers: "The increasing adoption of these victim words signals the gradual acquisition of a working ethic, of motives, rationales for action, images of victimizers and their victims, and assumptions about reality" (1985: 148).

We could also cite other works on various discourses and their effects: Cressey (1953) with embezzlers, particularly the "vocabulary of motives" such as rationalizations found in the work environment that justify or excuse embezzlement; Sykes and Matza (1957), with their idea of "techniques of neutralization"; Matza (1964) with his idea of neutralizations found in peer groups; Arrigo (1996) in his research on discourses that justify legal commitment to psychiatric institutions, to name a few (see also the "applications" section in part 2 of this book).

Given the negative effects of discourse, we want to now look at the positive potentials. We already have seen the importance of various television campaigns to curtail various forms of violence: a public service announcement shows a potential flare up between two high-school students, and then the message, "just walk away"; an anti-drug commercial says "say no to drugs"; an antirape commercial says, "no means no!"; and an antialcohol commercial says "don't drink and drive." The effectiveness of these various rhetorics have yet to be fully understood. However, there does seem to be a link to the potential ceasing of otherwise spiraling phenomena that may lead to abrupt violent episodes.

Consider, for example Katz's study (1988) of "righteous slaughter." Confronted with humiliation, an attack on moral self-worth, the subject may envision a future where the humiliation would no longer exist, the escape option, or he may also attempt to abolish it by conjuring up various culturally stable narratives (1988: 24-5). According to Katz:

> He tries to abolish the unbearable awful feeling by reciting folk recipes: "time heals all wounds"; "he's drunk, he doesn't mean it and won't remember it"; "she's upset because of her period"; "life goes on"; "I don't need him, I'll leave"; or "I'll move, and my new associates won't know about my past." (1988: 25)

Katz also stresses that even these at times do not work, even when one may resort to "counting to ten," a form of a "time-out" rhetoric. We pick up on this theme to indicate that Katz's investigations are suggestive in indicating that, first, certain narrative devices may in fact curtail escalating or spiraling emotional states that abruptly end in rage and attack, and, second, at times even these narrative devices do not work. The latter notwithstanding, we nevertheless want to push ahead to suggest perhaps a form of minimizing much of this spiraling phenomena and abrupt end in violence.

The implications of the research on discourse and narrative constructions are that various rhetorics may be functional in minimizing some form of escalating and abrupt violence in various settings. We would therefore suggest the development of a "peace rhetoric" or a "peace discourse." Campaigns in the media and within the school system could focus on these rhetorics with attached imageries that sustain them. Thus the Symbolic and Imaginary Orders, to follow Lacan (see chapters 2, 3), are mutually implicated in this process. Returning to figure 3, we could envision the butterfly factor, "peace rhetoric" or the "peace discourse," as offsetting the effects of postmodern society, attacks on moral self-worth, and diminished life chances. However, we cannot remain optimistic that most forms of violence will be curtailed. Clearly, the structural components of a postmodern society need to be dealt with. Our suggestion, if more limited, would be a short range crisis-intervention tool that should not be envisioned as supporting the contemporary arrangements in society with their structurally defined life chances and vulnerabilities. We do not, however, subscribe to some romantic revolutionary's ideal of letting the system collapse with the various contradictions in order to allow the "good" society to appear. To use Van den Haag's idea, we cannot wait while a barn is burning with children inside when we do have available buckets of water. Attempts at eradicating escalating violence in various interpersonal situations are worthy and should be developed.

Our synthesis suggests that given the continuous emergence of localities of interpersonal communication where differences will appear, and that these differences may be initiated and/or amplified by the effects of our normal factor (postmodern society and its effects), splitting factor (assault on moral self-worth), and bias factor (the effects of differential life chance), that a peace rhetoric sufficiently stabilized within various cultural spaces may militate against the continued spiraling nature found where emotions run high and sometimes abruptly change into violent attack. This would be portrayed in figure 3 as the "pocket" that emerges, the "third position." From seemingly polarized positions, we find that we may create a viable option. Bimodal behavior changes into trimodal forms.

What we are suggesting is that, consistent with the works such as Katz's (1988) and Matza's (1969), which indicate that at a certain moment in the escalation process the person finds him/herself now more object than subject, that creating time intervals, time-lags, may provide the pause necessary to return the "pacified" subject into one of a reclaimed subject position.

Of course, the question of the "escape option" remains somewhat problematic. Katz, for example, says that "the lives of those who are higher in the social class system are likely to be so thoroughly different that not just the response but the emergence and shape of humiliation may also be radically different" (1988: 46-7). Clearly, we need further investigations that focus on this issue. It may be, in the end, for a peace rhetoric to work it needs to be culturally sensitive and socioeconomically targeted. Doing ethnographic work with teenagers in the schools and their hanging-out places would help, for example, in understanding negative rhetorics and escape options, and how to devise peace rhetorics. These peace rhetorics would be in the form of "contingent universalities"; that is, subject to continuous examination, change, deletion, and substitution. Just as clearly, life chance must be changed to allow those further down the economic ladder greater opportunities for self- and community-actualization.

DISCUSSION
Catastrophe theory has strengths and weaknesses. It must be carefully applied when examining social-science phenomena. Explanation is its goal, not prediction.

Catastrophe theory can be used for hypothesis testing (Zeeman, 1977: 332-56; Oliva, Day and MacMillan, 1988: 384-86; Baack and Cullen, 1994: 218-24), theorem construction, modeling (Thom, 1975), and for establishing laws of transformation summarizing experimental results (see for example, our iterative polynomials in chapter 11). Baack and Cullen (1994: 224) have even suggested that "catastrophe theory has the potential to act as a 'middle range' theory..." described by Merton (1968). These "middle range" theories "consolidate empirical findings and are sufficiently abstract to deal with a range of social behaviors and social structures" (Baack and Cullen, 1994: 224). In criminology, catastrophe theory appears very well situated to explain many of the discontinuities that appear in interpersonal encounters where spiraling phenomena sometimes lead to an abrupt violent ending. Doing postmodern criminology may find a useful conceptual tool for the investigation and perhaps alleviation of interpersonal violence in various contexts.

Catastrophe theory, when applied to the social sciences, also has some limitations. First, collapsing multivariate factors into univariate ones may produce the loss of important information (Oliva, Day and MacMillan, 1988: 375). A way of overcoming this potential problem has been developed (Oliva, et al., 1987). They treat the various control parameters as latent and can measure each variable, whether univariate or multivariate measurements.

Second, in applying catastrophe theory to the social sciences we assume that the mathematical relationships connecting the control parameters to the behavioral surface follow the "classification theorem" (Casti, 1994: 79). This is somewhat similar to the "fanciful" part of Gregersen and Sailer's examination of iterative polynomials (see chapter 11).

Third, the generic models are limited to the assumptions of outcomes being point attractors resulting from a "smooth dynamical system" (Casti, 1994: 79). In other words, the generic models of the seven basic catastrophes assume point attractors as the outcome basins. Of course, chaos theory indicates that other attractors exist: cyclical/periodic, quasiperiodic torus, and strange attractors. Dynamic systems following chaos principles show that even very small changes (perturbations) of control parameters may produce qualitatively different outcomes and these end states may be both unpredictable and unstable. Catastrophe is in need of a reconceptualization to account for these other outcomes. Lacking this development, catastrophe theory will be limited to only certain dynamical systems that manifest point attractors. However, Casti makes the case for the use of approximations to generic catastrophe models in studying otherwise inapplicable dynamic social phenomena with a certain amount of qualified success (1994: 81).

Fourth, catastrophe theory may be overly preoccupied with the local level rather than having global significance (Casti, 1994: 80-1). That is, mathematical "jumps" may not be experienced as such in the social world.

They may indeed exist, but may be so small as to be of insignificant consequence for human subjects going about their everyday business.

Fifth, we must presuppose that the coordinate systems being applied in the mathematical model coincide with our measurement of control parameters and behavioral parameters (Casti, 1994: 79-80). Otherwise we must use a transposition, similar to our use of iterative polynomials in chapter 11. And of course, the assumption is that this is indeed possible. We might consider, here, for a moment, Lacan's many usages of algorithms, ideographs, and mathemes that should be used more intuitively, or even poetically, rather than strictly mathematically.

Given these limitations there are some exciting potential developments in reformulation, integration, synthesis of the generic catastrophe models. One potential direction might take our notion of COREL sets (Henry and Milovanovic, 1996) and show how these constitutive interrelational sets are composed of nonlinear iterative loops, which codeterminously produce effects. Our control parameters, therefore, would need to be reconceptualized in terms of a network of COREL sets producing some effect on the behavioral plane. We may still, indeed, witness the discontinuities, folds, and pockets that develop with this reformulated conceptualization. We have some confidence that this is a worthwhile direction for future investigation and certainly will be pursing it.

In our exposition we have indicated the usefulness of catastrophe theory for both understanding the onset of deviance, as well as for a possible way of advancing the conciliatory model of social control toward the end of peacemaking and social justice. Many illuminating insights could follow this direction in doing a postmodern criminology.

CONCLUSION

Catastrophe theory has been identified by Lyotard (1984) as one of the elements of doing postmodern investigations. We have pursued this call in indicating how postmodern criminology can be advanced with these conceptual tools of inquiry. Much further refinement is needed. But we do see applications to both an understanding of certain forms of crimes as well to the development of a peace rhetoric.

Conclusion: Toward the New Orderly (Dis)Order

There once seemed to be a sure way from here to there. Post-Enlightenment thought had projected the path. The new modernist sciences with their notions of the individual, the juridic subject, linear causality, inputs with proportional effects, the value of global knowledge, the neutrality of language and its liberating potentials, the unfolding of history, objectivity, empiricism, the calculus, and so forth, seemed to have clearly pointed the way. Modernist criminology, too, embraced this metaphysics only to find that the path was not the linear one hoped for. Postmodernist thought has undermined the core assumptions guiding this dream machine.

Postmodernist thought, perhaps finding its scion in Jacques Lacan and his integrative work, is offering a new direction. But a clear path it is not. Chaos and catastrophe theory have indicated that continuities and discontinuities can exist side by side, determinism and indeterminism are indeed compatible. The very notion of causation and agency has been fundamentally redeveloped. Modernist criminology has been somewhat unreceptive to opening the doors to the academe. And indeed, postmodernist thought forces the reconsideration of the key assumptions guiding its enterprise. Surely, however, debate will begin. Just as surely, the new insights generated from the necessary dialogue will uncover the factors behind repressive configurations that perpetuate the diminishment of the human spirit. And postmodernist's contribution to social justice will be substantial.

This book has provided some of the themes of doing postmodern criminology. And this work is indeed demanding. Much integration and synthesis is needed. Topology and chaos theory, psychoanalytic semiotics, catastrophe theory, critical theory and much more need to be further developed. The contributions of feminist analysis, critical race theory, dialogical pedagogy, and constitutive theory, among others, will surely invigorate critical scholarship.

In this book we provided an alternative view of the person, the decentered subject. The "speaking being" is intimately connected with the discourse within which it is situated. "Reality" is discursively codetermined. Our notion of constitutive interrelational sets (COREL sets) expanded on this idea. We showed that those in struggle often inadvertently reconstitute forms of domination. To more adequately deal with the dialectics of struggle, we offered the notion of transpraxis as a more sustainable notion rooted more in Nietzsche than in Hegel's master-slave dialectic and the notion of praxis. We moved on to more suggestive, and, no doubt, what will be seen as more controversial analysis rooted heavily in an integration of chaos, catastrophe, and psychoanalytic semiotic theory.

This latter work, being more suggestive and bordering speculative, will surely generate alternative hypotheses building, testing, and refinement, including even deletions. And so it should be. The implications of chaos theory are that a more desirable society is one in which far-from-equilibrium conditions prevail, where dissipative structures are in continuity with each other, where point and limit attractors give way to torus and strange attractors, where the subject is always in process, where sensitivities to initial conditions and the work of iteration continuously produce the unexpected, and where determinacy lives side by side with indeterminacy. This is the new (dis)order. And here lies hope for the better society, one in which community, solidarity, and agency may flourish, bringing out the highest potentialities of the human spirit and soul.

Many questions remain unanswered. What will be the new ethics of this society? What notions of "responsibility" should exist? How will the "bad" disproportionate effects be dealt with? How do we begin to set in motion the movement toward societal far-from-equilibrium conditions? How will the new discourses, replacement discourses, assure some communication, sensitivity, and tolerance across differences? How will new alliance formations both push forth contingent universalities and at the same time be sensitive to the various groups' more particular interests? And how will excesses be dealt with? After all, we are not naive to the effects of excessive investors in harm towards others. The struggle for a better society is the guiding force of our work. Let this book be a contribution for the better society to come.

References

Abel, R. 1982a. "A Socialist Approach to Risk." *Maryland Law Review* 41: 695-754.

———. 1982b. "Torts." In D. Kairys (ed.), *The Politiccs of Law*, pp. 185-200. New York: Pantheon Books.

Abraham, F.D. 1992. *A Visual Introduction to Dynamical Systems Theory for Psychology.* Santa Cruz, CA: Aerial Press.

Althusser, L. 1971. *Lenin and Philosophy.* New York: Monthy Review Press.

American Law Institute.1985. *Model Penal Code and Commentaries.* Philadelphia, PA: The American Law Institute.

Anderson, D.J. 1986. *Curbing the Abuses of Inmate Litigation.* College Park, MD: American Correctional Association.

Andrews, D.A., I. Zinger, R. Hoge, J. Bonta, P. Gendreau, and F. Cullen. 1990. "Does Correctional Treatment Work?" *Journal of Criminology* 28: 369-404.

Aronowitz, S., and H.A. Giroux. 1985. *Education under Siege.* South Hadley, MA: Bergin and Garvey.

———. 1992. *Postmodern Education.* Minneapolis, MN: University of Minnesota Press.

Arrigo, B. 1993a. "The Insanity Defense: A Study in Psychoanalytic Semiotics and Chaos Theory." Paper presented at the 7th Annual Round Table on Law and Semiotics, Reading, PA.

———. 1993b. "An Experientially-Informed Feminist Jurisprudence." *Humanity and Society* 17(1): 28-47.

———. 1993c. *Madness, Language and the Law.* Albany, NY: Harrow and Heston.

———. 1994. "The Insanity Defense." In R. Kevelson (ed.), *The Eyes of Justice.* New York: Peter Lang.

———. 1995a. "The Peripheral Core of Law and Criminology: On Postmodern Social Theory and Conceptual Integration." *Justice Quarterly* 12(3): 447-72.

———. 1995b. "Deconstructing Classroom Instruction: Theoretical and Methodological Contributions of the Postmodern Sciences for Crimino-Legal Education." *Social Pathology* 1(2): 115-148.

———. 1996. *The Contours of Psychiatric Justice: A Postmodern Critique of Mental Illness, Criminal Insanity, and the Law.* New York: Garland.

Athens, L. 1989. *The Creation of Dangerous Violent Criminals.* New York: Routledge.

Baack, D., and J.B. Cullen. 1994. "A Catastrophe Theory Model of Technological and Structural Change." *Journal of High Technology Management Research* 3: 125-45.

Baker, P. 1993. "Chaos, Order and Sociological Theory." *Sociological Inquiry* 63(2): 123-49.

Bakhtin, M. 1981. *The Dialogical Imagination.* Austin, TX: University of Texas Press.

Balbus, I. 1977. *The Dialectics of Legal Repression: Black Rebels before the American Criminal Courts.* New Brunswick, NJ: Transaction Books.

Balint, M. 1957. *The Doctor, His Patient, and the Illness.* New York: International Universities Press.

Balkin, J.M. 1987. "Deconstructive Practice and Legal Theory." *Yale Law Journal* 96(4): 743-86.

Banchoff, T. 1990. *Beyond the Third Dimension.* New York: Scientific American Library.

Bankowski, Z., and G. Mungham. 1976. *Images of Law.* London: Routledge and Kegan Paul.

Bannister, S., and D. Milovanovic. 1990. "The Necessity Defense, Substantive Justice and Oppositional Linguistic Praxis." *International Journal of the Sociology of Law* 18(2): 179-98.

Barak, G. 1988. "Newsmaking Criminology: Reflections on the Media, Intellectuals, and Crime." *Justice Quarterly* 5: 565-87.

———. 1991. "Homelessness and the Case for Community-Based Initiatives: The Emergence of a Model Shelter as a Short-Term Response to the Deepening Crisis in Housing." In H. Pepinsky and R. Quinney (eds.), *Criminology as Peacemaking.* Bloomington, IN: Indiana University Press.

———. 1993. "Media, Crime, and Justice: A Case for Constitutive Criminology," *Humanity and Society* 17(3): 272-96.

Barak, G., and B. Bohm. 1989. "The Crimes of the Homeless or the Crime of Homelessness." *Contemporary Crisis* 13: 275-88.

Barr, S. 1964. *Experiments in Topology.* New York: Dover Publications.

Barthes, R. 1974. *S/Z.* New York: Hill and Wang.

Bartlett, K., and R. Kennedy. 1991a. "Introduction," in K. Bartlett and R. Kennedy (eds.), *Feminist Legal Theory.* Oxford: Westview Press, 1-11.

———. 1991b. "Feminist Legal Methods," in K. Bartlett and R. Kennedy (eds.), *Feminist Legal Theory.* Oxford: Westview Press, pp. 370-403.

Barton, S. 1994. "Chaos, Self-Organization, and Psychology." *American Psychologist* 49(1): 5-14.

Baskin, D. 1988. "Community Mediation and the Public/Private Problem." *Social Justice* 15(1): 98-115.

Baudrillard, J. 1981. *For a Critique of the Political Economy of the Sign.* St. Louis, MO: Telos Press.

———. 1988. *Simulacra and Simulations.* New York: Semiotext(e).

Benedict, H. 1992. *Virgin or Vamp: How the Press Covers Sex Crimes.* New York: Oxford University Press.

Bennet, L., and Feldman, M. 1981. *Reconstructing Reality in the Courtroom.* New Brunswick, NJ: Rutgers University Press.

Benveniste, E. 1971. *Problems in General Linguistics.* Coral Gables, Fla.: University of Miami Press.

Bergson, H. 1958. *Time and Free Will.* New York: Harper and Row.

Berry, M. 1994. "Quantum Physics on the Edge of Chaos." In N. Hall (ed.), *Exploring Chaos.* New York: W.W. Norton.

Bianchi, H., and R. van Swaaningen, eds. 1986. *Abolitionism: Towards a Non-Repressive Approach to Crime.* Amsterdam: Free Press.

Bigman, P. 1979. *Discretion, Determinate Sentencing and the Illinois Prisoner Review Board: A Shotgun Wedding.* Chicago: Chicago Law Enforcement Study Group Report/John Howard Association.

Black, D. J. 1976. *The Behavior of Law.* New York: Academic Press.

———. 1983. "Crime as Social Control." *American Sociological Review* 48: 34-45.

———. 1989. *Sociological Justice.* New York: Oxford University Press.

Blum, A. 1974. *Theorizing.* London: Heinemann.

Blumstein, A. et al. 1974. "The Honoring of Accounts." *American Sociological Review* 39: 551-566.

Bohm, D. 1980. *Wholeness and the Implicate Order*. New York: ARK.

Bohm, D., and F.D. Peat. 1987. *Science, Order, and Creativity*. New York: Bantam Books.

⸺. 1980. *Wholeness and the Implicate Order*. New York: ARK.

Bourdieu, P. 1977. *Outline of a Theory of Practice*. New York: Cambridge University Press.

⸺. 1987. "The Force of Law: Toward a Sociology of the Juridical Field." *The Hastings Law Journal* 38: 814-53.

⸺. 1989. "Social Space and Symbolic Power." *Social Theory* 7:14-25.

Box, S. 1987. *Recession, Crime and Punishment*. London: Macmillan.

Box, S., and C. Hale. 1986. "Unemployment, Crime and Imprisonment and the Enduring Problem of Prison Overcrowding" in R. Matthews and J. Young, *Confronting Crime*. London: Sage.

Boyle, F. 1985a. "Defending Nonviolent Civil Disobedience against the Reagan Administration under International Law." *Crime and Social Justice* 24: 110-34.

⸺. 1985b. "The Politics of Reason: Critical Legal Theory and Local Social Thought." *University of Pennsylvania Law Review* 133: 685-780.

⸺. 1987. *Defending Civil Resistanse Under International Law*. Transnational.

Bracher, M. 1988. "Lacan's Theory of the Four Discourses." *Prose Studies* 11: 32-49.

⸺. 1993. *Lacan, Discourse and Social Change*. Ithaca, NY: Cornell University Press.

Braidotti, R. 1990. "The Politics of Ontological Difference," in T. Brennan (ed.), *Between Feminism and Psychoanalysis*. New York: Routledge, pp. 89-105.

Brakel, S.J. 1987. "Prison Reform Litigation: Has the Revolution Gone Too Far?" *Corrections Today* 49:16-68.

Braswell, M. 1990. "Peacemaking: A Missing Link in Criminology." *The Criminologist* 15(1): 3-5.

Brecht, B. 1964. *Baal, A Man's a Man, and The Elephant Calf*. New York: Grover Press.

Brennan, T. (ed.). 1989. *Between Feminism and Psychoanalysis*. New York: Routledge.

⸺. 1993. *History after Lacan*. New York: Routledge.

Briggs, J., and D. Peat. 1989. *Turbulent Mirror*. New York: Harper and Row.

Brigham, J. 1987. "Right, Rage, and Remedy: Forms of Law in Political Discourse," *Studies in American Political Development* 2: 303-16.

Brigham, J., and C. Harrington. 1987. "Right, Rage and Remedy: Forms of Law in Political Discourse." *Studies in American Political Development* 2: 303-316.

⸺. 1989. "Realism and Its Consequences: An Inquiry into Contemporary Sociolegal Research." *International Journal of the Sociology of Law* 17: 41-62.

Brion, D. 1991. "The Chaotic Law of Tort: Legal Formalism and the Problem of Indeterminacy." In R. Kevelson (ed.), *Peirce and Law*, pp. 45-77. New York: Peter Lang.

Burt, C. 1985. "Rule 9 (a) and Its Impact on Habeas Corpus Litigation." *New England Journal of Criminal and Civil Confinement* 11: 363-94.

Butler, J. 1990. *Gender Trouble*. New York: Routledge.

⸺. 1992. "Contingent Foundations: Feminism and the Question of 'Postmodernism.'" In J. Butler and J.W. Scott (eds.), *Feminists Theorize the Political*. London: Routledge.

⸺. 1993. *Bodies that Matter*. New York: Routledge.

Butz, M. 1991. "Fractal Dimensionality and Paradigms." *The Social Dynamicist* 2(4): 4-7.

⸺. 1992a. "The Fractal Nature of the Development of the Self." *Psychological Reports* 71: 1043-63.

⸺. 1992b. "Systematic Family Therapy and Symbolic Chaos." *Humanity and Society* 17(2): 200-22.

————. 1992c. "Chaos, An Omen of Transcendence in the Psychotherapeutic Process." *Psychological Reports* 71: 827-43.

Cain, M. 1989. *Growing Up Good: Policing Behaviour of Girls in Europe*. London: Sage.

Camus, A. 1955. *The Myth of Sisyphus*. New York: Vintage Books.

————. 1956. *The Rebel: An Essay on Man in Revolt*. New York: Vintage Books.

————. 1958. *Caligula and Three Other Plays*. New York: Vintage Books.

Capra, F. 1982. *The Turning Point*. New York: Simon and Schuster.

Carlen, P. 1990. "Women, Crime, Feminism and Realism." *Social Justice* 17(4): 106-23.

Carneiro, R. 1987. "The Evolution of Complexity in Human Sciences and Its Mathematical Expression." *International Journal of Comparative Sociology* 28(3-4): 111-27.

Casti, J. 1994. *Complexification*. New York: Harper Perennial.

Caudill, D. 1992a. "Lacan and Law: Networking with the Big O[ther]." *Studies in Psychoanalytic Theory* 1(1): 25-55.

————. 1992b. "'Name-of-the-Father' and the Logic of Psychosis: Lacan's Law and Ours." *Legal Studies Forum* 16(4): 23-46.

————. 1992c. "Jacques Lacan and Our State of Affairs: Preliminary Remarks on Law as Other." In R. Kevelson (ed.), *Law and the Human Sciences*. New York: Peter Lang, pp. 95-113.

Chaubard, J.-F. 1984. *Le Noeud dit du Fantasme*.

Chesney-Lynd, M. 1986. "Women and Crime: The Female Offender." *Signs: Journal of Women in Culture and Society* 121: 78-96.

Christie, N. 1981. *Limits to Pain*. Oxford: Martin Robertson.

Cicourel, A. 1968. *The Social Organization of Juvenile Justice*. New York: John Wiley & Sons.

Cixous, H. 1990. *Reading with Clarice Lispector*. Minneapolis, MN: University of Minnesota Press.

————. 1986. *The Newly Born Woman*. Minneapolis, MN: University of Minnesota Press.

Clement, C. 1983. *The Lives and Legends of Jacques Lacan*. New York: Columbia University Press.

Cohen, S. 1985. *Visions of Social Control*. Oxford: Polity Press.

————. 1988. *Against Criminology*. New Brunswick, NJ: Transaction Books.

Collins, H. 1982. *Marxism and Law*. New York: Oxford University Press.

Committee to End the Marion Lockdown.1988. *Can't Jail the Spirit: Political Prisoners in the U.S., A Collection of Biographies*. Committee to End the Marion Lockdown 343 S. Dearborn, Suite 1607, Chicago, IL, U.S.A. 60604.

Coombe, R.J. 1989. "Room for Manoeuver: Toward a Theory of Practice in Critical Legal Studies." *Law and Social Inquiry* 14: 69-121.

Cornell, D. 1991. *Beyond Accommodation: Ethical Feminism, Deconstruction and the Law*. New York: Routledge.

————. 1993. *Transformations: Recollective Imagination and Sexual Difference*. New York: Routledge.

Crenshaw, K.W. 1993. "Beyond Racism and Misogyny: Black Feminism and 2 Live Crew." In M.J. Matsuda, C.R. Lawrence, R. Delgado, and K.W. Crenshaw (eds.), *Words That Wound*, 111-32. San Francisco: Westview Press.

Cressey, D. 1953. *Other People's Money*. Glencoe, Ill.: The Free Press.

————. 1970. "The Respectable Criminal." In J. Short (ed.) *Modern Criminals*. New York: Transactions/Aldine.

Cullen, J. 1994. "Decentralization in Growth and Decline: A Catastrophe Theory Approach." *Behavioral Science* 39: 213-27.

Currie, D. 1986. "Female Criminality: A Crisis in Feminist Theory." In B. MacLean (ed.), *The Political Economy of Crime*. Scarborough, Ontario: Prentice-Hall.

————. 1989. "Women and the State: A Statement on Feminist Theory." *The Critical Criminologist* (Spring):4-5.

————. 1990. "Battered Women and the State: From the Failure of Theory to a Theory of Failure." *Journal of Human Justice* 1: 77-96.

————. 1993. "Unhiding the Hidden: Race, Class, and Gender in the Construction of Knowledge," *Humanity and Society* 17(1): 3-27.

Currie, D., B. MacLean, and D. Milovanovic. 1992. "Three Traditions of Critical Justice Inquiry: Class, Gender and Discourse." In D. Currie and B. MacLean (eds.), *Struggle for Equality: Re-Thinking the Administration of Justice.* Toronto: Garamond Press.

Daly, K., and M. Chesney-Lynd.1987. "Discrimination in the Criminal Courts: Family, Gender, and the Problem of Equal Treatment." *Social Forces* 66: 152-175.

————. 1988. "Feminism and Criminology." *Justice Quarterly* 5: 497-538.

Daniels, A. 1970. "Normal Mental Illness and Understandable Excuses." *American Behavioral Scientist* 14: 167-184.

Danner, M.J.E. 1989. "Socalist Feminism: A Brief Introduction." *Critical Criminologist* (Summer):1-2.

de Haan, W. 1986. "Abolitionism and the Politics of Bad Conscience." In H. Bianchi and R. van Swaaningen (eds.), *Abolitionism: Towards a Non-Repressive Approach to Crime.* Amsterdam: Free Press.

————. 1990. *The Politics of Redress: Crime, Punishment and Penal Abolition.* Boston: Unwin Hyman.

DeKeseredy, W., and B. MacLean. 1990. Researching Women Abuse in Canada: A Realistic Critique of the Conflict Tactics Scale. *Canadian Review of Social Policy* 25: 19-27.

————. 1991. "Exploring the Gender, Class, and Race Dimension of Victimization: A Realist Critique of the Canadian Urban Victimization Survey. *International Journal of Offender Therapy and Comparative Criminology* 35(2): 143-61.

Deleuze, G. 1983. *Nietzsche and Philosophy.* New York: Columbia University Press.

————. 1988. *Foucault.* Minneapolis, MN: University of Minnesota Press.

Deleuze, G., and F. Guattari. 1986. *Kafka: Toward a Minor Literature.* Minneapolis, MN: University of Minnesota Press.

————. 1987. *A Thousand Plateaus.* Minneapolis, MN: University of Minnesota Press.

Delgado, R. (ed.). 1995. *Critical Race Theory.* New York: Temple University Press.

Dennis, D. 1989. "Richard Quinney: An interview, 8/1/89." *Critical Criminologist* (Summer): 11-14.

Derrida, J. 1973. *Speech and Phenomena.* Evanston, IL: Northwestern University Press.

————. 1976. *Of Grammatology.* Baltimore, MD: Johns Hopkins.

————. 1978. "Structure, Sign and Play in the Discourse of the Human Sciences." In *Writing and Difference.* A. Bass, trans. Chicago: University of Chicago Press.

————. 1981. *Positions.* Chicago: University of Chicago Press.

————. 1988. *Limited Inc.,* trans. S. Weber. Evanston, IL: Northwestern University Press.

de Saussure, F. 1974. *Course in General Linguistics.* London: Fontana.

Dews, P. 1987. *Logics of Disintegration.* New York: Verso.

DiJulio, J. 1987. *Governing Prisons: A Comparative Study of Correctional Management.* New York: The Free Press.

Dore, L.K. 1995. "Downward Adjustment and the Slippery Slope: The Use of Duress in Defense of Battered Offenders." *Ohio State Law Journal* 56(3):665-766.

Duffee, D. 1980. *Correctional Management: Change and Control in Correctional Organizations.* Englewood Cliffs, NJ: Prentice Hall.

Ebert, T. 1991a. "Writing in the Political: Resistance (Post)Modernism." *Legal Studies Forum* 15(4): 291-303.

————. 1991b. "Political Semiosis in/of American Cultural Studies." *The American Journal of Semiotics* 8: 113-35.

Einstadter, W. 1989. "Asymmetries of Control: Technologies of Surveillance in the the Area of Privacy." Paper presented to Society for the Study of Social Problems, San Francisco, August.

Elliot, D.S. 1994. "1993 Presidential Address: Serious Violent Offenders: Onset, Developmental Course and Termination." *Criminology* 32(1): 1-21.

Emerson, R. 1969. *Judging Delinquents.* Aldine Publishing.

Esslin, M. 1961. *The Theatre of the Absurd.* New York: Anchor Books.

Fairchild, E. S. 1977. "Politicization of the Criminal Offender." *Criminology* 15: 287-318.

Federal Judicial Center. 1980. *Recommended Procedures for Handling Prisoner Civil Rights Cases in the Federal Courts.* Washington, DC: The Federal Judicial Center.

Feigenbaum, M. 1980. "Universal Behavior in Nonlinear Systems." *Los Alamos Science* 1: 4-27.

Ferrell, J. 1993. *Crimes of Style: Urban Graffiti and the Politics of Criminality.* New York: Garland Publishing.

———. 1995a. "Urban Graffiti: Crime, Control, and Resistance," *Youth and Society* 27: 73-79.

———. 1995b. "Adrenalin, Pleasure, and Criminological Verstehen." Paper presented at the Annual Meeting of the American Society of Criminology, Boston, Mass., November.

Fink, B. 1995. *The Lacanian Subject.* Princeton, N J: Princeton University Press.

Fitzgerald. M. 1977. *Prisoners in Revolt.* Harmondsworth, UK: Pelican Books.

Fitzpatrick, P. 1984. "Law and Societies." *Osgood Hall Law Journal* 22: 115-138.

———. 1988. "The Rise of Informalism." In R. Matthews (ed.), *Informal Justice.* London: Sage.

Foucault, M. 1973. *The Order of Things.* New York: Vintage Books.

———. 1977. *Discipline and Punish.* New York: Pantheon Books.

———. 1978. *The History of Sexuality: Vol 1. An Introduction.* New York: Random House.

———. 1980. *Power/Knowledge: Selected Interviews and Other Writings 1972-77.* C. Gordon (ed.). N.Y.: Pantheon Books.

Frechet, M., and K. Fan. 1967. *Initiation to Combinatorial Topology,* H. Eves, trans. Boston, MA: Prindle, Weber and Schmidt.

Freire, P. 1972. *Pedagogy of the Oppressed.* New York: Herder and Herder.

———. 1985. *The Politics of Education.* South Hadley, MA: Bergin and Garvey.

Freud, S. 1965 [1900]. *The Interpretation of Dreams.* New York: Avon Books.

Friedrichs, D. 1986. "Critical Legal Studies and the Critique of Criminal Justice." *Criminal Justice Review* 12: 11-15.

———. 1989. "Critical Criminology and Critical Legal Studies." *The Critical Criminologist* 2(2): 7-8.

Gardner, M.R. 1976. "The Renaissance of Retribution—An Examination of Doing Justice." *Wisconsin Law Review* 1: 117-34.

Geertz, C. 1983. *Local Knowledge: Further Essays in Interpretive Anthropology.* New York: Basic Books.

Gellman, S. 1991. "Sticks and Stones Can Put You in Jail, But Can Words Increase Your Sentence? Constitutional and Policy Dilemmas of Ethnic Intimidation Laws." *UCLA Law Review* 39: 333-96.

Gelsthorpe, L., and A. Morris. 1988. "Feminism and Criminology in Britain." *British Journal of Criminology* 28: 93-110.

Gibson, W. 1984. *Neuromancer.* New York: Ace.

Giddens, A. 1984. *The Constitution of Society.* Oxford: Polity Press.

Gilsinan, J. 1982. *Doing Justice: How the System Works — As Seen by the Participants.* Englewood Cliffs, NJ: Prentice-Hall.

Giroux, H. 1992. *Border Crossings.* New York: Routledge.

Gleick, J. 1987. *Chaos: Making a New Science*. New York: Viking.

Glogowski, J. 1990. "The Therapeutic Effect of Psychoanalysis: The Intervention of Lacan." In P. Hogan and L. Pandit (eds.), *Criticism and Lacan*, pp. 159-79. London: University of Georgia Press.

Godel, K. 1962. "On Formally Undecidable Propositions." In R.B. Braitewaite (ed.), *'Principia Mathematica' and Related Systems*, pp. 173-98. New York: Basic Books.

Goffman, E. 1961. *Asylums: Essays in the Social Situation of Mental Patients and Other Inmates*. Garden City, NY: Anchor.

———. 1974. *Frame Analysis*. New York: Harper & Row.

———. 1981. *Forms of Talk*. Oxford: Basil Blackwell.

Gold, J.Z. 1979. "Prison Escape and Defenses Based on Conditions: A Theory of Social Preference." *California Law Review* 67: 1183-1204.

Golden, R., and M. McConnell. 1986. *Sanctuary: The New Underground Railroad*. Maryknoll, NY: Orbis Books.

Goodrich, P. 1984. "Law and Language: An Historical and Critical Introduction." *Journal of Law and Society* 11: 173-206.

———. 1990. *Languages of Law: From Logics of Memory to Nomadic Masks*. London: Weidenfeld and Nicolson.

Goodwin, G. A. 1971. "On Transcending the Absurd." *American Journal of Sociology* 76: 831-46.

Gramsci, A. 1971. *Prison Notebooks*. London: Lawrence and Wishart.

Granon-Lafont. J. 1985. *La Topologie Ordinaire de Jacques Lacan*. Paris: Point Hors Ligne.

———. 1990. *Topologie Lacanienne et Clinique Analytique*. Paris: Point Hors Ligne..

Grant, J. 1993. *Fundamental Feminism: Contesting the Core Concepts of Feminist Theory*. New York: Routledge.

Greenberg, D. F. (ed.). 1981. *Crime and Capitalism*. Palo Alto, CA: Mayfield Publishing

Gregersen, H., and L. Sailer. 1993. "Chaos Theory and Its Implications for Social Science Research. *Human Relations* 46(7): 777-802.

Greimas, A. 1987. *On Meaning*. Minneapolis, MN: University of Minnesota Press.

———. 1990. *The Social Sciences: A Semiotic View*. Minneapolis, MN: University of Minnesota Press.

Grosz, E. 1990. *Jacques Lacan: A Feminist Introduction*. New York: Routledge.

Groves, C. 1991. "Us and Them." In B. Maclean and D. Milovanovic (eds.), *New Directions in Critical Criminology*. Vancouver: The Collective Press, pp. 111-12.

Haas, J. 1986. "Appendix 3, Commentary on the Arizona Indictments," In R. Golden and M. McConnell, *Sanctuary: The New Underground Railroad*. Maryknoll, NY: Orbis Books: Maryknoll.

Habermas, Jurgen. 1984. *The Theory of Communicative Action. Vol. 1: Reason and the Rationalization of Society*. Boston: Beacon Press.

———. 1987. *The Theory of Communicative Action. Vol. 2: Lifeworld and System: A Critique of Functionalist Reason*. Boston: Beacon Press.

Hall, J. 1960. *General Principles of Criminal Law*. 2nd Edition. New York: Bobbs-Merrill.

Halleck, S. 1967. *Psychiatry and the Dilemmas of Crime*. Berkeley, CA: University of California Press.

Handler, J. 1992. "The Presidential Address, Law and Society: Postmodernism, Protest, and the New Social Movement." *Law and Society Review* 26(4): 697-731.

Harraway, D. 1991. "Situated Knowledges." In D. Harraway, *Simians, Cyborgs and Women*, pp. 183-201. New York: Routledge.

Harrington, C. 1988. "Moving from Integrative to Constitutive Theories of Law." *Law and Society Review* 22: 963-7.

Harrington, C., and S. Merry. 1988. "Ideological Production: The Making of Community Mediation." *Law and Society Review* 22: 709-735.

Harrington, C., and B. Yngvesson. 1990. "Interpretive Sociolegal Research." *Law and Social Inquiry* 15: 135-148.

Harris, A. 1991. "Race and Essentialism in Feminist Legal Theory." In K. Bartlett and R. Kennedy (eds.), *Feminist Legal Theory*, pp. 235-62. Oxford: Westview Press.

Harris, M.K. 1987. "Moving into the New Millenium: Toward a Feminist Vision of Justice." *The Prison Journal* 67: 27-38.

Harry, H., and J. Thomas. 1988. "The Dialectics of Prisoner Litigation: Reformist Idealism or Social Praxis?" *Social Justice* 15: 48-71

Hayles, K. 1990. *Chaos Bound: Orderly Disorder in Contemporary Literature and Science.* Ithaca, NY: Cornell University Press.

———. (ed.). 1991. *Chaos and Order: Complex Dynamics in Literature and Science.* Chicago: University of Chicago Press.

Held, B. 1995. *Back to Reality.* New York: W.W. Norton.

Henderson, L. 1983. *The Fourth Dimension and Non-Euclidean Geometry in Modern Art.* Princeton, NJ: Princeton University Press.

Henry, S. 1976. "Fencing with Accounts: The Language of Moral Bridging." *The British Journal of Law and Society* 3: 91-100.

———. 1978. *The Hidden Economy.* Oxford: Martin Robertson.

———. 1983. *Private Justice.* London: Routledge and Kegan Paul.

———. 1985. "Community Justice, Capitalist Society and Human Agency: The Dialectics of Collective Law in the Cooperative." *Law and Society Review* 19: 301-325.

———. 1987. "Private Justice and the Policing of Labor: The Dialectics of Industrial Discipline." In C. Shearing and P. Stenning (eds.), *Private Policing.* Beverly Hills, CA: Sage.

———. 1988a. "Can the Hidden Economy Be Revolutionary?" *Social Justice* 15: 29-60.

———. 1988b. "Rules, Rulers and Ruled in Egalitarian Collectives: Deviance and Social Control in Cooperatives." In J.G. Flanagan and S. Rayner (eds.), *Rules. Decisions, and Egalitarian Societies.* Aldershot, United Kingdom: Avebury.

———. 1989a. "Constitutive Criminology: The Missing Link." *The Critical Criminologist* (Summer): 9, 12.

———. 1989b. "Justice on the Margin: Can Alternative Justice Be Different?" *The Howard Journal of Criminal Justice* 28: 255-271.

Henry, S., and D. Milovanovic. 1991. "Constitutive Criminology." *Criminology* 29: 293-315.

———. 1993a. "Back to Basics: A Postmodern Redefinition of Crime." *The Critical Criminologist* 5(2/3): 1-2, 6, 12.

———. 1993b. "The Constitution of Constitutive Criminology: A Postmodern Approach to Criminological Theory." In D. Nelkin (ed.), *The Futures of Criminology.* London: Sage Publications.

———. 1996. *Constitutive Criminology.* London: Sage.

Hilbert, D., and S. Cohn-Vossen. 1952. *Geometry and the Imagination.* New York: Chelsea.

Hobsbawm, E. J. 1969. *Bandits.* London: George Weidenfeld and Nicolson.

Hosticka, C. 1979. "We Don't Care about What Happened. We Only Care About What Is Going to Happen: Lawyer-Client Negotiations of Reality." *Social Problems* 26: 599-611.

Howe, A. 1994. *Punish and Critique.* London: Routlege.

Hunt, A. 1987. "The Critique of Law: What Is 'Critical' About Critical Legal Theory?" *Journal of Law and Society* 14: 5-19.

———. 1993. *Explorations in Law and Society: Toward a Constitutive Theory of Law.* New York: Routledge.

Irigaray, L. 1985. *Speculum of the Other Woman.* Ithaca, NY: Cornell University Press.

Irwin, J. 1970. *The Felon*. Englewood Cliffs, NJ: Prentice Hall.

———. 1980. *Prisons in Turmoil*. Boston, MA: Little, Brown.

Jackson, B. 1985. *Semiotics and Legal Theory*. New York: Routledge and Kegan Paul.

———. 1988. *Law, Fact and Narrative Coherence*. Merseyside, United Kingdom.: Deborah Charles Publications.

Jackson, G. 1970. *Soledad Brother: The Prison Letters of George Jackson*. New York: Coward-McCann.

Jacobs, J.B. 1983a. "Sentencing by Prison Personnel." *UCLA Law Review* 30: 217 70.

———. 1983b. *New Perspectives on Prisons and Imprisonment*. Ithaca, NY: Cornell University Press.

Jakobson, R. 1971. "Two Aspects of Language and Two Types of Aphasic Disorders." In R. Jakobson and M. Halle, *Fundamentals of Language*. Paris: Mouton.

Jameson, F. 1984. "Postmodernism, or the Cultural Logic of Capital." *New Left Review* 15: 146-162.

JanMohammed, A.R. 1993. "Some Implications of Paulo Freire's Border Pedagogy." *Cultural Studies* 7(1): 107-17.

Jantsch, E. 1980. *The Self-Organizing Universe*. NY: Pergamon Press.

Jefferson, T. 1990. *The Case for Paramilitary Policing*. Milton Keynes, United Kingdom: Open University Press.

Jessop, B. 1990. *State Theory: Putting the Capitalist State in Its Place*. Cambridge, MA: Polity Press.

———. 1982. *The Capitalist State*. New York: New York University Press.

John, J., Jr. 1987. *Governing Prisons: A Comparative Study of Correctional Management*. New York: The Free Press.

Jones, T., B. MacLean, and J. Young. 1986. *The Islington Crime Survey: Crime, Victimization, and Policing in Inner-City London*. Aldershot, United Kingdom: Gower Press.

Juranville, A. 1984. *Lacan et la Philosophie*. Paris: Presses Universitaires de France.

Kafka, F. 1972. *The Trial*. Harmondsworth, England: Penguin Books.

Kahne, M., and C. Schwartz. 1978. "Negotiating Trouble: The Social Construction and Management of Trouble in a College Psychiatric Context." *Social Problems* 25: 461-474.

Kaku, M. 1994. *Hyperspace*. New York: Oxford University Press.

Kalinich, D. B. 1986. *Power, Stability and Contraband: The Inmate Economy*. Prospect Heights, IL: Waveland Press.

Kaplan, M., and N. Kaplan. 1991. "The Self-Organization of Human Psychological Functioning." *Behavioral Science* 36: 161-78.

Katz, Jack. 1988. *The Seductions of Crime*. New York: Basic Books.

Keller, S. 1993. *In the Wake of Chaos*. Chicago: University of Chicago Press.

Kennedy, D. 1982. "Legal Education as Training for Hierarchy." In D. Kairys (ed.), *The Politics of Law: A Progressive Critique*, pp. 40-61. New York: Pantheon Books.

Kerruish, V. 1991. *Jurisprudence as Ideology*. NY: Routledge.

Kinsey, R., J. Lea, and J. Young. 1986. *Losing the Fight against Crime*. London: Basil Blackwell.

Klare, K. 1978. "Judicial Deradicalization of the Wagner Act and the Origins of Modern Legal Consciousness, 1937-1941." *Minnesota Law Review* 62: 265-339.

———. 1979. "Law-Making as Praxis." *Telos* 40:123-35.

———. 1993. "Power/Dressing: Regulation of Employee Appearance." *New England Law Review* 26(4): 1395-1451.

Klein, Dorie. 1973. "The Etiology of Female Crime: A Review of the Literature." *Issues in Criminology* 8:3-30.

Klockars, C. 1980. "The Contemporary Crisis of Marxist Criminology." In J. A. Inciardi (ed.), *Radical Criminology*. Beverly Hills, CA: Sage.

Knoespel, K. 1985. *Medieval Ovidian Commentary: Narcissus and the Invention of Personal History*. New York: Garland Publishing.

Knorr-Cetina, K., and A. Cicourel. 1981. *Advances in Social Theory and Methodology: Toward an Integration of Macro-and Micro-Sociologies*. London: Routledge and Kegan Paul.

Korn, R. 1988. "The Effects of Confinement in the High Security Unit at Lexington." *Social Justice* 15(1): 8-19.

Kosik, K. 1976. *Dialectics of the Concrete: A Study on Problems of Man and World*. Boston, MA: D. Reidel.

Kristeva, J. 1980. *Desire in Language*. New York: Columbia University Press.

————. 1984. *Revolution in Poetic Language*. New York: Columbia University Press.

Lab, S.P., and J.T. Whitehead. 1990. "From 'Nothing Works' to 'The Appropriate Works.'" *Journal of Criminology* 28: 405-417.

Lacan, J. 1962. *Seminar 9, L'Identification*, unpubl.

————. 1966-1967. *Seminar 14, La Logique du fantasme*, unpubl.

————. 1972. "Of Structure as an Inmixing of an Otherness Prerequisite to Any Subject Whatever." In R. Macksey and E. Donato (eds.), *The Structuralist Controversy*. Baltimore, MD: John Hopkins.

————. 1973. "L'Etourdit." *Scilicet* 4: 5-52.

————. 1973-1974. *Seminar 21, Les Non-Dupes Errent*, unpubl.

————. 1974-1975. *Seminar 22, Encore.*. Text edited by J.-A. Miller. *Ornicar?* 2 (1975): 87-105; 3 (1975): 95-110; 4 (1975): 91-106; 5 (1975): 15-66.

————. 1975-1976. *Seminar 23, Le Synthome*. Text edited by J-A. Miller. *Ornicar?* 6 (1976): 3-20; 7 (1976): 3-18; 8 (1976): 6- 20; 9 (1977): 32-40; 10 (1977): 5-12; 11 (1977): 2-9.

————. 1976-1977. *Le Synthome*, unpubl.

————. 1976. "Conferences et Entretiens dans des Universites Nord-Americaines." *Scilicet* 6/7: 5-63.

————. 1977. *Ecrit*. New York: Norton.

————. 1981. *The Four Fundamental Concepts of Psycho-Analysis*. New York: Norton.

————. 1985. *Feminine Sexuality*. New York: W.W. Norton and Pantheon Books.

————. 1987a. "Joyce le Symptome 1." In J. Aubert (ed.), *Joyce avec Lacan*, 21-9. Paris: Navarin.

————. 1987b. "Joyce le Symtome 2." In J. Aubert (ed.), *Joyce avec Lacan*, 31-48. Paris: Navarin.

————. 1987c. "Television." *October* 40: 7-50.

————. 1988. "The Purloined Letter." In J. Muller and W. Richardson (eds.), *The Purloined Poe*, pp. 28-54. Baltimore, MD: Johns Hopkins.

————. 1991a. *L'Envers de la Psychanalyse*. Paris: Editions du Seuil.

————. 1991b. *Le Transfert*. Paris, France: Editions du Seuil.

————. 1992. *The Ethics of Pyschoanalysis*. New York: Norton.

————. 1993. *The Seminar of Jacques Lacan: Book 111, The Psychoses*. Paris: Editions du Seuil.

Laclau, E., and C. Mouffe. 1985. *Hegemony and Socialist Strategy*. NY: Verso.

Landowski, E. 1991. "A Note on Meaning, Interaction and Narrativity." *International Journal of the Semiotics of Law* 11: 151-61.

Laurence, K. 1988. "Captive Souls: Portraits of People in Prison." *Social Justice* 15(1): 72-82.

Lecercle, J. 1985. *Philosophy through the Looking Glass: Language, Nonsense, Desire*. London: Hutchinson.

————. 1990. *The Violence of Language*. New York: Routledge.

Lee, J. 1990. *Jacques Lacan*. Amherst: MA: University of Massachusetts Press.

Leifer, R. 1989. "Understanding Organizational Transformation Using a Dissipative Structure Model." *Human Relations* 42: 899-916.

Lem, S. 1981. "Metafantasia: The Possibilities of Science Fiction." Trans. E. de Laczay and I. Csicsery-Ronary, *Science Fiction Studies* 8: 54-71.

———. 1984. *Microworlds*. San Diego, CA: Harcourt Brace, Jovanovich.

Lopez-Rivera, O.1989."Political Prisoners in the U.S." *Critical Criminologist* 1(2): 10-11.

Love, N. 1986. *Marx, Nietzsche, and Modernity*. New York: Columbia University Press.

Loye, D., and E. Riane. 1987. "Chaos and Transformation: Implications of Nonequilibrium Theory for Social Science and Society." *Behavioral Science* 32: 53-65.

Luhmann, N.A. 1985. *Sociological Theory of Law*. Boston: Routledge and Kegan Paul.

———.1992. "Operational Closure and Structural Coupling: The Differentiation of the Legal System." *Cardozza Law Review* 13(5): 1419-41.

Lukacs, G. 1971. *History and Class Consciousness*. London: Merlin Press.

Lyng, S. 1990. "Edgework: A Social Psychological Analysis of Voluntary Risk Taking." *American Journal of Sociology* 95(4): 851-86.

Lyotard, J.-F. 1984. *The Postmodern Condition*. Minneapolis, MN: University of Minnesota Press.

———. 1993. *Libidinal Economy*. Bloomington, IN: Indiana University Press.

———. 1972. "Of Structure as an Inmixing of an Otherness Prerequisite to Any Subject Whatever." In R. Macksey and E. Donato (eds.), *The Structuralist Controversy*. Baltimore: Johns Hopkins.

McCann, M. 1992. "Resistance, Reconstruction, and Romance in Legal Scholarship." *Law and Society Review* 26(4): 733-49.

McLaren, P. 1994a. "Postmodernism and the Death of Politics: A Brazilian Reprieve." In P. McLaren and C. Lankshear (eds.), *Politics of Liberation: Paths from Freire*, 193-215. New York: Routledge.

———. 1994b. "Multiculturalism and the Postmodern Critique." In H. Giroux and P. McLaren (eds.), *Between Borders*. New York: Routledge.

McLaren, P., and C. Lankshear. 1994. *Politics of Liberation*. London: Routledge.

MacLean, B. 1991. "In Partial Defense of Socialist Realism." *Crime, Law and Social Change: An International Journal* 15(3): 213-54.

McRobie, A., and M. Thompson. 1994. "Chaos, Catastrophes and Engineering." In N. Hall (ed.), *Exploring Chaos*. New York: W.W. Norton.

Mandel, D. 1995. "Chaos Theory, Sensitive Dependence, and the Logistic Equation." *American Psychologist* (February): 106-107.

Mandelbrot, B. 1983. *The Fractal Geometry of Nature*. New York: W.H. Freeman.

Manning, P. 1986. "Signwork." *Human Relations* 39: 283-308.

———. 1987. *Semiotics and Fieldwork*. Newbury Park, CA: Sage.

———. 1988. *Symbolic Communication: Signifying Calls and the Police Response*. Cambridge, MA: The MIT Press.

———. 1990a. "Semiotics and Postmodernism." In D. Dickens and A. Fontana (eds.), *Post Modernism and Sociology*. Chicago: University of Chicago Press.

———. 1990b. "Critical Semiotics Part II." *The Critical Criminologist*, 2 (1): 5-6, 16.

Marchante, R. 1992. "A Dissipative System-Model for Organization Transformation: The Emergence of a Far-From-Equilibrium Paradigm" (unpublished manuscript).

Marini, M. 1992. *Jacques Lacan*. New Brunswick, NJ: Rutgers University Press.

Martinson, R. 1974. "What Works? - Questions and Answers about Prison Reform." *The Public Interest* 35: 22-54.

Marx, G. 1988. *Undercover: Police Surveillance in America*. Berkeley, CA: University of California Press.

Marx, K. 1964. *Economic and Philosophic Manuscripts of 1844*. New York: International Publishers.

———. 1984. *The Eighteenth Brumaire of Louis Bonaparte, 1852*. K. Marx and F. Engels, Werke, in Eugene Kamenka (ed.), *The Portable Marx*. New York: Penguin.

Mastrofski, S., and R. Parks. 1990. "Improving Observational Studies of Police." *Journal of Criminology* 28: 475-496.

Matsuda, M. 1989. "When the First Quail Calls: Multiple Consciousness as Jurisprudential Method." *Women's Rights Law Reporter* 11: 7, 9.

Matsuda, M., C. Lawrence, R. Delgado, and K. Crenshaw. 1993. *Words that Wound.* Oxford: Westview Press.

Matthews, R., and J. Young, eds. 1986. *Confronting Crime.* London: Sage.

————.1987. "Taking Realist Criminology Seriously." *Contemporary Crisis* 11: 371-81.

Matza, D. 1964. *Delinquency and Drift.* New York: John Wiley.

————. 1969. *Becoming Deviant.* Englewood Cliffs, NJ: Prentice Hall.

Melville, S. 1987. "Psychoanalysis and the Place of Jouissance." *Critical Inquiry* 13: 349-70.

Merry, S. 1985. "Concepts of Law and Justice among Working-Class Americans: Ideology as Culture." *Legal Studies Forum* 9(1): 59-69.

Merton, R. 1968. *Social Theory and Social Structure.* New York: Free Press.

Mertz, E., and B. Weissbourd. 1985. "Legal Ideology and Linguistic Theory: Variability and Its Limits." In E. Mertz and B. Weissbourd (eds.), *Semiotic Mediation.* New York: Academic Press.

Messerschmidt, J.D. 1986. *Capitalism, Patriarchy and Crime: Toward a Socialist Feminist Criminology.* Lanham, MD.: Rowman and Littlefield.

Mika, H., and J. Thomas. 1987 "The Dialectics of Prisoner Litigation: Reformist Idealism or Social Praxis." *Social Justice* 15: 48-71.

Mills, C. W. 1940. "Situated Actions and Vocabularies of Motive." *American Sociological Review* 5: 904-13

————. 1959. *The Sociological Imagination.* New York: Oxford University Press.

Milovanovic, D. 1984. "Autonomy of the Legal Order, Ideology and the Structure of Legal Thought." In M. Schwartz and D. Friedrichs (eds.), *Humanistic Perspectives in Crime and Justice,* pp. 97-119. New Haven, CT:: Practitioner Press.

————. 1986. "Juridico-Linguistic Communicative Markets: Towards a Semiotic Analysis." *Contemporary Crises* 10: 281-304.

————. 1987. "The Political Economy of 'Liberty' and 'Property' Interests." *Legal Studies Forum* 11: 267-293.

————. 1988a. "Jailhouse Lawyers and Jailhouse Lawyering." *International Journal of the Sociology of Law* 16: 455-75.

————. 1988b. *A Primer in the Sociology of Law.* New York: Harrow and Heston.

————. 1988c. "Review Essay: Critical Legal Studies and the Assault on the Bastion." *Social Justice* 15(1): 161-172.

————. 1989a. "Critical Criminology and the Challenge of Post Modernism." *The Critical Criminologist* (Winter): 9-10, 17.

————. 1989b. *Weberian and Marxian Analysis of Law: Structure and Function of Law in a Capitalist Mode of Production.* Aldershot, Hampshire, UK: Gower.

————. 1990a. "Re-Thinking Subjectivity in Law and Ideology: A Semiotic Perspective." In D.Currie and B. MacLean (eds.), *Struggles for Equality: Re-Thinking the Administration of Justice.* Toronto: Garamon Press.

————. 1990b. "Repressive Formalism." In B. MacLean and D. Milovanovic (eds.), *Racism, Empiricism and Criminal Justice.* Vancouver, Canada: Collective Press.

————. 1991a. "Images of Unity and Disunity in the Juridic Subject and the Movement toward the Peacemaking Community." In H. Pepinsky and R. Quinney (eds.), *Criminology as Peacemaking,* 209-227. Bloomington, IN: Indiana University Press.

————. 1991b. "Schmarxism, Exorcism and Transpraxis." *The Critical Criminologist* 3(4): 5-6, 11-12.

————. 1992a. *Postmodern Law and Disorder: Psychoanalytic Semiotics, Chaos and Juridic Exegeses.* Liverpool, England: Deborah Charles Publications.

————. 1992b. "Re-Thinking Subvjectivity in Law and Ideology: A Critically Informed Psychoanalytic Semiotic View." *Journal of Human Justice* 4(1): 31-53.

————. 1993a. "Lacan, Chaos and Practical Discourse in Law." In R. Kevelson (ed.), *Flux, Complexity, Illusion in Law.* NY: Peter Lange.

————. 1993b. "Borromean Knots and the Constitution of Sense in Juridico-Discursive Production." *Legal Studies Forum* 17(2): 171-192.

————. 1993c. "Lacan's Four Discourses, Chaos and Cultural Criticism in Law." *Studies in Psychoanalytic Theory* 2(1): 3-23.

————. 1994a. "The Decentered Subject in Law." *Studies in Psychoanalytic Theory* 3(1): 93-127.

————. 1994b. *Sociology of Law.* 2nd ed. Albany, New York: Harrow and Heston.

————. 1994c. "The Postmodern Turn: Lacan, Psychoanalytic Semiotics, and the Construction of Subjectivity in Law." *Emory International Law Review* 8(1): 67-98.

————. 1995a. "Dueling Paradigms: Modernist v. Postmodernist." *Humanity and Society* 19(1): 1-22.

————. 1995b. "Affirmative Postmodern Criminology: Mapping the Terrain." Paper presented at the Annual Meeting of the American Society of Criminology, Boston, November 15-20.

————. 1995c. "Inscribing the Body with a Sign: Semiotics and Punishment." In R. Janikowski and D. Milovanovic (eds.), *Legality and Illegality: Semiotics, Postmodernism and Law.* New York: Peter Lang, pp. 47-78.

————. 1996. "Postmodern Criminology: Mapping the Terrain." *Justice Quarterly* 13(4): 567-610.

————. 1997. ed. *Chaos, Criminology, and Social Justice: The New Orderly(Dis)Order.* Westport, CT: Praeger.

Milovanovic, D., and S. Henry. 1991. "Constitutive Penology." *Social Justice* 18: 204-224.

Milovanovic, D., and J. Thomas. 1988. "The Ironies of Jailhouse Law." Unpublished manuscript.

————. 1989. "Overcoming the Absurd: Legal Struggle as Primitive Rebellion." *Social Problems* 36(1): 48-60.

Moi, T. (ed.). 1986. *The Kristeva Reader.* Oxford: Blackwell Publishers.

————. 1985. *Sexual Politics/Textual Politics.* London: Methuen.

Morrissey, E.R. 1985. "Power and Control Through Discourse: The Case of Drinking and Drinking Problems among Women." *Contemporary Crisis* 10: 57-79.

Mouffe, C. 1992. "Feminism, Citizenship and Radical Democratic Politics." In J. Butler and J. W. Scott (eds.), *Feminists Theorize the Political.* London: Routledge.

Mueller, J., and W. Richardson. 1982. *Lacan and Language: A Reader's Guide to Ecrits.* New York: International Universities Press.

Muir, W. 1977. *Police: Streetcorner Politicians.* Chicago: University of Chicago Press.

Murray, E. 1986. *Imaginative Thinking and Human Existence.* Pittsburgh: Duquesne University Press.

Nasio, J.-D. 1987. *Les Yeux de Laure.* Paris: Aubier.

Nelken, D. (ed.). 1995. *The Futures of Criminology.* London: Sage.

Newman, G. 1993. "Batman and Justice: The True Story." *Humanity and Society* 17(3): 297-320.

Nietzsche, F. 1980. *On the Advantages and Disadvantages of History for Life.* Indianapolis, IN: Hackett Publishing.

————. 1969. *The Genealogy of Morals.* Trans. W. Kaufman. New York: Vintage.

O'Malley, P., and S. Mugford. 1994. "Crime, Excitement, and Modernity." In G. Barak (ed.), *Varieties of Criminology.* Wesport, CT: Praeger.

Oliva, T., D. Day, and I. MacMillan. 1988. "A General Model of Competitive Dynamics."
    Academy of Management Review 13(3): 374-88.
Oliva, T., P. Michael, and H. Murthy. 1981. "A Preliminary Empirical Test of a Cusp
    Catastrophe Model in the Social Sciences." *Behavioral Science* 26: 153-162.
Pallas, J., and B. Barber. 1980. "From Riot to Revolution." In T. Platt and P. Takagi (eds.),
    *Punishment and Penal Discipline: Essays on the Prison and the Prisoners'
    Movement.* Berkeley, CA: Crime and Social Justice Associates, pp. 146-54.
Palmer, A. 1975. "Martinson Revisited." *Journal of Research in Crime and Delinquency*
    12: 133-52,
Palmer, J., W. 1985. *Constitutional Rights of Prisoners.* Cincinnati, OH: Anderson.
Pashukanis, E. 1978. *Law and Marxism.* C.J. Athur (ed.). London: Ink Links.
————. 1980. "The General Theory of Law and Marxism." In P. Beirne and R. Sharlet
    (eds.), *Pashukanis: Selected Writings on Marxism and Law.* New York:
    Academic Press.
Peak, D., and M. Frame. 1994. *Chaos under Control.* New York: W.H. Freeman.
Peat, D. 1988. *Superstrings and the Search for the Theory of Everything.* Chicago:
    Contemporary Books.
Pecheux, M. 1982. *Language, Semantics and Ideology.* New York: St. Martin's Press.
Peirce, C.S. 1923. *Chance, Love, and Logic.* New York: George Braziller.
————. 1934. *Pragmatism and Pragmaticism.* Cambridge, MA: Harvard University Press.
————. 1940. *The Philosophy of Peirce: Selected Writings.* J. Buchler (ed.). London:
    Routledge and Kegan Paul.
————. 1965. *The Collected Papers of Charles Sanders Peirce.* C. Hartshorne and P.
    Weiss (eds.). Cambridge, MA: Harvard University Press.
Peitgen, H.O., H. Jurgens, and D. Saupe. 1992. *Fractals for the Classroom.* NY: Springer-
    Verlag.
Penrose, R. 1989. *The Emperor's New Mind.* New York: Oxford University Press.
Pepinsky, H. 1986. "This Can't Be Peace: A Pessimist Looks at Punishment." In W.B.
    Groves and G. Newman (eds.), *Punishment and Privilege.* New York: Harrow
    and Heston.
————.1989. "Peacemaking in Criminology." *Critical Criminologist* (Summer): 6-10.
————.1991. *The Geometry of Violence and Democracy.* Bloomington, IN: Indiana
    University Press.
Pepinsky, H., and R. Quinney (eds.). 1991. *Criminology as Peacemaking.* Bloomington,
    IN: Indiana University Press.
Perkins, R. M. 1969. *Criminal Law.* Mineola, NY: The Foundation Press.
Pfohl, S. J. 1985. "Toward a Sociological Deconstruction of Social Problems." *Social
    Problems* 32: 228-232.
Pickover, C. 1988. "Pattern Formation and Chaos in Networks." *Communications of the
    ACM* 31(2): 136-51.
Pitkin, H. 1971. *Wittgenstein and Justice.* Berkeley: University of California Press.
Poulantzas, N. 1973. *Political Power and Social Class.* Atlantic Fields, NJ: Humanities
    Press.
————. 1978. *State Power and Socialism.* London: New Left Books.
Pribram, K. 1977. *Languages of the Brain.* Englewood Cliffs, NJ: Prentice-Hall.
Prigogine, I., and I. Stengers. 1984. *Order Out of Chaos.* New York: Bantam Books.
Quinney, R. 1988. "The Theory and Practice of Peacemaking in the Development of
    Radical Criminology." Paper presented to American Society of Criminology,
    Chicago, November.
Ragland, E. 1995. *Essays on the Pleasures of Death.* New York: Routledge.
Ragland-Sullivan, E. 1986. *Jacques Lacan and the Philosophy of Psychoanalysis.*
    Chicago: University of Illinois Press.

————.1990a. "Counting from O to 6: Lacan, Suture, and the Imaginary Order." In P. Hogan and L. Pandit (eds.), *Criticism and Lacan*. London: University of Georgia Press, pp. 31-63.

————. 1990b. "Lacan's Seminar on James Joyce: Writing as Symptom and 'Singular Solutions.'" In R. Feldstein and H. Sussman (eds.), *Psychoanalysis and...* New York: Routledge, pp. 67-86.

Rajchman, J. 1991. *Truth and Eros: Foucault, Lacan, and the Question of Ethics*. New York: Routledge.

Rapaport, H. 1990. "Effi Briest and La Chose Fredienne." In P. Hogan and L. Pandit (eds.), *Criticism and Lacan*. London: University of Gerogia Press, pp. 223-47.

Reed, A. W. 1980. "Guilt, Innocence, and Federalism in Habeas Corpus." *Cornell Law Review* 65: 1123-47.

Regnault, F. 1995. "The Name-of-the-Father." In R. Feldstein, B. Fink, and M. Jaanus (eds.), *Reading Seminar XI*. New York: State University of New York Press.

Ricoeur, P. 1973. "Creativity of Language." *Philosophy Today* 17: 97-112.

Rossi-Landi, F. 1983. *Language as Work and Trade: A Semiotic Homology for Linguistics and Economics*. South Hadley, MA: Bergin and Garvey.

Rothman, D.J. 1971. *Discovery of the Asylum: Social Order and Disorder in the Republic*. Boston: Little, Brown.

Rubington, E., and M. Weinberg (eds). 1968. *Deviance: The Interactionist Perspective*. New York: Macmillan.

Rucker, R. 1984. *The Fourth Dimension*. Boston: Houghton Mifflin Company.

Russell, F. 1956. *Foundations of Geometry*. NY: Dover Publications.

Salecl, R. 1993. "Crime as a Mode of Subjectivization: Lacan and the Law." *Law and Critique* 4(1): 3-20.

Salyer, L. 1989. "Captives of Law: Judicial Enforcement of the Chinese Exclusion Law." *Journal of American History* 76: 91-117.

————. 1991. "The Constitutive Nature of Law in American History." *Legal Studies Forum* 15(1): 61-64.

Sartre, J.P. 1955. *No Exit and Three Other Plays*. New York: Vintage Books.

Sarup, M. 1989. *Post-Structuralism and Postmodernism*. Athens, Georgia: University of Georgia Press.

————. 1992. *Jacques Lacan*. Toronto: University of Toronto Press.

Scheff, L. 1968. "Negotiating Reality: Notes on Power in the Assessment of Responsibility." *Social Problems* 16: 3-18.

Schutz, A. 1967. *The Phenomenology of the Social World*. Evanston, IL: Northwestern University Press.

Schwartz, M. 1989. "The Undercutting Edge of Criminology." *The Critical Criminologist* (Spring): 1-2, 5-6.

Schwartz, M., and D.O. Friedrichs. 1994. "Postmodern Thought and Criminological Discontent: New Metaphors for Understanding Violence." *Criminology* 32(2): 221-46.

Schwartz, M., and D. Milovanovic (eds.). 1996. *Race, Gender and Class in Criminology: The Intersection*. New York: Garland Publishing.

Schwendinger, J., and H. Schwendinger. 1983. *Rape and Inequality*. Newbury Park, CA: Sage.

————. 1985. *Adolescent Subcultures and Delinquency*. New York: Praeger.

Scott, S., and M. Lyman. 1970. "Accounts, Deviance and the Social Order." In J. Douglas (ed.), *Deviance and Respectability*. New York: Basic Books.

Sellers, S. 1991. *Language and Sexual Differences: Feminist Writing in France*. New York: St. Martin's Press.

Selva, L., and R. Bohm. 1987. "Law and Liberation: Toward an Oppositional Legal Discourse." *Legal Studies Forum* 11(3): 243-266.

Serres, M. 1982a. *Hermes: Literature, Science, Philosophy.* Baltimore, MD: Johns Hopkins.

————. 1982b. *The Parasite.* Baltimore: Johns Hopkins.

Shaw, R. 1981. "Strange Attractors, Chaotic Behavior, and Information Flow." *Zeitschrift fur Naturforschung* 36: 79-112.

Silverman, K. 1982. *The Subject of Semiotics.* New York: Oxford University Press.

Sinanoglu, O. 1981. "1- and 2-Topology of Reaction Networks." *Journal of Mathematical Physics* 22(7):1504-12.

Sinclair, M.B.W. 1987. "The Use of Evolution Theory in Law." *University of Detroit Law Review* 64: 451.

————. 1992. "Autopoiesis: Who Needs It?" *Legal Studies Forum* 16(1): 81-102.

Skriabine, P. 1989. "Clinique et Topologie." Unpublished Manuscript.

Smart, C. 1990. "Feminist Approaches to Criminology or Postmodern Woman Meets Atavistic Man." In L. Gelsthorpe and A. Morris (eds.), *Feminist Perspectives in Criminology.* London: Open University Press.

Smith, C., and D. Comer. 1994. "Self-Organization in Small Groups: A Study of Group Effectiveness within Non-Equilibrium Conditions." *Human Relations* 47(5): 553-81.

Smith, P. 1988. *Discerning the Subject.* Minneapolis, MN: University of Minnesota Press.

Soury, P. 1980. *Chains and Noeuds: Premiere Partie.* Paris: Fabrique avec l'aide de la Maison des Sciences de l'Homme.

Spivak, G. 1988. "Can the Subaltern Speak?" In C. Nelson and L. Grossberg (eds.), *Marxisms and the Interpretation of Culture.* London: MacMillan.

Stacy, H. 1996. "Legal Discourse and the Feminist Political Economy: Moving Beyond Sameness/Difference." *Australian Feminist Law Journal* 6 (forthcoming).

Stewart, I. 1989. *Does God Play with Dice?* New York: Basil Blackwell.

Sudnow, D. 1965. "Normal Crimes: Sociological Features of the Penal Code in a Public Defender Office." *Social Problems* 12: 255-276.

Swigert, V., and R. Farrell. 1976. *Murder, Inequality and the Law.* Massachusetts: Lexington Books.

Sykes, G.M., and Matza, D. 1957. "Techniques of Neutralization: A Theory of Delinquency." *American Sociological Review* 22: 664-70.

Talbot, M. 1991. *The Holographic Universe.* New York: Harper Collins.

Taylor, L. 1972. "The Significance of Interpretation of Replies to Motivational Questions: The Case of Sex Offenders." *Sociology* 6: 23-39.

Thom, R. 1975. *Structural Stability and Morphogenesis.* Reading, MA: W.A. Benjamin.

Thomas, J. 1984. "Law and Social Praxis: Prisoner Civil Rights Litigation and Structural Mediations." In S. Spitzer and A. Scull (eds.), *Research in Law, Deviance and Social Control* 6, 141-170. Greenwich, CT: JAI Press.

————. 1988. *Prisoner Litigation: The Paradox of the Jailhouse Lawyer.* Totowa, NJ: Rowman and Littlefield.

————. 1989. "Repackaging the Data: The 'Reality' of Prisoner Litigation." *New England Journal of Criminal and Civil Confinement* 15: 233-253.

Thomas, J., A. Aylward, M. Harry, and J. Blakemore. 1988. "Prison Disciplinary Proceedings: The Social Enactment of Power." Paper presented to the Midwest Criminal Justice Association, Chicago.

Thomas, J., K. Harris, and D. Keeler. 1987. "Issues and Misconceptions in Prisoner Litigation." *Criminology* 24: 901-19.

Thomas, J., and A. O'Maochatha. 1989. "Reassessing the Critical Metaphor: An Optimistic Revisionism View." *Justice Quarterly* 6: 143-172.

Unger, R.. 1987. *False Necessity.* New York: Cambridge University Press.

Useem, B., and P. A. Kimball. 1987. "A Theory of Prison Riots." *Theory and Society* 16: 87-122.

Vappereau, J.-M. 1988. *Etoffe.* Paris: Duculot a Gembiousx.

Volosinov, V. 1986. *Marxism and the Philosophy of Language*. Cambridge, MA: Harvard University Press.

Wald, K. 1980. "The San Quentin Six Case: Perspective and Analysis." In T. Platt and P. Takagi (eds.), *Punishment and Penal Discipline: Essays on the Prison and the Prisoners' Movement*, pp. 165-75. Berkeley, CA: Crime and Social Justice Associates.

Weber, M. 1978. *Economy and Society*. Two Volumes. G. Roth, G. Guenther, C.Wittich (eds). Berkeley, CA: University of California Press.

Weeks, J. 1985. *The Shape of Space*. New York: Marcel Dekker.

Weiss, R. P. 1987. "From 'Slugging Detectives' to 'Labor Relations.'" In C.D. Shearing and P.C. Stenning (eds.), *Private Policing*. Beverly Hills, CA: Sage.

Wheeler, S. 1961. "Socialization in Correctional Communities." *American Sociological Review* 26: 697-712.

White, H. 1973. *Metahistory*. Baltimore, MD: Johns Hopkins.

White, M., and D. Epston. 1990. *Literate Means to Therapeutic Ends*. Adelaide, Australia: Dulwich Centre Publications.

Whitehead, J.T., and S.P. Lab. 1989. "A Meta-Analysis of Juvenile Correctional Treatment." *Journal of Research in Crime and Delinquency* 26: 276-95.

Whorf, B. 1956. *Language, Thought and Reality*. Cambridge, MA: MIT Press.

Williams, R. 1987. "Taking Rights Aggressively: The Perils and Promise of Critical Legal Theory for Peoples of Color." *Law and Inequality* 5: 103-25.

———. 1991. "Deconstructing Gender." In K. Barlett and R. Kennedy (eds.), *Feminist Legal Theory*. Oxford: Westview Press, pp. 95-123.

Williamson, J. 1987. *Decoding Advertisement*. New York: Marion Boyars.

Willis II, M.A. 1991. "Inside Jackson: An Inmate's View of a Typical Morning at Southern Michigan Prison." *The Ann Arbor News*, May 19, p. C9.

Willis, P. 1977. *Learning to Labor*. Farnborough, United Kingdom: Saxon House.

Willis, P., and P. Corrigan. 1983. "Orders of Experience: The Differences of Working Class Cultural Forms." *Social Problems* 7: 85-102.

Winter, S. 1992. "For What It's Worth." *Law and Society Review* 26(4): 789-818.

Wolfgang, M. R., M. Figlio, and T. Sellin. 1972. *Delinquency in a Birth Cohort*. Chicago: University of Chicago Press.

Yngvessen, B. 1993. *Virtuous Citizens*. New York: Routledge.

Young, J. 1987. "The Tasks Facing a Realist Criminology." *Contemporary Crisis* 11: 337-56.

———. 1988. "Radical Criminology in Britain: The Emergence of a Competing Paradigm." *British Journal of Criminology* 28: 159-183.

———. 1989. *Realist Criminology*. London: Sage.

Young, T.R. 1991a. "Chaos and Crime: Nonlinear and Fractal Forms of Crime." *Critical Criminologist* 3(4): 3-4, 10-11.

———. 1991b. "The ABC of Crime: Nonlinear and Fractal Forms of Crime." *The Critical Criminologist* 3(4): 3-4, 13-14.

———. 1992. "Chaos Theory and Human Agency: Humanist Sociology in a Postmodern Era." *Humanity and Society* 16(4): 441-60.

———. 1994. Personal communication, November 29.

———. 1997. "Challenges: For Postmodern Criminology." In D. Milovanovic (ed.), *Chaos, Criminology and Social Justice: The New Orderly (Dis)Order*. Westport, CT: Praeger.

Zavarzadeh, M., and D. Morton. 1990. "Signs of Knowledge in the Contemporary Academy." *American Journal of Semiotics* 7(4): 149-60.

Zeeman, C. 1976. "Catastrophe Theory." *Scientific America* 234: 65-83.

———. 1977. *Catastrophe Theory: Selected Papers, 1972-1977*. London: Addison-Wesley Publishing Company.

Zita, J. 1987. "Pornography and the Male Imaginary." *Enclitic* 9: 28-44.

Zizek, S. 1989. *The Sublime Object of Ideology*. New York: Verso.
Zwerman, G. 1988. "Special Incapacitation: The Emergence of a New Correctional Facility for Women Political Prisoners." *Social Justice* 15(1): 31-47.
————. 1994. "Postmodern Law and Subjectivity." In D. Caudill and S. Gould (eds.), *Radical Philosophy of Law*. New York: Humanities Press.

CASES CITED

Bounds v. Smith, 430 U.S. 817 (1977).

Brown v. Board of Education 347 U.S. 483 (1954).

Chaplinski v. New Hampshire, 315 (1942).

Coffin v. Reichard, 143 F. 2d 443, 445 (9th Cir. 1944) cert. denied 325 U.S. 887 (1945).

EEOC v. Sears, Roebuck and Co., 628 F. Supp. 1264, 1302-08 (N.D. IL. 1986), aff'd, 839 F. 2d 302 (7th Cir. 1988).

Faretta v. California, 422 U.S. 806 (1975).

Gideon v. Wainright, 372 U.S. 335 (1963).

Holt v. Sarver, 300 F. Supp. 825. E.D. Ark. (1969).

Jackson v. Elrod et al., 86-C-1817, N.D. IL. 1986.

Johnson v. Avery, 393 U.S. 806 (1969

Lightfoot et al. v. Walker et al., 486 F. Supp. 504, 1980.

People v. Brown, Nos. 78CM2520-78CM2540 (Cir.Ct. of Lake County, IL. January 1979).

People v. Harmon, 220 N.W. 2d 212 (1974) .

People v. Jarka, Nos. 2170, 2196 2212, 2214, 2236-2238 (Cir. Ct. of Lake County, IL. April 1985).

People v. Lovercamp, 43 Cal. App. 3d 823, 118 Cal. Rptr. 110 (1974).

People v. Streeter, Nos. 85-108644, 85-108645, 85-108648, 85-108649, 85-108652, 85-120323, 85-120326, 85-120327 (Cir. Ct. of Cook County, IL. May 1985).

People v. Unger, 66 Ill. 2d 333 (1977).

People v. Whitson, 127 Ill.App. 3d 999 (3rd Dist. 1984).

R.A.V., Petitioner v. City of St. Paul, Minnesota (1992).

R. v. Butler, 1 S.C.R. 452 (1992) [Canadian].

Ruffin v. Commonwealth (1871).

Ruiz v. Estell, 650 F. 2d 555 (Fifth Cir. 1981).

State v. Mouer, Nos. 77-246-77-324 (Columbia Co. Dist. Ct., 12-16 Dec. 1977).

State v. Whisman, 575 P.2d 1005 (1978).

Surocco v. Geary, 3 Cal. 69 (1853).

Texas v. Johnson, 491 U.S. 397 (1989).

United States v. Ashton, 24 F.Cas. 873 (No. 14, 470) (C.D. Mass. 1834).

United States v. Bailey, 444 U.S. 394 (1980).

United States Ex Rel Hunley v. Godinez, 784 F. Supp. 1992.

United States v. Wyler, 526 F. Supp. 76 (S.D.N.Y. 1981), aff'd 697 F. 2d. 301 (2d Cir. 1981).

Valvano v. McGrath, 325 F. Supp. 408 (1980).

Wolff v. McDonnell, 418 U.S. 539 (1974).

Woods v. Aldworth, 84-C-7745, N.D. IL. 1984.

Younger v. Gilmore, 404 U.S. 15 (1971).

INDEX

law-of-the-father, 36, 38, 45, 47, 182, 216
le champ de la réalité, 34, 36; see also field of reality
le sinthome, 66-71, 75, 215
Lecercle, J. 11, 13, 14, 74, 92, 199
Lee, J. 11, 24, 29, 40, 44, 47, 48, 172
Legal narrative constructions, 38
legal realists, 21, 157
Leifer, R. 6, 7, 42, 53
Lem, S. 19
limit attractors, 7, 8, 53, 190, 218, 238
linear reading, 13
linguistic coordinate systems, 12, 13, 15, 57, 58, 62, 65, 69, 71, 166, 199, 227, 231, 232
linguistic coordinates, 102, 107, 110, 146, 147
linguistic relativity principle, 12
local indeterminacy, 8, 190, 213
local knowledge,15, 47, 52, 197, 199
logocentricism, 5, 91
losange, 32
Love, N. 22, 48
Luhmann, N. 5, 6, 22, 83
Lukacs, G. 128
Lyng, S. 174, 176, 180, 218, 225
Lyotard, J.F. 4, 6, 15, 16, 20, 25, 42, 221, 223, 236

MacLean, B. 92
major literature, 11, 13, 15
Mandel, D. 193
Mandelbrot, 7, 18, 19, 20, 191, 212, 217
Mandelbrot Set, 205-211, 218
Manning, P. 22, 83, 86, 88, 89, 91, 92, 161, 163, 165, 167, 197, 199
manque d'être, 172, 174
manque-à-être, 30
Marini, M. 29, 172

Martinson, R. 157
Marx, K. 4, 22, 28, 66, 72, 80, 87 87, 142, 151, 165
master discourse, 12, 200, 202
master signifiers, 10, 11, 12, 15, 35, 46, 47, 52, 53, 54, 55, 57, 69, 71, 72, 73, 75, 197, 198, 199, 200, 201, 202, 203
Mastrofski, S. 157, 163
Matsuda, M. 10, 44, 197, 209, 213
Matthews, R. 92
Matza, D. 158, 174, 175, 179, 181, 184, 195, 196, 218, 225, 232
McCann, M. 25, 27
McLaren, P. 8, 11, 22, 23, 24, 202
McRobie, A. 224
Melville, S. 48
Merry, S. 86, 92
Merton, R. 235
Messerschmidt, J. 92
metaphor, 8, 12, 29, 30, 31, 32, 36, 38, 39, 47, 61, 65, 74, 174, 178-182, 214
metonymy, 12, 30, 36, 38, 39, 47, 61, 65, 74, 178-179, 182
Mika, H. 122, 126, 161
Mills, C.W. 158, 164
Milovanovic, D. 4, 6, 7, 10, 11, 12, 13, 15, 16, 18, 19, 21, 23, 24, 27, 28, 30, 37, 38, 41, 42, 46, 47, 52, 53, 54, 55, 57, 58, 59, 60, 61, 69, 74, 75, 77, 80, 81, 83, 88, 89, 91, 92, 110, 112, 113, 115, 118, 120, 126, 130, 133, 151, 153, 154, 157, 161, 165, 167, 168, 170, 172, 173, 175, 178, 181, 183, 194, 197, 198, 199, 203, 213, 215, 218, 225, 236
mimeses, 22, 23, 49, 212
minor literature, 11, 12, 14, 53
mirror stage, 37